Computer Graphics

Dr.J. Gladson Maria Britto

G. Shankar

M. Sadhasivam

Published by

BONFRING®
Intellectual Integrity

Computer Graphics

ISBN 978-93-92537-09-7

Author

Dr.J. Gladson Maria Britto

G. Shankar

M. Sadhasivam

Bonfring

309, 5th Street Extension, Gandhipuram,

Coimbatore-641 012.

Tamil Nadu, India.

E-mail: info@bonfring.org

Website: www.bonfring.org

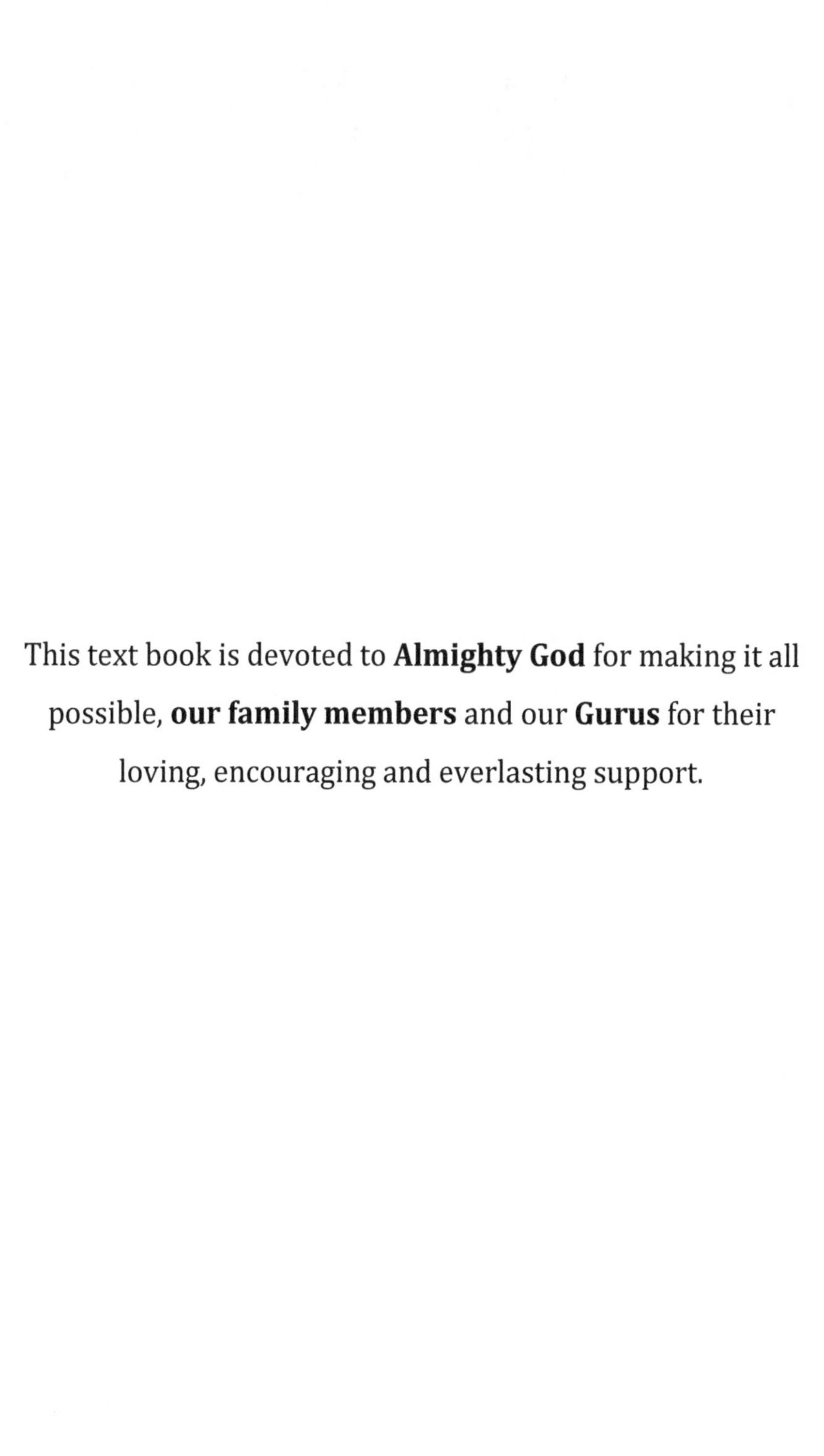

This text book is devoted to **Almighty God** for making it all possible, **our family members** and our **Gurus** for their loving, encouraging and everlasting support.

Acknowledgement

First and foremost, I thank, the Almighty God for endowing his immense blessing that helped me in each step of my progress towards the successful completion of this text book **"Computer Graphics"**.

I owe a warm debt of gratitude to my co-authors for their guidance, noval ideas, inspiration and brilliant discussions at every stage of this work. From my bottom of heart I thank him for made this as a good research work.

It is my privilege to thank the management and the staff of the Department of Computer Science & Engineering of our college for their constant support and cooperation to complete the text book.

Most importantly, none of this would have been possible without the love and patience of our family. Words alone cannot describe the encouragement, affection and our parent, wife and children; I thank them for all the help, care and moral support provided throughout this work.

Dr.J. Gladson Maria Britto

G. Shankar

M. Sadhasivam

Preface

This book, **Computer Graphics,** presents many of the important ideas of computer graphics to students, researchers, and practitioners. Several of these ideas are not new: They have already appeared in widely available scholarly publications, technical reports, textbooks, and lay-press articles.

The aim of this text book is to provide an introduction of fundamental concepts and theory of computer graphics. Here topics covered includes graphics systems and input devices; geometric representations and 2D/3D transformations; viewing and projections; illumination and color models; animation; rendering and implementation; visible surface detection; Our aim has been to treat ideas with as much sophistication as possible (which includes omitting ideas that are no longer as important as they once were), while still introducing beginning students to the subject lucidly and gracefully.

After reading this book I am sure, you acquire familiarity with the relevant concepts and mathematics of computer graphics. Be able to design basic graphics application programs, including animation and be able to design applications that display graphic images to given specifications.

TABLE OF CONTENTS

1. Introduction to Computer Graphics

Computer graphics is an art of drawing pictures, lines, charts, etc. using computers with the help of programming. Computer graphics is made up of number of pixels. Computer graphics may be defined as a pictorial representation or graphical representation of objects in a computer.

Basically there are two types of computer graphics namely.

a) Interactive Computer Graphics.

b) Non-Interactive Computer Graphics.

Interactive Computer Graphics: Interactive Computer Graphics involves a two way communication between computer and user. Here the observer is given some control over the image by providing him with an input device for example the video game controller of the ping pong game. This helps him to signal his request to the computer.

The computer on receiving signals from the input device can modify the displayed picture appropriately. To the user it appears that the picture is changing instantaneously in response to his commands. He can give a series of commands, each one generating a graphical response from the computer. In this way he maintains a conversation, or dialogue, with the computer.

Non-Interactive Computer Graphics: In non-interactive computer graphics otherwise known as passive computer graphics. It is the computer graphics in which user does not have any kind of control over the image. Image is merely the product of static stored program and will work according to the instructions given in the program linearly. The image is totally under the control of program instructions not under the user. Example: screen savers.

1.1. Applications of Computer Graphics

Computer Aided Design (CAD)

A major use of computer graphics is in design processes, particularly for engineering and architectural systems, but almost all products are now computer designed. Generally referred to as CAD, computer-aided design methods are now routinely used in the design of buildings, automobiles, aircraft, watercraft, spacecraft, computers, textiles, and many, many other products.

Presentation Graphics

Presentation graphics is used to produce illustrations for reports or to generate 35-mm slides or transparencies for use with projectors. Presentation graphics is commonly used to summarize financial, statistical, mathematical, scientific, and economic data for research reports, managerial reports, consumer information bulletins, and other types of reports. Workstation devices and service bureaus exist for converting screen displays into 35-mm slides or overhead transparencies for use in presentations. Typical examples of presentation graphics are bar charts, line graphs, surface graphs, pie charts, and other displays showing relationships between multiple parameters.

Computer Art

Computer graphics methods are widely used in both fine art and commercial art applications. Artists use a variety of computer methods, including special-purpose hardware, artist's paintbrush, other paint packages, specially developed software, symbolic mathematics packages, CAD packages, desktop publishing software, and animation packages that provide facilities for designing object shapes and specifying object motions.

Entertainment

Computer graphics methods am now commonly used in making motion pictures, music videos, and television shows. Sometimes the graphics scenes are displayed by themselves, and sometimes graphics objects are combined with the actors and live scenes.

Education and Training

Computer-generated models of physical, financial, and economic systems are often used as educational aids. Models of physical systems, physiological systems, population trends, or equipment, such as the color coded diagram, can help trainees to understand the operation of the system.

For some training applications, special systems are designed. Examples of such specialized systems are the simulators for practice sessions or training of ship captains, aircraft pilots, heavy-equipment operators, and air traffic control personnel. Some simulators have no video screens; for example, a flight simulator with only a control panel for instrument flying.

Visualization

Scientists, engineers, medical personnel, business analysts, and others often need to analyse large amounts of information or to study the behaviour of certain processes. Numerical simulations carried out on supercomputers frequently produce data files containing thousands and even millions of data values. Similarly, satellite cameras and other sources are amassing large data files faster than they can be interpreted. Scanning these large sets of numbers to determine trends and relationships is a tedious and ineffective process. But if the data are converted to a visual form, the trends and patterns are often immediately apparent.

Image Processing

Image processing, on the other hand, applies techniques to modify or interpret existing pictures, such as photographs and TV scans. Two principal applications of image processing are (1) improving picture quality and (2) machine perception of visual information, as used in robotics. To apply image processing methods, we first digitize a photograph or other picture into an image file. Then digital methods can be applied to rearrange picture parts, to enhance color separations, or to improve the quality of shading.

Graphical User Interface

A major component of a graphical interface is a window manager that allows a user to display multiple- window areas. Each window can contain a different process that can contain graphical or non-graphical displays. To make a particular window active, we simply click in that window using an interactive pointing device.

1.2.   Video Display Devices

The primary output device in a graphics system is a video monitor. The operation of most video monitors is based on the standard cathode-ray tube (CRT) design, but several other technologies exist and solid-state monitors may eventually predominate.

Refresh Cathode Ray Tube

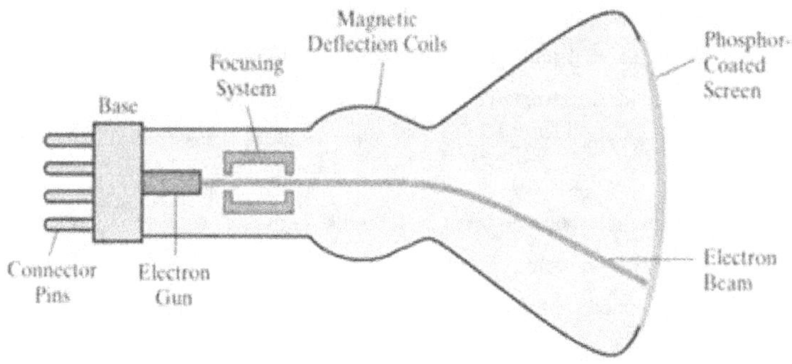

Fig. 1.1: Basic Design of a Magnetic-deflection CRT

Figure 1.1 illustrates the basic operation of, a CRT. A beam of electrons (cathode rays), emitted by an electron gun, passes through focusing and deflection systems that direct the beam toward specified positions on the phosphor-coated screen. The phosphor then emits a small spot of light at each position contacted by the electron beam. Because the light emitted by the phosphor fades very rapidly, some method is needed for maintaining the screen picture. One way to keep the phosphor glowing is to redraw the picture repeatedly by quickly directing the electron beam back over the same points. This type of display is called a refresh CRT.

The primary components of an electron gun in a CRT are the heated metal cathode and a control grid (Fig. 1.2). Heat is supplied to the cathode by directing a current through a coil of wire, called the filament, inside the cylindrical cathode structure. This causes electrons to be 'boiled off" the hot cathode surface. In the vacuum inside the CRT envelope, the free, negatively charged electrons are then accelerated toward the phosphor coating by a high positive voltage. The accelerating voltage can be generated with a positively charged metal coating on the inside of the CRT envelope near the phosphor screen, or an accelerating anode can be used, as in Fig. 1.2. Sometimes the electron gun is built to contain the accelerating anode and focusing system within the same unit. Intensity of the electron beam is controlled by setting voltage levels on the control grid, which is a metal cylinder that fits over the cathode. A high negative voltage applied to the control grid will shut off the beam by repelling electrons and stopping them from passing through the small hole at the end of the control grid structure. A smaller negative voltage on the control grid simply decreases the number of electrons passing through. Since the amount of light emitted by the phosphor coating depends on the number of electrons striking the screen, we control the brightness of a display by varying the voltage on the control grid. The focusing system in a CRT is needed to force the electron beam to converge into a small spot as it strikes the phosphor. Otherwise, the electrons would repel each other, and the beam would spread out as it approaches the screen. Focusing is accomplished with either electric or magnetic fields. Electrostatic focusing is commonly used in television and computer graphics monitors. With electrostatic focusing, the electron beam passes through a positively charged metal cylinder that forms an electrostatic lens, as shown in Fig. 1.2. The action of the electrostatic lens focuses the electron beam at the center of the screen, in exactly the same way that an optical lens focuses a beam of height at a particular focal distance. Similar lens focusing effects can be accomplished with a magnetic field set up by a coil mounted around the outside of the CRT envelope. Magnetic lens focusing produces the smallest spot size on the screen and is used in special purpose devices.

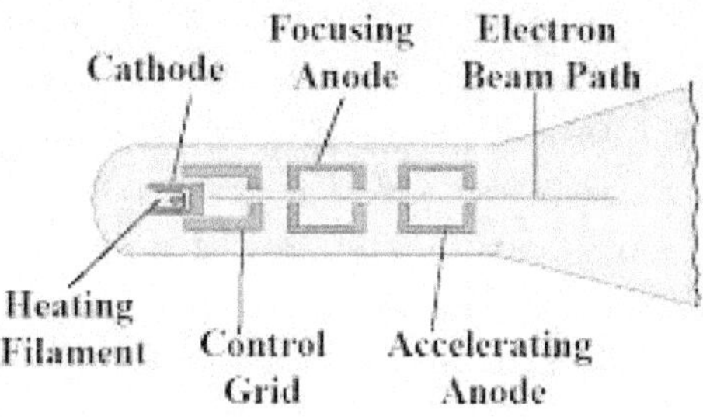

Figure 1.2: Operation of an Electron Gun with an Accelerating Anode

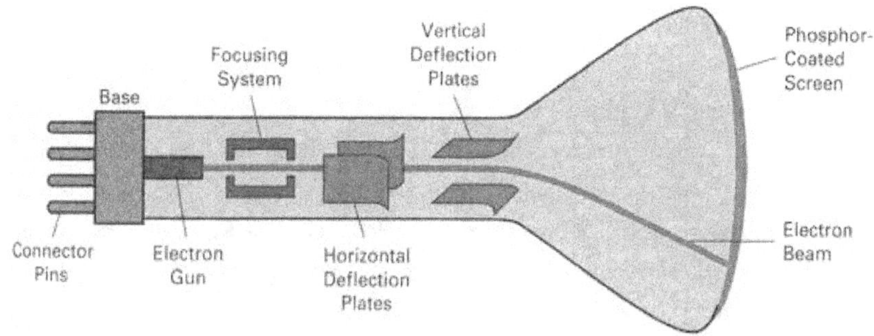

Figure 1.3: Electrostatic Deflection of the Electron Beam in a CRT

As with focusing, deflection of the electron beam can be controlled either with electric fields or with magnetic fields. Cathode-ray tubes are now commonly constructed with magnetic deflection coils mounted on the outside of the CRT envelope, as illustrated in Fig. 1.1. Two pairs of coils are used, with the coils in each pair mounted on opposite sides of the neck of the CRT envelope. One pair is mounted on the top and bottom of the neck, and the other pair is mounted on opposite sides of the neck. The magnetic, field produced by each pair of coils results in a transverse deflection force that is perpendicular both to the direction of the magnetic field and to the direction of travel of the electron beam. Horizontal deflection is accomplished with one pair of coils, and vertical deflection by the other pair. The proper deflection amounts are attained by adjusting the current through the coils. When electrostatic deflection is used, two pairs of parallel plates are mounted inside the CRT envelope. One pair of plates is mounted horizontally to control the vertical deflection, and the other pair is mounted vertically to control horizontal deflection (Fig. 1.3).

Spots of light are produced on the screen by the transfer of the CRT beam energy to the phosphor. When the electrons in the beam collide with the phosphor coating, they are stopped and their kinetic energy is absorbed by the phosphor. Part of the beam energy is converted by friction into heat energy, and the remainder causes electrons in the phosphor atoms to move up to higher quantum-energy levels. After a short time, the "excited phosphor electrons begin dropping back to their stable ground state, giving up their extra energy as small quantum's of Light energy. What we see on the screen is the combined effect of all the electron light emissions: a glowing spot that quickly fades after all the excited phosphor electrons have returned to their ground energy level. The frequency (or color) of the light emitted by the phosphor is proportional to the energy difference between the excited quantum state and the ground state.

Raster-Scan Displays

The most common type of graphics monitor employing a CRT is the raster-scan display, based on television technology. In a raster-scan system, the electron beam is swept across the screen, one row at a time from top to bottom. As the electron beam moves across each row, the beam intensity is turned on and off to create a pattern of illuminated spots. Picture definition is stored in a memory area called the refresh buffer or frame buffer. This memory area holds the set of intensity values for all the screen points. Stored intensity values are then retrieved from the refresh buffer and "painted" on the screen one row (scan line) at a time (Fig. 1.4). Each screen point is referred to as a pixel or pel (shortened forms of picture element). The capability of a raster-scan system to store intensity information for each screen point makes it well suited for the realistic display of scenes containing subtle shading and color patterns. Home television sets and printers are examples of other systems using raster-scan methods.

Intensity range for pixel positions depends on the capability of the raster system. In a simple black-and- white system, each screen point is either on or off, so only one bit per pixel is needed to control the intensity of screen positions. For a bi-level system, a bit value of 1 indicates that the electron beam is to be turn4 on at that position, and a value of 0 indicates that the beam intensity is to be off. Additional bits are needed when color and intensity variations can be displayed. Up to 24 bits per pixel are included in high-quality systems, which can require several megabytes of storage for the frame buffer, depending on the resolution of the system.

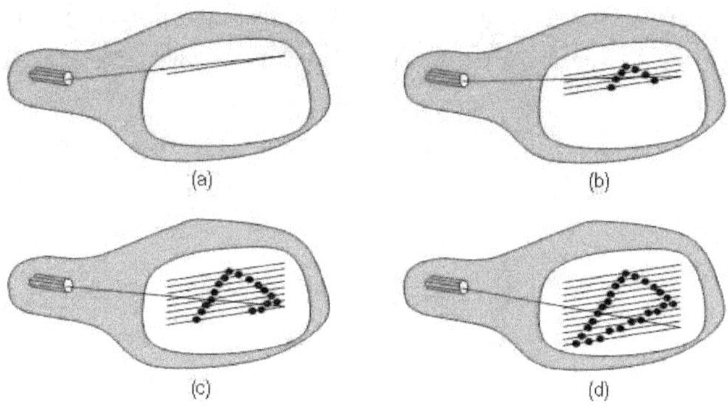

Figure 1.4: A Raster-scan System displays an Object as a Set of Discrete Points Across each scan Line

A system with 24 bits per pixel and a screen resolution of 1024 bv 1024 requires 3 megabytes of storage for the frame buffer. On a black-and-white system with one bit per pixel, the frame buffer is commonly called a bitmap. For systems with multiple bits per pixel, the frame buffer is often referred to as a pixmap. Refreshing on raster- scan displays is carried out at the rate of 60 to 80 frames per second, although some systems are designed for higher refresh rates. Sometimes, refresh rates are described in units of cycles per second, or Hertz (Hz), where a cycle corresponds to one frame.

Random-Scan Displays

When operated as a random-scan display unit, a CRT has the electron beam directed only to the parts of the screen where a picture is to be drawn. Random scan monitors draw a picture one line at a time and for this reason are also referred to as vector displays (or stroke-writing or calligraphic displays). The component lines of a picture can be drawn and refreshed by a random-scan system in any specified order (Fig. 1.5). A pen plotter operates in a similar way and is an example of a random-scan, hard-copy device. Refresh rate on a random-scan system depends on the number of lines to be displayed. Picture definition is now stored as a set of line drawing commands in an area of memory referred to as the refresh display file. Sometimes the refresh display file is called the display list, display program, or simply the refresh buffer. To display a specified picture, the system cycles through the set of commands in the display file, drawing each component line in turn. After all line drawing commands have been processed, the system cycles back to the first line command in the list.

Random-scan displays are designed to draw all the component lines of a picture 30 to 60 times each second. High quality vector systems are capable of handling approximately 100,000 "short" lines at this refresh rate. When a small set of lines is to be displayed, each refresh cycle is delayed to avoid refresh rates greater than 60 frames per second. Otherwise, faster refreshing of the set of lines could be out the phosphor. Random-scan systems are designed for line drawing applications and cannot display realistic shaded scenes.

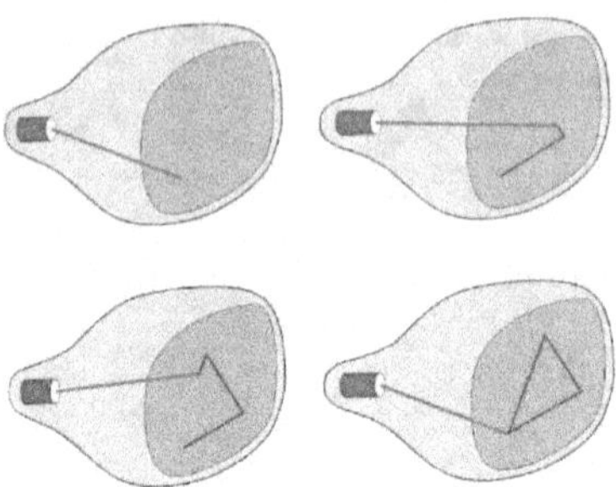

Figure 1.5: A Random-scan System Draws the Component Lines of an Object in any order Specified

Since picture definition is stored as a set of line drawing instructions and not as a set of Intensity values for all screen points, vector displays generally have higher resolution than raster systems. Also, vector displays produce smooth line drawings because the CRT beam directly follows the line path. A raster system, in contrast, produces jagged lines that are plotted as discrete point sets.

Color CRT Monitors

A CRT monitor displays color pictures by using a combination of phosphors that emit different-colored light. By combining the emitted light from the different phosphors, a range of colors can be generated. The two basic techniques for producing color displays with a CRT are the beam-penetration method and the shadow-mask method.

The beam-penetration method for displaying color pictures has been used with random-scan monitors. Two layers of phosphor, usually red and green, are coated onto the inside of the CRT screen, and the displayed color depends on how far the electron beam penetrates into the phosphor layers. A beam of slow electrons excites only the outer red layer. A beam of very fast electrons penetrates through the red layer and excites the inner green layer. At intermediate beam speeds, combinations of red and green light are emitted to show two additional colors, orange and yellow. The speed of the electrons, and hence the screen color at any point, is controlled by the beam- acceleration voltage. Beam penetration has been an inexpensive way to produce color in random-scan monitors, but only four colors are possible, and the quality of pictures is not as good as with other methods.

Shadow-mask methods are commonly used in raster scan systems (including color TV) because they produce a much wider range of colors than the beam penetration method. A shadow-mask CRT has three phosphor color dots at each pixel position. One phosphor dot emits a red light, another emits a green light, and the third emits a blue light. This type of CRT has three electron guns, one for each color dot, and a shadow-mask grid just behind the phosphor-coated screen. Figure 1.6 illustrates the delta-delta shadow-mask method, commonly used in color CRT systems. The three electron beams are deflected and focused as a group onto the shadow mask, which contains a series of holes aligned with the phosphor-dot patterns. When the three beams pass through a hole in the shadow mask, they activate a dot method, commonly used in color CRT systems. The three electron beams are deflected and focused as a group onto the shadow mask, which contains a series of holes aligned with the phosphor-dot patterns. When the three beams pass through a hole in the shadow mask, they activate a dot triangle, which appears as a small color spot on the screen. The phosphor dots in the triangles are arranged so that each electron beam can activate only its corresponding color dot when it passes through the shadow mask. Another configuration for the three electron guns is an in-line arrangement in which the three electron guns, and the corresponding red-green- blue color dots on the screen, are aligned along one scan line instead of in a triangular pattern. This in-line arrangement of electron guns is easier to keep in alignment and is commonly used in high-resolution color CRT's.

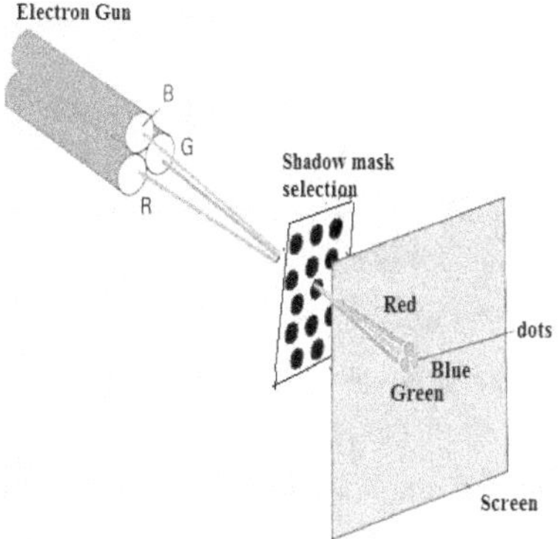

Figure 1.6: Operation of a Delta-delta, Shadow-mask CRT

We obtain color variations in a shadow-mask CRT by varying the intensity levels of the three electron beams. By turning off the red and green guns, we get only the color coming from the blue phosphor. Other combinations of beam intensities produce a small light spot for each pixel position, since our eyes tend to merge the three colors into one composite. The color we see depends on the amount of excitation of the red, green, and blue phosphors. A white (or gray) area is the result of activating all three dots with equal intensity. Yellow is produced with the green and red dots only, magenta is produced with the blue and red dots, and cyan shows up when blue and green are activated equally. In some low-cost systems, the electron beam can only be set to on or off, limiting displays to eight colors. More sophisticated systems can set intermediate intensity levels for the electron beams, allowing several million different colors to be generated.

Direct-View Storage Tubes

An alternative method for maintaining a screen image is to store the picture information inside the CRT instead of refreshing the screen. A direct-view storage tube (DVST) stores the picture information as a charge distribution just behind the phosphor-coated screen. Two electron guns are used in a DVST. One, the primary gun, is used to store the picture pattern; the second, the flood gun, maintains the picture display.

A DVST monitor has both disadvantages and advantages compared to the refresh CRT. Because no refreshing is needed, very complex pictures can be displayed at very high resolutions without flicker. Disadvantages of DVST systems are that they ordinarily do not display color and that selected parts of a picture cannot he erased. To eliminate a picture section, the entire screen must be erased and the modified picture redrawn. The erasing and redrawing process can take several seconds for a complex picture. For these reasons, storage displays have been largely replaced by raster systems.

Flat-Panel Displays

The term Flat-panel display refers to a class of video devices that have reduced volume, weight, and power requirements compared to a CRT. A significant feature of flat-panel displays is that they are thinner than CRTs, and we can hang them on walls or wear them on our wrists. Since we can even write on some flat-panel displays, they will soon be available as pocket notepads. Current uses for flat-panel displays include small TV monitors, calculators, pocket video games, laptop computers, armrest viewing of movies on airlines, as advertisement boards in elevators, and as graphics displays in applications requiring rugged, portable monitors.

We can separate flat-panel displays into two categories: emissive displays and non-emissive displays. The emissive displays (or emitters) are devices that convert electrical energy into light. Plasma panels, thin-film electroluminescent displays, and Light-emitting diodes are examples of emissive displays. Flat CRTs have also been devised, in which electron beams arts accelerated parallel to the screen, then deflected 90' to the screen. But flat CRTs have not proved to be as successful as other emissive devices. Non-emissive displays (or non-emitters) use optical effects to convert sunlight or light from some other source into graphics patterns. The most important example of a non-emissive flat-panel display is a liquid-crystal device.

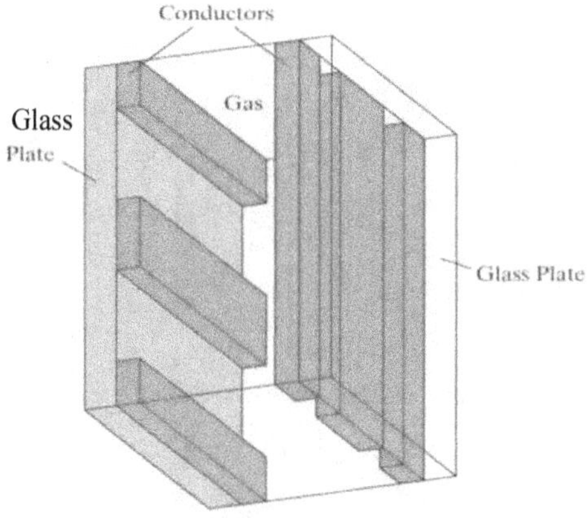

Figure 1.7: Basic Design of a Plasma-panel display Device

Plasma panels, also called gas- discharge displays, are constructed by filling the region between two glass plates with a mixture of gases that usually includes neon. A series of vertical conducting ribbons is placed on one glass panel, and a set of horizontal ribbons is built into the other Glass panel (Fig. 1.7). Firing voltages applied to a pair of horizontal and vertical conductors cause the gas at the intersection of the two conductors to break down into a glowing plasma of electrons and ions. Picture definition is stored in a refresh buffer, and the firing voltages are applied to refresh the pixel positions (at the intersections of the conductors) 60 times per second. Alternating-current methods are used to provide faster application of the firing voltages, and thus brighter displays. Separation between pixels is provided by the electric field of the conductors.

Thin-film electroluminescent displays are similar in construction to a plasma panel. The difference is that the region between the glass plates is filled with a phosphor, such as zinc sulphide doped with manganese, instead of a gas (Fig. 1.8). When a sufficiently high voltage is applied to a pair of crossing electrodes, the phosphor becomes a conductor in the area of the intersection of the two electrodes. Electrical energy is then absorbed by the manganese atoms, which then release the energy as a spot of light similar to the glowing plasma effect in a plasma panel. Electroluminescent displays require more power than plasma panels, and good color and gray scale displays are hard to achieve.

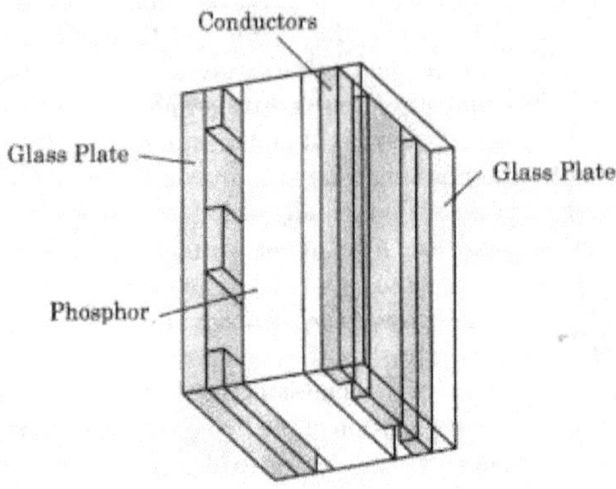

Figure 1.8: Basic Design of a Thin-film Electroluminescent display Device

Liquid Crystal Display (LCD) are commonly used in small systems, such as calculator, and portable, laptop computers. These non-emissive devices produce a picture by passing polarized light from the surroundings are from an internal light source through a liquid-crystal material that can be aligned to either block or transmit the light.

The term liquid crystal refers to the fact that these compounds have a crystalline arrangement of molecules, yet they flow like a liquid. Flat-panel displays commonly use nematic (threadlike) liquid-crystal compounds that tend to keep the long axes of the rod-shaped molecules aligned. A flat-panel display can then be constructed with a nematic liquid crystal, as demonstrated in Fig. 1.9. Two glass plates, each containing a light polarizer at right angles to the-other plate, sandwich the liquid-crystal material. Rows of horizontal transparent conductors are built into one glass plate, and columns of vertical conductors are put into the other plate. The intersection of two conductors defines a pixel position. Normally, the molecules are aligned as shown in the "on state" of Fig. 1.9. Polarized light passing through the material is twisted so that it will pass through the opposite polarizer. The light is then reflected back to the viewer. To turn off the pixel, we apply a voltage to the two intersecting conductors to align the molecules so that the light is not twisted. This type of flat-panel device is referred to as a passive-matrix LCD. Picture definitions are stored in a refresh buffer, and the screen is refreshed at the rate of 60 frames per second, as in the emissive devices. Back lighting is also commonly applied using solid-state electronic devices, so that the system is not completely dependent on outside light sources. Colors can be displayed by using different materials or dyes and by placing a triad of color pixels at each screen location. Another method for constructing LCD's is to place a transistor at each pixel location, using thin-film transistor technology. The transistors are used to control the voltage at pixel locations and to prevent charge from gradually leaking out of the liquid-crystal cells. These devices are called active-matrix displays.

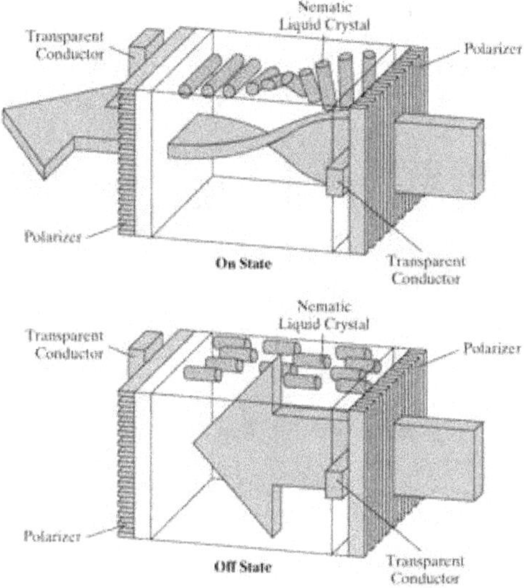

Figure 1.9: The Light-twisting, Shutter effect used in the Design of most Liquid Crystal Display Devices

Three-Dimensional Viewing Devices

Graphics monitors for the display of three-dimensional scenes have been devised using a technique that reflects a CRT image from a vibrating, flexible mirror. The operation of such a system is demonstrated in Fig. 1.10. As the varifocal mirror vibrates, it changes focal length. These vibrations are synchronized with the display of an object on a CRT so that each point on the object is reflected from the mirror into a spatial position corresponding to the distance of that point from a specified viewing position. This allows us to walk around an object or scene and view it from different sides.

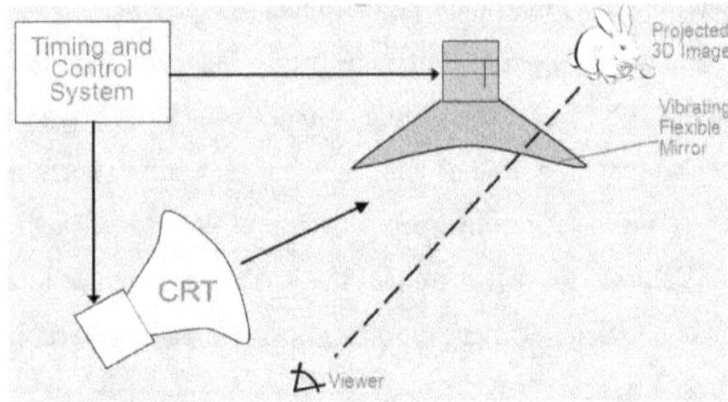

Figure 1.10: Operation 3-D viewing Device

1.3.   Raster-scan Systems

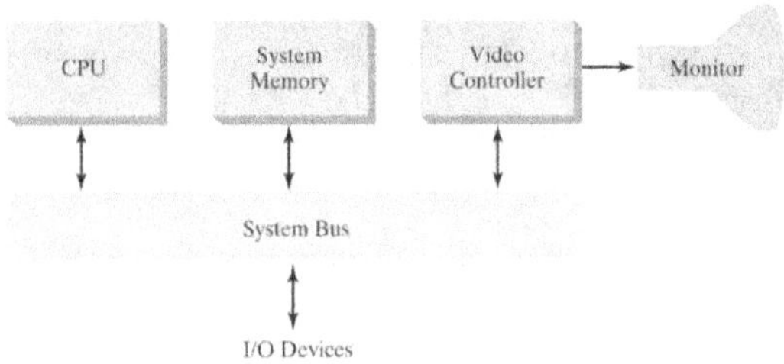

Figure 1.11: Architecture of a Simple Raster Graphics System

Interactive raster graphics systems typically employ several processing units. In addition to the central processing unit, or CPU, a special-purpose processor, called the video controller or display controller, is used to control the operation of the display device. Organization of a simple raster system is shown in Fig. 1.11. Here, the frame buffer can be anywhere in the system memory, and the video controller accesses the frame buffer to refresh the screen. In addition to the video controller, more sophisticated raster systems employ other processors as coprocessors and accelerators to implement various graphics operations.

Video Controller

Figure 1.12 shows a commonly used organization for raster systems. A fixed area of the system memory is reserved for the frame buffer, and the video controller is given direct access to the frame-buffer memory.

Frame-buffer locations, and the corresponding screen positions, are referenced in Cartesian coordinates. For many graphics monitors, the coordinate origin is defined at the lower left screen comer (Fig. 1.13).

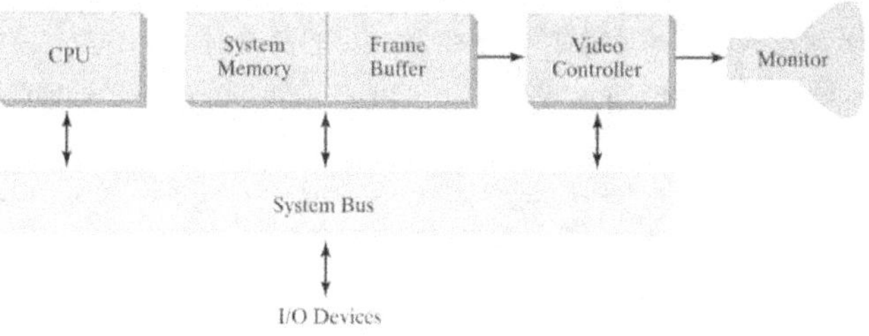

Figure 1.12: Architecture of a Raster System

The screen surface is then represented as the first quadrant of a two-dimensional system, with positive x values increasing to the right and positive y values increasing from bottom to top. (On some personal computers, the coordinate origin is referenced at the upper left comer of the screen, so the y values are inverted) Scan lines are then labeled from ymax, at the top of the screen to 0 at the bottom. Along each scan line, screen pixel positions are labeled from 0 to xmax. Since the screen must be refreshed at the rate of 60 frames per second, the simple procedure illustrated in Fig. 1.13 cannot be accommodated by typical RAM chips. The cycle time is too slow.

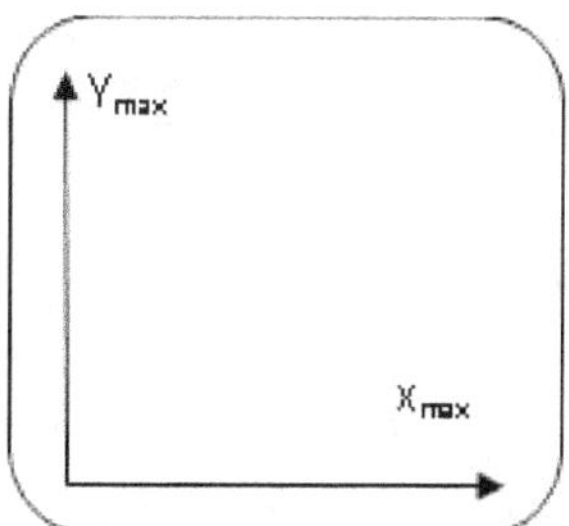

Figure 1.13: The Origin of the Coordinate System

To speed up pixel processing, video controllers can retrieve multiple pixel values from the refresh buffer on each pass. The multiple pixel intensities are then stored in a separate register and used to control the CRT beam intensity for a group of adjacent pixels. When that group of pixels has been processed, the next block of pixel values is retrieved from the frame buffer.

A number of other operations can be performed by the video controller, besides the basic refreshing operations. For various applications, the video controller can retrieve pixel intensities from different memory areas on different refresh cycles. In high quality systems, for example, two frame buffers are often provided so that one buffer can be used for refreshing while the other is being filled with intensity values. Then the two buffers can switch roles. This provides a fast mechanism-for generating real-time animations, since different views of moving objects can be successively loaded into the refresh buffers. Also, some transformations can be accomplished by the video controller. Areas of the screen can be enlarged, reduced, or moved from one location to another during the refresh cycles. In addition, the video controller often contains a lookup table, so that pixel values in the frame buffer are used to access the lookup table instead of controlling the CRT beam intensity directly.

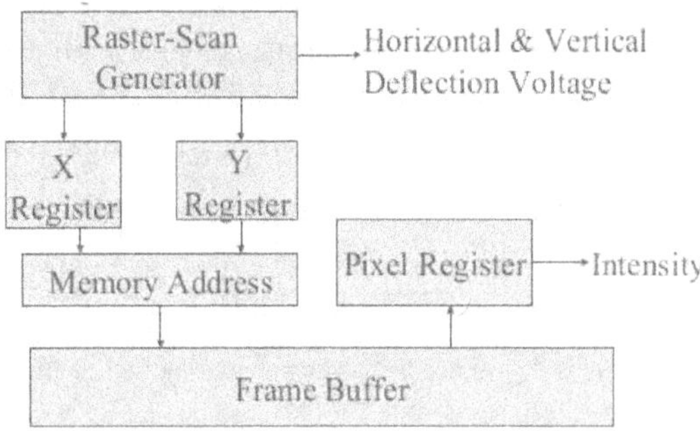

Figure 1.14: Basic Video-controller Refresh Operations

Raster-Scan Display Processor

Figure 1.15 shows one way to set up the organization of a raster system containing a separate display processor, sometimes referred to as a graphics controller or a display coprocessor. The purpose of the display processor is to free the CPU from the graphics chores. In addition to the system memory, a separate display processor memory area can also be provided. A major task of the display processor is digitizing a picture definition given in an application program into a set of pixel-intensity values for storage in the frame buffer. This digitization process is called scan conversion. Graphics commands specifying straight lines and other geometric objects are scan converted into a set of discrete intensity points. Scan converting a straight-line segment, for example, means that we have to locate the pixel positions closest to the line path and store the intensity for each position in the frame buffer. Similar methods are used for scan converting curved lines and polygon outlines.

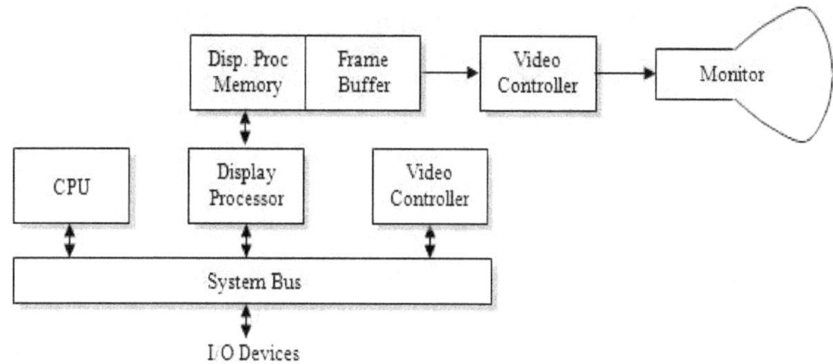

Figure 1.15: Architecture of a Raster-graphics System with a display Processor

1.4.   Random-scan Systems

The organization of a simple random-scan (vector) system is shown in Fig. 1.16. An application program is input and stored in the system memory along with a graphics package. Graphics commands in the application program are translated by the graphics package into a display file stored in the system memory. This display file is then accessed by the display processor to refresh the screen. The display processor cycles through each command in the display file program once during every refresh cycle. Sometimes the display processor in a random-scan system is referred to as a display processing unit or a graphics controller.

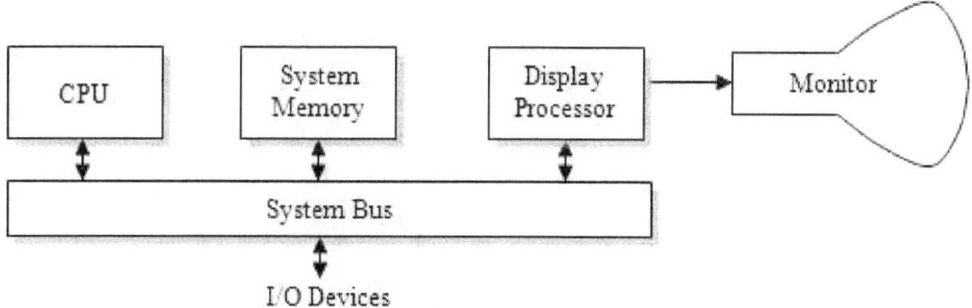

Figure 1.16: Architecture of a Simple Random Scan System

Graphics patterns are drawn on a random-scan system by directing the electron beam along the component lines of the picture. Lines are defined by the values for their coordinate endpoints, and these input coordinate values are converted to x and y deflection voltages. A scene is then drawn one line at a time by positioning the beam to fill in the line between specified endpoints.

1.5.   Graphics Monitors and Workstations

Most graphics monitors today operate as raster scan displays, and here we survey a few of the many graphics hardware configurations available. Graphics systems range from small general-purpose computer systems with graphics capabilities to sophisticated full color systems that are designed specifically for graphics applications. A typical screen resolution for personal Computer systems, such as the Apple Quadra, is 640 by 480, although screen resolution and other system capabilities vary depending on the size and cost of the system. Diagonal screen dimensions for general-purpose personal computer systems can range from 12 to 21 inches, and allowable color selections range from 16 to over 32,000. For workstations specifically designed for graphics applications, such as the systems, typical screen resolution is 1280 by 1024, with a screen diagonal of 16 inches or more. Graphics workstations can be configured with from 8 to 24 bits per pixel (full-color systems), with higher screen resolutions, faster processors, and other options available in high-end systems. A high-definition graphics monitor used in applications such as air traffic control, simulation, medical imaging, and CAD. This system has a diagonal screen size of 27 inches, resolutions ranging from 2048 by 1536 to 2560 by 2048, with refresh rates of 80 Hz or 60 Hz non-interlaced. A multi-screen system called the Media Wall, provides a large "wall-sized display area. This system is designed for applications that require large area displays in brightly lighted environments, such as at trade shows, conventions, retail stores, museums, or passenger terminals. Media Wall operates by splitting images into a number of Sections and distributing the sections over an array of monitors or projectors using a graphics adapter and satellite control units. An array of up to 5 by 5 monitors, each with a resolution of 640 by 480, can be used in the Media Wall to provide an overall resolution of 3200 by 2400 for either static scenes or animations. Scenes can be displayed behind mullions, or the mullions can be eliminated to display a continuous picture with no breaks between the various sections. Many graphics workstations, such as some of those are configured with two monitors. One monitor can be used to show all features of an object or scene, while the second monitor displays the detail in some part of the picture. Another use for dual-monitor systems is to view a picture on one monitor and display graphics options (menus) for manipulating the picture components on the other monitor.

1.6.   Input Devices

Various devices are available for data input on graphics workstations. Most systems have a keyboard and one or more additional devices specially designed for interactive input. These include a mouse, trackball, spaceball, joystick, digitizers, dials, and button boxes. Some other input devices used in particular applications are data gloves, touch panels, image scanners, and voice systems.

Keyboards

An alphanumeric keyboard on a graphics system is used primarily as a device for entering text strings. The keyboard is an efficient device for inputting such nongraphic data as picture labels associated with a graphics display. Keyboards can also be provided with features to facilitate entry of screen coordinates, menu selections, or graphics functions. Cursor-control keys and function keys are common features on general purpose keyboards. Function keys allow users to enter frequently used operations in a single keystroke, and cursor-control keys can be used to select displayed objects or coordinate positions by positioning the screen cursor. Other types of cursor- positioning devices, such as a trackball or joystick, are included on some keyboards

Mouse

A mouse is small hand-held box used to position the screen cursor. Wheels or rollers on the bottom of the mouse can be used to record the amount and direction of movement. Another method for detecting mouse motion is with an optical sensor. For these systems, the mouse is moved over a special mouse pad that has a grid of horizontal and vertical lines. The optical sensor detects movement across the lines in the grid.

Trackball and Spaceball

A trackball is a ball that can be rotated with the fingers or palm of the hand, to produce screen-cursor movement. Potentiometers, attached to the ball, measure the amount and direction of rotation. Trackballs are often mounted on keyboards or other devices such as the Z mouse.

While a trackball is a two-dimensional positioning device, a spaceball provides six degrees of freedom. Unlike the trackball, a spaceball does not actually move. Strain gauges measure the amount of pressure applied to the spaceball to provide input for spatial positioning and orientation as the ball is pushed or pulled in various directions. Spaceballs are used for three-dimensional positioning and selection operations in virtual-reality systems, modeling, animation, CAD, and other applications.

Joysticks

A joystick consists of a small, vertical lever (called the stick) mounted on a base that is used to steer the screen cursor around. Most joysticks select screen positions with actual stick movement; others respond to pressure on the stick. Some joysticks are mounted on a keyboard; others function as stand-alone units.

Data Glove

A data glove that can be used to grasp a "virtual" object. The glove is constructed with a series of sensors that detect hand and finger motions. Electromagnetic coupling between transmitting antennas and receiving antennas is used to provide information about the position and orientation of the hand. The transmitting and receiving antennas can each be structured as a set of three mutually perpendicular coils, forming a three- dimensional Cartesian coordinate system. Input from the glove can be used to position or manipulate objects in a virtual scene. A two-dimensional projection of the scene can be viewed on a video monitor, or a three-dimensional projection can be viewed with a headset.

Digitizers

A common device for drawing, painting, or interactively selecting coordinate positions on an object is a digitizer. These devices can be used to input coordinate values in either a two-dimensional or a three-dimensional space. Typically, a digitizer is used to scan over a drawing or object and to input a set of discrete coordinate positions, which can be joined with straight-line segments to approximate the curve or surface shapes.

One type of digitizer is the graphics tablet (also referred to as a data tablet), which is used to input two-dimensional coordinates by activating a hand cursor or stylus at selected positions on a flat surface. A hand cursor contains cross hairs for sighting positions, while a stylus is a pencil-shaped device that is pointed at positions on the tablet.

Image Scanners

Drawings, graphs, color and black-and-white photos, or text can be stored for computer processing with an image scanner by passing an optical scanning mechanism over the information to be stored. The gradations of gray scale or color are then recorded and stored in an array. Once we have the internal representation of a picture, we can apply transformations to rotate, scale, or crop the picture to a particular screen area. We can also apply various image-processing methods to modify the array representation of the picture. For scanned text input, various editing operations can be performed on the stored documents. Some scanners are able to scan either graphical representations or text, and they come in a variety of sizes and capabilities.

Touch Panels

Touch panels allow displayed objects or screen positions to be selected with the touch of a finger. A typical application of touch panels is for the selection of processing options that are represented with graphical icons. Some systems, such as the plasma panels are designed with touch screens. Other systems can be adapted for touch input by fitting a transparent device with a touch sensing mechanism over the video monitor screen. Touch input can be recorded using optical, electrical, or acoustical methods.

Light Pens

Such pencil-shaped devices are used to select screen positions by detecting the light coming from points on the CRT screen. They are sensitive to the short burst of light emitted from the phosphor coating at the instant the electron beam strikes a particular point. Other Light sources, such as the background light in the room, are usually not detected by a light pen. An activated light pen, pointed at a spot on the screen as the electron beam lights up that spot, generates an electrical pulse that causes the coordinate position of the electron beam to be recorded. As with cursor-positioning devices, recorded Light-pen coordinates can be used to position an object or to select a processing option.

Voice Systems

Speech recognizers are used in some graphics workstations as input devices to accept voice commands The voice-system input can be used to initiate graphics operations or to enter data. These systems operate by matching an input against a predefined dictionary of words and phrase. A dictionary is set up for a particular operator by having, the operator speak the command words to be used into the system. Each word is spoke? Several times, and the system analyzes the word and establishes a frequency pattern for that word in the dictionary along with the corresponding function to be performed. Later, when a voice command is given, the system searches the dictionary for a frequency-pattern match.

2. Output Primitives

2.1. Points and Lines

Point plotting is accomplished by converting a single coordinate position furnished by an application program into appropriate operations for the output device in use. With a CRT monitor, for example, the electron beam is turned on to illuminate the screen phosphor at the selected location. How the electron beam is positioned depends on the display technology. A random-scan (vector) system stores point-plotting instructions in the display list, and coordinate values in these instructions are converted to deflection voltages that position the electron beam at the screen locations to be plotted during each refresh cycle. For a black and white raster system, on the other hand, a point is plotted by setting the bit value corresponding to a specified screen position within the frame buffer to 1. Then, as the electron beam sweeps across each horizontal scan line, it emits a burst of electrons (plots a point) whenever a value of 1 is encountered in the frame buffer. With an RGB system, the frame buffer is loaded with the color codes for the intensities that are to be displayed at the screen pixel positions.

Line drawing is accomplished by calculating intermediate positions along the line path between two specified endpoint positions. An output device is then directed to fill in these positions between the endpoints. For analog devices, such as a vector pen plotter or a random-scan display, a straight line can be drawn smoothly from one endpoint to the other. Linearly varying horizontal and vertical deflection voltages are generated that are proportional to the required changes in the x and y directions to produce the smooth line.

2.2. Line-Drawing Algorithms

The Cartesian slope-intercept equation for a straight line is

$$y = m.\, x + b \qquad (2.1)$$

with m representing the slope of the line and b as the y intercept. Given that the two endpoints of a he segment are specified at positions (x1, y1) and (x2, y2), as shown in Fig. 2.1, we can determine values for the slope m and y intercept b with the following calculations,

$$m = \frac{y_2 - y_1}{x_2 - x_1} \qquad (2.2)$$

$$b = y_1 - m \cdot x_1 \qquad (2.3)$$

Algorithms for displaying straight lines are based on the line equation 2.1 and the calculations given in Eqn. 2.2 and 2.3. For any given x interval Δx along a line, we can compute the corresponding y interval from

Δy Eq.2.2 as

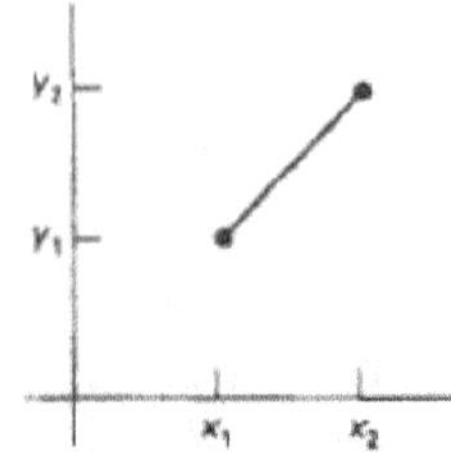

Figure 2.1: Line Path

$$\Delta y = m\, \Delta x \qquad (2.4)$$

Similarly, we can obtain the x interval Δx corresponding to a specified Δy as,

$$\Delta x = \frac{\Delta y}{m} \qquad (2.5)$$

These equations form the basis for determining deflection voltages in analog devices. For lines with slope magnitudes $|\, m\, | < 1$, Δx can be set proportional to a small horizontal deflection voltage and the corresponding vertical deflection is then set proportional to Δy as calculated from Eq.2.4. For lines whose slopes have magnitudes $|\, m\, | > 1$, Δy can be set proportional to a small vertical deflection voltage with the corresponding horizontal deflection voltage set proportional to Δx, calculated from Eq. 2.5. For lines with $m = 1$, $\Delta x = \Delta y$ and the horizontal and vertical deflections voltages are equal. In each case, a smooth line with slope m is generated between the specified endpoints.

DDA Algorithm

The *digital differential analyzer (DDA)* is a scan-conversion line algorithm based on calculating either Δy or Δx, using Eq. 2.4 or Eq. 2.5. We sample the line at unit intervals in one coordinate and determine corresponding integer values nearest the line path for the other coordinate.

Consider first a line with positive slope, as shown in Fig. 2.1. If the slope is less than or equal to 1, we sample at unit x intervals $(\Delta x = 1)$ and compute each successive y value as,

$$y_{k+1} = y_k + m \qquad (2.6)$$

Subscript k takes integer values starting from 1, for the first point, and increases by 1 until the final endpoint is reached. Since m can be any real number between 0 and 1, the calculated y values must be rounded to the nearest integer.

For lines with a positive slope greater than 1, we reverse the roles of x and y. That is, we sample at unit

y intervals $(\Delta y = 1)$ and calculate each succeeding x value as,

$$x_{k+1} = x_k + \frac{1}{m}$$

(2.7)

Equations 2.6 and 2.7 are based on the assumption that lines are to be processed from the left endpoint to the right endpoint (Fig. 2.1). If this processing is reversed, so that the starting endpoint is at the right, then either we have $\Delta x = -1$ and

$$y_{k+1} = y_k - m$$

(2.8)

or (when the slope is greater than 1) we have $\Delta y = -1$ with

$$x_{k+1} = x_k - \frac{1}{m}$$

(2.9)

Equations 2.6 through 2.9 can also be used to calculate pixel positions along a line with negative slope. If the absolute value of the slope is less than 1 and the start endpoint is at the left, we set $\Delta x = 1$ and calculate y values with Eq. 2.6. When the start endpoint is at the right (for the same slope), we set $\Delta x = -1$ and obtain y positions from Eq. 2.8. Similarly, when the absolute value of a negative slope is water than 1, we use $\Delta y = -1$ and Eq. 2.9 or we use $\Delta y = 1$ and Eq. 2.7.

Bresenham's Line Algorithm

To illustrate Brsenham's approach, we-first consider the scan-conversion process for lines with positive slope less than 1. Pixel positions along a line path are then determined by sampling at unit x intervals. Starting from the left endpoint (x_0, y_0) of a given line, we step to each successive column $(x$ position) and plot the pixel whose scan-line y value is closest to the line path. Assuming we have determined that the pixel at (x_k, y_k) is to be displayed, we next need to decide which pixel to plot in column x_{k+1}. Our choices are the pixels at positions (x_k+1, y_k) and (x_k+1, y_k+1).

At sampling position x_{k+1}, we label vertical pixel separations from the mathematical line path as d1 and d2. They coordinate on the mathematical line at pixel column position x_k+1 is calculated as

$$y = m (x_k + 1) + b \qquad\qquad (2.10)$$

Then,

$d1 = y - yk$

$\quad = m (x_k + 1) + b - yk$

and

$d2 = (y_k + 1) - y$

$\quad = y_k + 1 - m (x_k + 1) - b$

The difference between these two separations is,

$$d1 - d2 = 2m (x_k + 1) - 2y_k + 2b - 1 \qquad (2.11)$$

A decision parameter pk for the kth step in the line algorithm can be obtained by rearranging Eq. 2.11 so that it involves only integer calculations. We accomplish this by substituting $m = \Delta y / \Delta x$, where Δy and Δx are the vertical and horizontal separations of the endpoint positions, and defining:

$pk = \Delta x(d1 - d2)$

$$\quad = 2\Delta y \cdot x_k - 2\Delta x \cdot y_k + c \qquad\qquad (2.12)$$

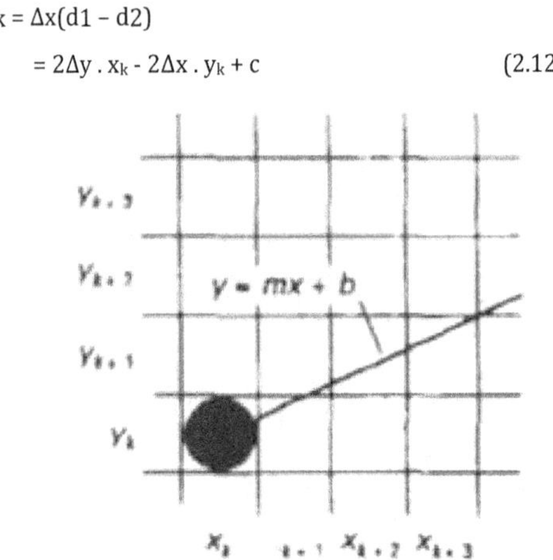

Figure 2.2: A Pixel in Column x_k on Scan Line y_k

The sign of p_k is the same as the sign of d1 – d2, since $\Delta x > 0$ for our example. Parameter c is constant and has the value $2\Delta y + \Delta x(2b - 1)$,

Which is independent of pixel position and will be eliminated in the recursive calculations for p_k. If the pixel at y_k is closer to the line path than the pixel at y_k +1 (that is, d1 < d2), then decision parameter p_k is negative. In that case, we plot the lower pixel; otherwise, we plot the upper pixel. Coordinate changes along the line occur in unit steps in either the x or y directions. Therefore, we can obtain the values of successive decision parameters using incremental integer calculations. At step k + 1, the decision parameter is evaluated from Eq. 2.12 as

$$p_{k+1} = 2\Delta y \,.\, x_{k+1} - 2\Delta x \,.\, y_{k+1} + c$$

Subtracting Eq. 2.12 from the preceding equation, we have,

$$p_{k+1} - p_k = 2\Delta y \,(x_{k+1} - x_k) - 2\Delta x \,(y_{x+1} - y_k)$$

but $x_{k+1} = x_k + 1$, so that,

$$p_{k+1} = p_k + 2\Delta y - 2\Delta x \,(y_{x+1} - y_k) \qquad\qquad (2.13)$$

where the term $y_{k+1} - y_k$ is either 0 or 1, depending on the sign of parameter p_k. This recursive calculation of decision parameters is performed at each integer x position, starting at the left coordinate endpoint of the line. The first parameter, p_0, is evaluated from Eq. 2.12 at the starting pixel position (x_0, y_0) and with m evaluated as $\Delta y / \Delta x$:

$$p_0 = 2\Delta y - \Delta x \qquad\qquad (2.14)$$

We can summarize Bresenham line drawing for a line with a positive slope less than 1 in the following listed steps. The constants $2\Delta y$ and $2\Delta y - 2\Delta x$ are calculated once for each line to be scan converted, so the arithmetic involves only integer addition and subtraction of these two constants.

Bresenham's Line-Drawing Algorithm for $| m | < 1$

1. Input the two line endpoints and store the left endpoint in (x_0, y_0)

2. Load (x_0, y_0) into the frame buffer; that is, plot the first point.

3. Calculate constants Δx, Δy, $2\Delta y$, and $2\Delta y - 2\Delta x$, and obtain the starting value for the decision parameter as

$$p_0 = 2\Delta y - \Delta x$$

4. At each x_k along the line, starting at $k = 0$, perform the following test:

If $P_k < 0$, the next point to plot is (x_{k+1}, y_k) and

$$p_{k+1} = p_k + 2\Delta y$$

Otherwise, the next point to plot is $(x_k + 1, y_k + 1)$ and

$$p_{k+1} = p_k + 2\Delta y - 2\Delta x$$

5. Repeat step 4 Δx times.

Parallel Line Algorithms

The line-generating algorithms we have discussed so far determine pixel positions sequentially. With a parallel computer, we can calculate pixel positions along a line path simultaneously by partitioning the computations among the various processors available. Given n_p processors, we can set up a parallel Bresenham line algorithm by subdividing the line path into n_p partitions and simultaneously generating line segments in each of the subintervals. For a line with slope $0 < m < 1$ and left endpoint coordinate position *(x0, y0)*, we partition the line along the positive *x* direction.

The distance between beginning x positions of adjacent partitions can be calculated as

$$\Delta x_p = \frac{\Delta x + n_p - 1}{n_p}$$

$$(2.15)$$

where Δx is the width of the line, and the value for partition width Δxp is computed using integer division. Numbering the partitions, and the processor as 0, 1, 2, up to n_p-1, we calculate the starting x coordinate for the kth partition as

$$x_k = x_0 + k \, \Delta x_p \qquad\qquad (2.16)$$

To apply Bresenham's algorithm over the partitions, we need the initial value for the y coordinate and the initial value for the decision parameter in each partition. The change Δyp in the y direction over each partition is calculated from the line slope m and partition width Δxp.

$$\Delta y_p = m\Delta x_p \qquad\qquad (2.17)$$

At the kth partition, the starting y coordinate is then,

$$y_k = y_0 + \text{round}(k\Delta y_p) \qquad\qquad (2.18)$$

The initial decision parameter for Bresenham's algorithm at the start of the kth subinterval is obtained from Eq. 2.12:

$$P_k = (k\Delta x_p)\,(2\Delta y) - \text{round}(k\Delta y_p)\,(2\Delta x) + 2\Delta y - \Delta x \qquad\qquad (2.19)$$

Each processor then calculates pixel positions over its assigned subinterval using the starting decision parameter value for that subinterval and the starting coordinates (xk, yk) We can also reduce the floating-point calculations to integer arithmetic in the computations for starting values yk and pk by substituting m = Δy / Δx and rearranging terms. The extension of the parallel Bresenham algorithm to a line with slope greater than 1 is achieved by partitioning the line in the y direction and calculating beginning x values for the partitions. For negative slopes, we increment coordinate values in one direction and decrement in the other.

where

$$A = \frac{-\Delta y}{linelength}$$

$$B = \frac{\Delta x}{linelength}$$

$$C = \frac{x_0 \Delta y - y_0 \Delta x}{linelength}$$

with

$$linelength = \sqrt{\Delta x^2 + \Delta y^2}$$

Another way to set up parallel algorithms on raster systems is to assign each processor to a particular group of screen pixels. With a sufficient number of processors, we can assign each processor to one pixel within some screen region. This approach can be adapted to line display by assigning one processor to each of the pixels within the limits of the line coordinate extents and calculating pixel distances from the line path. The number of pixels within the bounding box of a line is Δx. Δy. Perpendicular distance d from the line to a pixel with coordinates (x, y) is obtained with the calculation

$$d = Ax + By + c \qquad (2.20)$$

Once the constants A, B, and C have been evaluated for the line, each processor needs to perform two multiplications and two additions to compute the pixel distance d. A pixel is plotted if d is less than a specified line-thickness parameter.

2.3. Circle-Generating Algorithms

Since the circle is a frequently used component in pictures and graphs, a procedure for generating either full circles or circular arcs is included in most graphics packages.

Properties of Circles

A circle is defined as the set of points that are all at a given distance r from a center position (xc, yc) (Fig. 2.3). This distance relationship is expressed by the Pythagorean theorem in Cartesian coordinates as

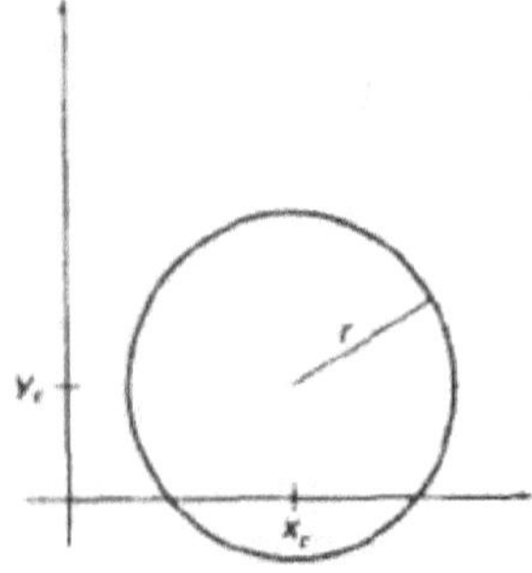

Figure 2.3: Circle with Center Coordinates(x_c, y_c) and Radius r

$$(x - x_c)^2 + (y - y_c)^2 = r^2 \qquad (2.20)$$

We could use this equation to calculate the position of points on a circle circumference by stepping along the x axis in unit steps from $x_c - r$ to $x_c + r$ and calculating the corresponding y values at each position as

$$y = y_c \pm \sqrt{r^2 - (x_c - x)^2} \qquad (2.21)$$

But this is not the best method for generating a circle. One problem with this approach is that it involves considerable computation at each step. Moreover, the spacing between plotted pixel positions is not uniform, as demonstrated in Fig. 2.4

We could adjust the spacing by interchanging x and y (stepping through y values and calculating x values) whenever the absolute value of the slope of the circle is greater than 1.

Another way to eliminate the unequal spacing shown in Fig. 2.4 is to calculate points along the circular boundary using polar coordinates r and θ

(Fig. 2.3). Expressing the circle equation in parametric polar form yields the pair of equations

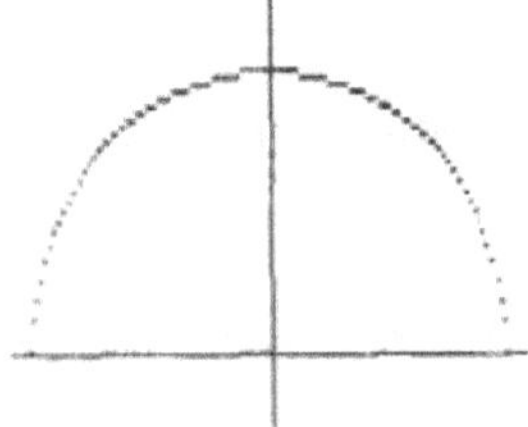

Figure 2.4: Positive Half of a Cycle

$$x = x_c + r \cos \theta$$

$$y = y_c + r \sin \theta \qquad\qquad (2.22)$$

When a display is generated with these equations using a fixed angular step size, a circle is plotted with equally spaced points along the circumference. The step size chosen for θ depends on the application and the display device.

Computation can be reduced by considering the symmetry of circles. The shape of the circle is similar in each quadrant. We can generate the circle in the second quadrant of the xy plane by noting that the two circle sections are symmetric with respect plotted with respect to the y axis. And circle sections in the third and fourth quadrants can be obtained from sections in the first and second quadrants by considering symmetry about the x axis. We can take this one step further and note that there is also symmetry between octants. Circle sections in adjacent octants within one quadrant are symmetric with respect to the 45^0 line dividing the two octants. These symmetry conditions are illustrated in Fig. 2.5, where a point at position (x, y) on a one-eighth circle sector is mapped into the seven circle points in the other octants of the xy plane. Taking advantage of the circle symmetry in this way we can generate all pixel positions around a circle by calculating only the points within the sector from x = 0 to x = y.

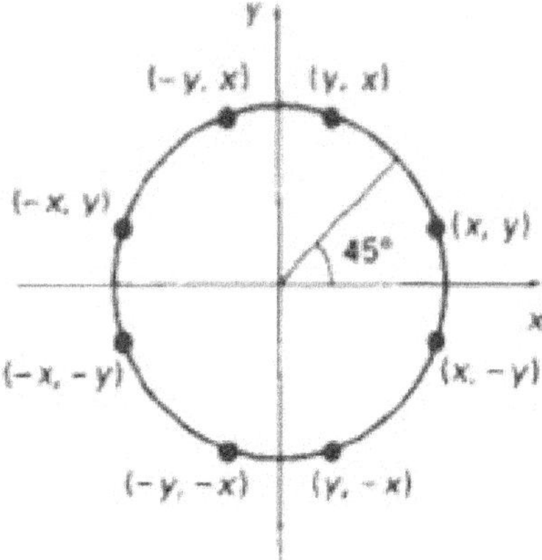

Figure 2.5: Symmetry of a Circle. Calculation of a Circle Point (x, y) in One Octant Yields the Circle Points shown for the other Seven Octants

Midpoint Circle Algorithm

As in the raster line algorithm, we sample at unit intervals and determine the closest pixel position to the specified circle path at each step. For a given radius r and screen center position (xc, yc), we can first set up our algorithm to calculate pixel positions around a circle path centered at the coordinate origin (0,0). Then each calculated position (x, y) is moved to its proper screen position by adding xc to x and yc to y. Along the circle section from x = 0 to x = y in the first quadrant, the slope of the curve varies from 0 to -1. Therefore, we can take unit steps in the positive x direction over this octant and use a decision parameter to determine which of the two possible y positions is closer to the circle path at each step. Positions in the other seven octants are then obtained by symmetry.

To apply the midpoint method, we define a circle function:

$$fcircle(x,y) = x^2 + y^2 - r^2 \qquad (2.23)$$

Any point (x, y) on the boundary of the circle with radius r satisfies the equation fcircle(x,y) = 0. If the point is in the interior of the circle, the circle function is negative. And if the point is outside the circle, the circle function is positive. To summarize, the relative position of any point (x. v) can be determined by checking the sign of the circle function:

$$f_{circle}(x, y) \begin{cases} < 0, & \text{if } (x, y) \text{ is inside the circle boundary} \\ = 0, & \text{if } (x, y) \text{ is on the circle boundary} \\ > 0, & \text{if } (x, y) \text{ is outside the circle boundary} \end{cases} \qquad (2.24)$$

The circle-function test are performed for the mid-positions between pixels near the circle path at each sampling step. Thus, the circle function is the decision parameter in the midpoint algorithm, and we can set up incremental calculations for this function as we did in the line algorithm.

The midpoint between the two candidate pixels at Sampling position x_k + 1. Assuming we have just plotted the pixel at (x_k, y_k), we next need to determine whether the pixel at position $(x_k + 1, y_k)$ or the one at position $(x_k + 1, y_k - 1)$ is closer to the circle. Our decision parameter is the circle function evaluated at the midpoint between these two pixels:

$$p_k = f_{circle}\left(x_k + 1, y_k - \frac{1}{2}\right)$$

$$= (x_k + 1)^2 + \left(y_k - \frac{1}{2}\right)^2 - r^2 \qquad (2.25)$$

If pk < 0, this midpoint is inside the circle and the pixel on scan line yk is closer to the circle boundary.

Otherwise, the mid-position is outside or on the circle boundary, and we select the pixel on scanline $y_k - 1$.

Successive decision parameters are obtained using incremental calculations. We obtain a recursive expression for the next decision parameter by evaluating the circle function at sampling position $x_{k+1} + 1 = x_k + 2$,

$$p_{k+1} = f_{circle}\left(x_{k+1} + 1, y_{k+1} - \frac{1}{2}\right)$$

$$= [(x_k + 1) + 1]^2 + \left(y_{k+1} - \frac{1}{2}\right)^2 - r^2$$

Or

$$p_{k+1} = p_k + 2(x_k + 1) + (y_{k+1}^2 - y_k^2) - (y_{k+1} - y_k) + 1$$

where y_{k+1} is either y_k or yk-1, depending on the sign of pk.

$$2x_{k+1} = 2x_k + 2$$

$$2y_{k+1} = 2y_k - 2 \tag{2.26}$$

Increments for obtaining p_{k+1} are either $2x_{k+1} + 1$ (if p_k is negative) or $2x_{k+1} + 1 - 2y_{k+1}$. Evaluation of the terms $2x_{k+1}$ and $2y_{k+1}$ can also be done incrementally as

The initial decision parameter is obtained by evaluating the circle function at the start position $(x_0, y_0) = (0, r)$:

$$p_0 = f_{circle}\left(1, r - \frac{1}{2}\right)$$

$$= 1 + \left(r - \frac{1}{2}\right)^2 - r^2$$

Or

$$p_0 = \frac{5}{4} - r \tag{2.27}$$

If the radius r is specified as an integer, we can simply round p_0 to $p_0 = 1 - r$ (for r an integer) since all increments are integers.

Midpoint Circle Algorithm

1. Input radius r and circle center (x_c, y_c), and obtain the first point on the circumference of a circle centered on the origin as

$$(x_0, y_0) = (0, r)$$

2. Calculate the initial value of the decision parameter as

$$p_0 = \frac{5}{4} - r$$

3. At each x_k position, starting at $k = 0$, perform the following test: If $p_k < 0$, the next point along the circle centered on $(0, 0)$ is (x_{k+1}, y_k) and

$$p_{k+1} = p_k + 2x_{k+1} + 1$$

Otherwise, the next point along the circle is $(x_k + 1, y_k - 1)$ and

$$p_{k+1} = p_k + 2x_{k+1} + 1 - 2y_{k+1}$$

where $2x_{k+1} = 2x_k + 2$ and $2y_{k+1} = 2y_k - 2$.
4. Determine symmetry points in the other seven octants.
5. Move each calculated pixel position (x, y) onto the circular path centered on (x_c, y_c) and plot the coordinate values:

$$x = x + x_c \qquad y = y + y_c$$

6. Repeat steps 3 through 5 until $x \geq y$.

2.4. Ellipse-Generating Algorithms

Properties of Ellipses

An ellipse is defined as the set of points such that the sum of the distances from two fixed positions (foci) is the same for all points (Fig. 2.6). If the distances to the two foci from any point P = (x, y) on the ellipse are labeled d1 and d2, then the general equation of an ellipse can be stated as,

$$d1 + d2 = \text{constant} \tag{2.28}$$

Expressing distances d1 and d2 in terms of the focal coordinates

$F_1 = (x_1, y_1)$ and $F_2 = (x_2, y_2)$, we have

$$\sqrt{(x - x_1)^2 + (y - y_1)^2} + \sqrt{(x - x_2)^2 + (y - y_2)^2} = \text{constant} \tag{2.29}$$

By squaring this equation, isolating the remaining radical, and then squaring again, we can rewrite the general ellipse equation in the form where the coefficients A, B, C, D, E, and F are evaluated in terms of the focal coordinates and the dimensions of the major and minor axes of the ellipse. The major axis is the straight line segment extending from one side of the ellipse to the other through the foci. The minor axis spans the shorter dimension of the ellipse, bisecting the major axis at the halfway position (ellipse center) between the two foci.

$$Ax^2 + By^2 + Cxy + Dx + Ey + F = 0 \qquad (2.30)$$

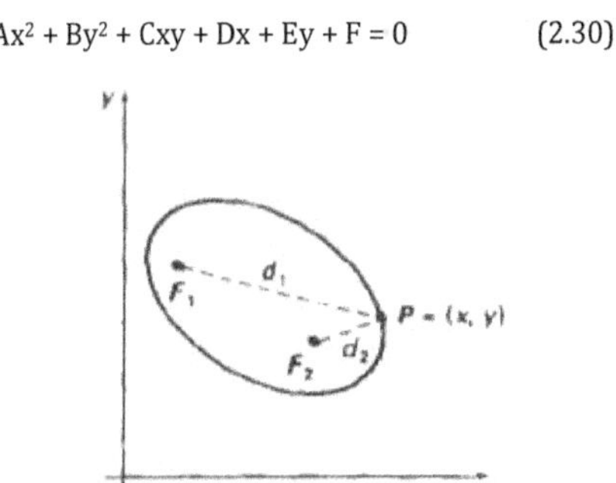

Figure 2.6: Ellipse Generated about Foci F1 and F2

Ellipse equations are greatly simplified if the major and minor axes are oriented to align with the coordinate axes. In Fig. 2.7, we show an ellipse in "standard position" with major and minor axes oriented parallel to the x and y axes. Parameter r_x for this example labels the semi-major axis, and parameter r_y, labels the semi-minor axis. The equation of the ellipse shown in Fig. 2.7 can be written in terms of the ellipse center coordinates and parameters r_x and r_y as

$$\left(\frac{x - x_c}{r_x}\right)^2 + \left(\frac{y - y_c}{r_y}\right)^2 = 1 \qquad (2.31)$$

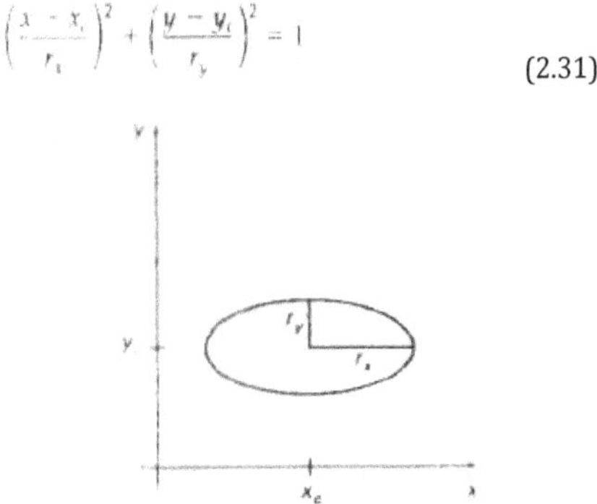

Figure 2.7: Ellipse Centered at (xc, yc)

Using polar coordinates r and 0. We can also describe the ellipse in standard position with the parametric equations:

$$x = xc + rx + \cos\theta \qquad\qquad (2.32)$$

$$y = yc + ry + \sin\theta$$

Symmetry considerations can be used to further reduce computations. An ellipse in standard position is symmetric between quadrants, but unlike a circle, it is not symmetric between the two octants of a quadrant. Thus, we must calculate pixel positions along the elliptical arc throughout one quadrant, then we obtain positions in the remaining three quadrants by symmetry (Fig 2.8).

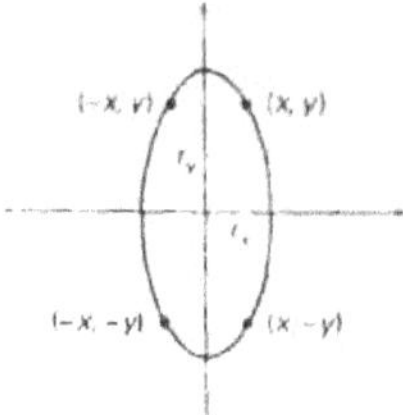

Figure 2.8: Symmetry of an Ellipse Calculation of a Point (x, y)

2.5. Mid-point Ellipse Algorithm

Given parameters r_x, r_y and (x_c, y_c), we determine points (x, y) for an ellipse in standard position centered on the origin, and then we shift the points so the ellipse is centered at (x_c, y_c). We also to display the ellipse in nonstandard position, we could then rotate the ellipse about its center coordinates to reorient the major and minor axes.

The mid-point ellipse method is applied throughout the first quadrant in two parts. Figure 2.9 shows the division of the first quadrant according to the slope, of an ellipse with $r_x < r_y$. We process this quadrant by taking unit steps in the x direction where the slope of the curve has a magnitude less than 1, and taking unit steps in the direction where the slop has a magnitude greater than 1.

Regions 1 and 2 (Fig. 2.9), can he processed in various ways. We can start at position $(0. r_y)$ and step clockwise along the elliptical path in the first quadrant, shifting from unit steps in x to unit steps in y when the slope becomes less than -1.

Alternatively, we could start at $(r_x, 0)$ and select points in a counter clockwise order, shifting from unit steps in y to unit steps in x when the slope becomes greater than -1. With parallel processors, we could calculate pixel positions in the two regions simultaneously. As an example of a sequential implementation of the midpoint algorithm, we take the start position at $(0, r_y)$ and step along the ellipse path in clockwise order throughout the first quadrant. We define an ellipse function from Eq. 2.31 with $(x_c, y_c) = (0,0)$ as

$$f_{ellipse}(x, y) = r_y^2 x^2 + r_x^2 y^2 - r_x^2 r_y^2$$

(2.33)

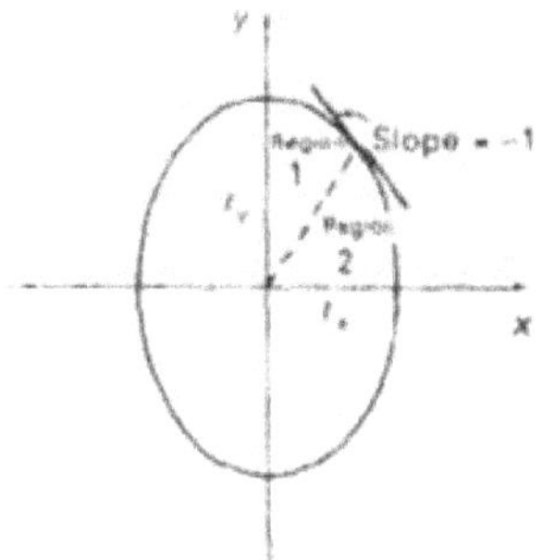

Figure 2.9: Ellipse Processing Regions

which has the following properties,

$$f_{ellipse}(x, y) \begin{cases} < 0, & \text{if } (x, y) \text{ is inside the ellipse boundary} \\ = 0, & \text{if } (x, y) \text{ is on the ellipse boundary} \\ > 0, & \text{if } (x, y) \text{ is outside the ellipse boundary} \end{cases}$$

(2.34)

Thus, the ellipse function fellipse(x, y) serves as the decision parameter in the mid-point algorithm. At each sampling position, we select the next pixel along the ellipse path according to the sign of the ellipse function evaluated at the midpoint between the two candidate pixels.

Starting at $(0, r_y)$, we take unit steps in the x direction until we reach the boundary between region 1 and region 2 Fig. 2.9. Then we switch to unit steps in the y direction over the remainder of the curve in the first quadrant. At each step, we need to test the value of the slope of the curve. The ellipse slope is calculated from Eq. 2.33 as,

$$\frac{dy}{dx} = -\frac{2r_y^2 x}{2r_x^2 y}$$

(2.35)

At the boundary between region 1 and region 2, dy/dx = - 1 and

$$2r_y^2 x = 2r_x^2 y$$

Therefore, we move out of region 1 whenever,

$$2r_y^2 x \geq 2r_x^2 y$$

(2.36)

Assuming position (x_k, y_k) has been selected at the previous step, we determine the next position along the ellipse path by evaluating the decision parameter (that is, the ellipse function 2.33) at this midpoint:

$$p1_k = f_{ellipse}\left(x_k + 1, y_k - \frac{1}{2}\right)$$

$$= r_y^2(x_k + 1)^2 + r_x^2\left(y_k - \frac{1}{2}\right)^2 - r_x^2 r_y^2 \tag{2.37}$$

If $p1_k < 0$, the midpoint is inside the ellipse and the pixel on scan line y, is closer to the ellipse boundary. Otherwise, the mid-position is outside or on the ellipse boundary, and we select the pixel on scan line yk - 1. At the next sampling position $(x_{k+1} + 1 = x_k + 2)$, the decision parameter for region 1 is evaluated as

$$p1_{k+1} = f_{ellipse}\left(x_{k+1} + 1, y_{k+1} - \frac{1}{2}\right)$$

$$= r_y^2[(x_k + 1) + 1]^2 + r_x^2\left(y_{k+1} - \frac{1}{2}\right)^2 - r_x^2 r_y^2$$

Or

$$p1_{k+1} = p1_k + 2r_y^2(x_k + 1) + r_y^2 + r_x^2\left[\left(y_{k+1} - \frac{1}{2}\right)^2 - \left(y_k - \frac{1}{2}\right)^2\right] \tag{2.38}$$

where y_{k+1} is either y_k, or $y_k - 1$, depending on the sign of $p1_k$.

Decision parameters are incremented by the following amounts:

$$increment = \begin{cases} 2r_y^2 x_{k+1} + r_y^2, & \text{if } p1_k < 0 \\ 2r_y^2 x_{k+1} + r_y^2 - 2r_x^2 y_{k+1}, & \text{if } p1_k \geq 0 \end{cases}$$

As in the circle algorithm, increments for the decision parameters can be calculated using only addition and subtraction, since values for the terms $2r_y^2 x$ and $2r_x^2 y$ can also be obtained incrementally. At the initial position $(0, r_y)$, the two terms evaluate to

$$2r_y^2 x = 0 \tag{2.39}$$

$$2r_x^2 y = 2r_x^2 r_y \tag{2.40}$$

As x and y are incremented, updated values are obtained by adding $2r_y^2$ to Eq. 2.39 and subtracting $2r_x^2$ from eq. 2.40. The updated values are compared at each step, and we move from region 1 to region 2 when condition Eq. 2.36 is satisfied.

In region 1, the initial value of the decision parameter is obtained by evaluating the ellipse function at the start position (x0 , y0) = (0, ry),

$$p1_0 = f_{ellipse}\left(1, r_y - \frac{1}{2}\right)$$

$$= r_y^2 + r_x^2\left(r_y - \frac{1}{2}\right)^2 - r_x^2 r_y^2$$

Or

$$p1_0 = r_y^2 - r_x^2 r_y + \frac{1}{4} r_x^2 \tag{2.41}$$

Over region 2, we sample at unit steps in the negative y direction, and the midpoint is now taken between horizontal pixels at each step. For this region, the decision parameter is evaluated as

$$p2_k = f_{ellipse}\left(x_k + \frac{1}{2}, y_k - 1\right)$$

$$= r_y^2\left(x_k + \frac{1}{2}\right)^2 + r_x^2(y_k - 1)^2 - r_x^2 r_y^2 \tag{2.42}$$

If $p2_k > 0$, the mid-position is outside the ellipse boundary, and we select the pixel at xk. If $p2_k \leq 0$, the midpoint is inside or on the ellipse boundary, and we select pixel position x_{k+1}.

To determine the relationship between successive decision parameters in region 2, we evaluate the ellipse function at the next sampling step $y_{k+1} + 1 = y_k + 2$.

$$p2_{k+1} = f_{ellipse}\left(x_{k+1} + \frac{1}{2}, y_{k+1} - 1\right)$$

$$= r_y^2\left(x_{k+1} + \frac{1}{2}\right)^2 + r_x^2[(y_k - 1) - 1]^2 - r_x^2 r_y^2 \tag{2.43}$$

Or

$$p2_{k+1} = p2_k - 2r_x^2(y_k - 1) + r_x^2 + r_y^2\left[\left(x_{k+1} + \frac{1}{2}\right)^2 - \left(x_k + \frac{1}{2}\right)^2\right] \tag{2.44}$$

with x_{k+1} set either to x_k or to $x_k + 1$, depending on the sign of $p2_k$. When we enter region 2, the initial position (x0, y0) is taken as the last position selected in region 1 and the initial derision parameter in region 2 is then

$$p2_0 = f_{ellipse}\left(x_0 + \frac{1}{2}, y_0 - 1\right)$$

$$= r_y^2\left(x_0 + \frac{1}{2}\right) + r_x^2(y_0 - 1)^2 - r_x^2 r_y^2$$

(2.45)

To simplify the calculation of $p2_0$ we could select pixel positions in counter clockwise order starting at $(r_x, 0)$. Unit steps would then be taken in the positive y direction up to the last position selected in region 1.

Midpoint Ellipse Algorithm

Assuming r_x, r_y and the ellipse center are given in integer screen coordinates, we only need incremental integer calculations to determine values for the decision parameters in the midpoint ellipse algorithm. The increments r_x^2, r_y^2, $2r_x^2$ and $2r_y^2$ are evaluated once at the beginning of the procedure. A summary of the midpoint ellipse algorithm is listed in the following steps:

1. Input r_x, r_y and ellipse center (x_c, y_c), and obtain the first point on an ellipse centered on the origin as

$$(x_0, y_0) = (0, r_y)$$

2. Calculate the initial value of the decision parameter in region 1 as

$$p1_0 = r_y^2 - r_x^2 r_y + \frac{1}{4}r_x^2$$

3. At each x_k position in region 1, starting at $k = 0$, perform the following test: If $p1_k < 0$, the next point along the ellipse centered on $(0, 0)$ is $(x_{,k+1}, y_k)$ and

$$p1_{k+1} = p1_k + 2r_y^2 x_{k+1} + r_y^2$$

Otherwise, the next point along the circle is (x_k+1, y_k-1) and

$$p1_{k+1} = p1_k + 2r_y^2 x_{k+1} - 2r_x^2 y_{k+1} + r_y^2$$

With

$$2r_y^2 x_{k+1} = 2r_y^2 x_k + 2r_y^2. \qquad 2r_x^2 y_{k+1} = 2r_x^2 y_k - 2r_x^2$$

and continue until $2ry^2 x \geq 2rx^2 y$.

4. Calculate the initial value of the decision parameter in region 2 using the last point (x_0, y_0) calculated in region 1 as

$$p2_0 = r_y^2\left(x_0 + \frac{1}{2}\right)^2 + r_x^2(y_0 - 1)^2 - r_x^2 r_y^2$$

5. At each y_k position in region 2, starting at k = 0, perform the following test: If $p2_k > 0$, the next point along the ellipse centered on (0, 0) is $(x_k, y_k - 1)$ and

$$p2_{k+1} = p2_k - 2r_x^2 y_{k+1} + r_x^2$$

Otherwise, the next point along the circle is $(x_k + 1, y_k - 1)$ and

$$p2_{k+1} = p2_k + 2r_y^2 x_{k+1} - 2r_x^2 y_{k+1} + r_x^2$$

6. Determine symmetry points in the other three quadrants.

7. Move each calculated pixel position (x, y) onto the elliptical path centered on (x_c, y_c) and plot the coordinate values:

$$x = x + x_c$$

$$y = y + y_c$$

8. Repeat the steps for region 1 until $2r_y^2 x \geq 2r_x^2 y$.

2.6.   Filled-area Primitives

A standard output primitive in general graphics packages is a solid-color or patterned polygon area. Other kinds of area primitives are sometimes available, but polygons are easier to process since they have linear boundaries.

There are two basic approaches to area filling on raster systems. One way to fill an area is to determine the overlap intervals for scan lines that cross the area. Another method for area filling is to start from a given interior position and paint outward from this point until we encounter the specified boundary conditions. The scan-line approach is typically used in general graphics packages to fill polygons, circles, ellipses, and other simple curves. All methods starting from an interior point are useful with more complex boundaries and in interactive painting systems.

Scan-Line Polygon Fill Algorithm

Figure 2.10 illustrates the scan-line procedure for solid filling of polygon areas. For each scan line crossing a polygon, the area-fill algorithm locates the intersection points of the scan line with the polygon edges. These intersection points are then sorted from left to right, and the corresponding frame buffer positions between each intersection pair are set to the specified fill color. In the example of Fig. 2.10, the four pixel intersection positions with the polygon boundaries define two stretches of interior pixels from $x = 10$ to $x = 14$ and from $x = 18$ to x = 24.

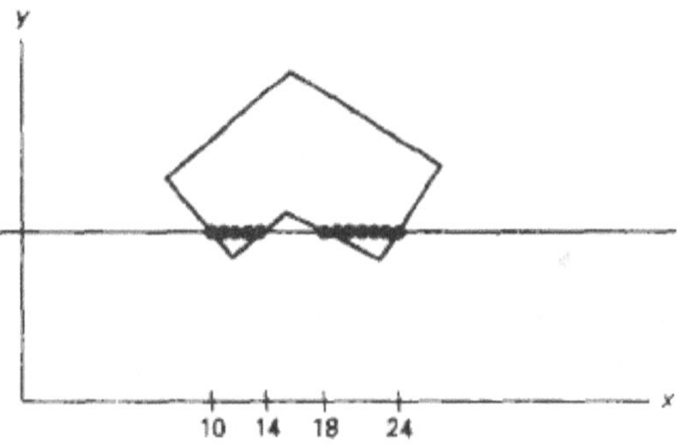

2.10: Interior Pixels along a Scan Line

Some scan-line intersections at polygon vertices require special handling. A scan line passing through a vertex intersects two polygon edges at that position, adding two points to the list of intersections for the scan line. Fig. 2.11 shows two scan lines at positions y and y' that intersect edge endpoints. Scan line y intersects five polygon edges. Scan line y', however, intersects an even number of edges although it also passes through a vertex. Intersection points along scan line y' correctly identify the interior pixel spans. But with scan line y, we need to do some additional processing to determine the correct interior points.

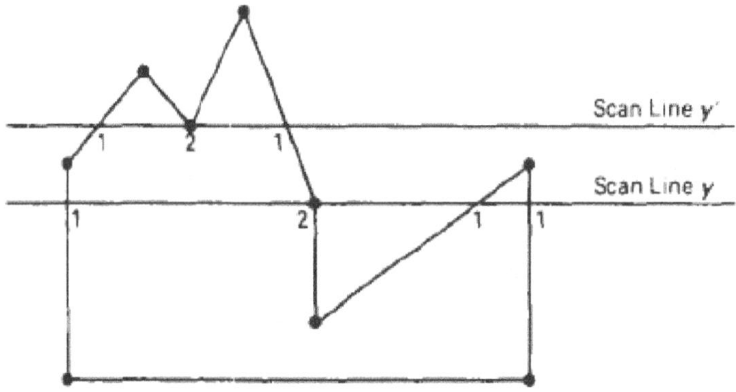

Figure 2.11: Intersection Points along Scan Lines that Intersect Polygon Vertices

The topological difference between scan line y and scan line y' in Fig. 2.11 is identified by noting the position of the intersecting edges relative to the scan line. For scan line y, the two intersecting edges sharing a vertex are on opposite sides of the scan line. But for scan line y', the two intersecting edges are both above the scan line. Thus, the vertices that require additional processing are those that have connecting edges on opposite sides of the scan line.

We can identify these vertices by tracing around the polygon boundary either in clockwise or counter clockwise order and observing the relative changes in vertex y coordinates as we move from one edge to the next. If the endpoint y values of two consecutive edges monotonically increase or decrease, we need to count the middle vertex as a single intersection point for any scan line passing through that vertex. Otherwise, the shared vertex represents a local extremum (minimum or maximum) on the polygon boundary, and the two edge intersections with the scan line passing through that vertex can be added to the intersection list.

Calculations performed in scan-conversion and other graphics algorithms typically take advantage of various *coherence* properties of a scene that is to be displayed. What we mean by *coherence* is simply that the properties of one part of a scene are related in some way to other parts of the scene so that the relationship can be used to reduce processing. Coherence methods often involve incremental calculations applied along a single scan line or between successive scan lines. In determining edge intersections, we can set up incremental coordinate calculations along any edge by exploiting the fact that the slope of the edge is constant from one scan line to the next. Fig 2.12 two successive scan lines crossing a left edge of a polygon. The slope of this polygon boundary line can be expressed in terms of the scan-line intersection coordinates:

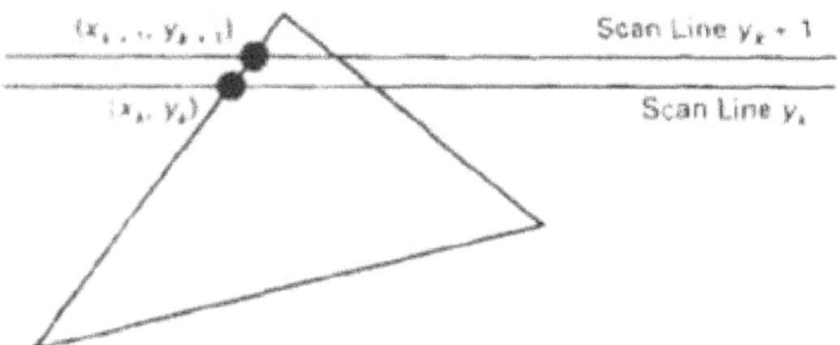

Figure 2.12: Two Successive Scan Lines Intersecting a Polygon Boundary

$$m = \frac{y_{k+1} - y_k}{x_{k+1} - x_k}$$

Since the change in *y* coordinates between the two scan lines is simply

$$y_{k+1} - y_k = 1$$

The x-intersection value xk+1, on the upper scan line can be determined from the x-intersection value *xk* on the preceding scan line as

$$x_{k+1} = x_k + \frac{1}{m}$$

Each successive x intercept can thus be calculated by adding the inverse of the slope and rounding to the nearest integer.

An obvious parallel implementation of the fill algorithm is to assign each scan line crossing the polygon area to a separate processor. Edge-intersection calculations are then performed independently. Along an edge with slope m, the intersection xk value for scan line k above the initial scan line can be calculated as

$$x_k = x_0 + \frac{k}{m}$$

In a sequential fill algorithm, the increment of x values by the amount $1/m$ along an edge can be accomplished with integer operations by recalling that the slope m is the ratio of two integers:

$$m = \frac{\Delta y}{\Delta x}$$

where Δx and Δy are the differences between the edge endpoint x and y coordinate values. Thus, incremental calculations of x intercepts along an edge for successive scan lines can be expressed as

$$x_{k+1} = x_k + \frac{\Delta x}{\Delta y}$$

Using this equation, we can perform integer evaluation of the x intercepts by initializing a counter to 0, then incrementing the counter by the value of Δx each time we move up to a new scan line. Whenever the counter value becomes equal to or greater than Δy, we increment the current x intersection value by 1 and decrease the counter by the value Δy. This procedure is equivalent to maintaining integer and fractional parts for x intercepts and incrementing the fractional part until we reach the next integer value.

Boundary-Fill Algorithm

Another approach to area filling is to start at a point inside a region and paint the interior outward toward the boundary. If the boundary is specified in a single color, the fill algorithm proceeds outward pixel by pixel until the boundary color is encountered. This method, called the boundary-fill algorithm, is particularly useful in interactive painting packages, where interior points are easily selected. Using a graphics tablet or other interactive device, an artist or designer can sketch a figure outline, select a fill color or pattern from a color menu, and pick an interior point. The system then paints the figure interior. To display a solid color region (with no border), the designer can choose the fill color to be the same as the boundary color.

A boundary-fill procedure accepts as input the coordinates of an interior point *(x, y)*, a fill color, and a boundary color. Starting from (x, y), the procedure tests neighboring positions to determine whether they are of the boundary color. If not, they are painted with the fill color, and their neighbors are tested. This process continues until all pixels up to the boundary color for the area have been tested. Both inner and outer boundaries can be set up to specify an area, and some examples of defining regions for boundary fill are shown in Fig. 2.13.

Figure 2.14 shows two methods for proceeding to neighboring pixels from the current test position. In Fig. 2.14(a), four neighboring points are tested. These are the pixel positions that are right, left, above, and below the current pixel. Areas filled by this method are called 4-connected. The second method, shown in Fig. 2.14(b), is used to fill more complex figures. Here the set of neighboring positions to be tested includes the four diagonal pixels. Fill methods using this approach are called 8-connected. An 8-conneded boundary-fill algorithm would correctly fill the interior of the area defined but a 4-connected boundary-fill algorithm produces the partial fill.

Figure 2.13: Example Color Boundaries for a Boundary-fill Procedure

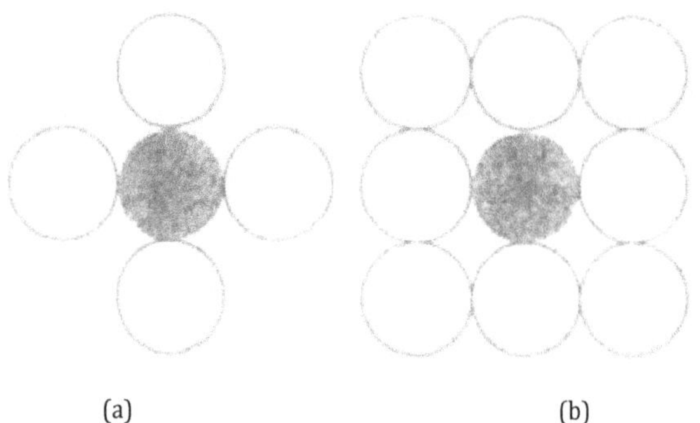

<table>
<tr><td>(a)</td><td>(b)</td></tr>
</table>

Figure 2.14: Fill Methods Applied to a 4-Connected Area (a) and to an 8-Connected Area (b)

Flood-Fill Algorithm

Sometimes we want to fill in (or recolor) an area that is not defined within a single color boundary.

Fig. 2.15 shows an area bordered by several different color regions. We can paint such areas by replacing a specified interior color instead of searching for a boundary color value. This approach is called a flood-fill algorithm. We start from a specified interior point (x, y) and reassign all pixel values that are currently set to a given interior color with the desired fill color. If the area we want to paint has more than one interior color, we can first reassign pixel values *so* that all interior points have the same color. Using either a 4-connected or 8-connected approach, we then step through pixel positions until all interior points have been repainted. The following procedure flood fills a 4-connected region recursively, starting from the input position.

Figure 2.15: An Area defined within Multiple Color Boundaries

3. Two – Dimensional Geometric Transformations

3.1. Basic Transformations

3.1.1. *Translation*

A translation is applied to an object by repositioning it along a straight-line path from one coordinate location to another. We translate a two-dimensional point by adding translation distances, t_x and t_y to the original coordinate position (x, y) to move the point to a new position (x', y')

$$x' = x + t_x, \ y' = y + t_y. \qquad (3.1)$$

The translation distance pair (t_x, t_y) is called a translation vector or shift vector.

We can express the translation equations as a single matrix equation by using column vectors to represent coordinate positions and the translation vector:

$$P = \begin{bmatrix} x_1 \\ x_2 \end{bmatrix}, P' = \begin{bmatrix} x_1 \\ x_2 \end{bmatrix}, T = \begin{bmatrix} t_x \\ t_y \end{bmatrix} \qquad (3.2)$$

This allows us to write the two-dimensional translation equations in the matrix form:

$$P' = P + T \qquad (3.3)$$

Sometimes matrix-transformation equations are expressed in terms of coordinate row vectors instead of column vectors. In this case, we would write the matrix representations as $P = [x \ y]$ and $T = [t_x, \ t_y]$. Since the column-vector representation for a point is standard mathematical notation, and since many graphics packages, for example, GKS and PHIGS, also use the column-vector representation, we will follow this convention.

Translation is a *rigid-body transformation* that moves objects without deformation. That is, every point on the object is translated by the same amount. A straight Line segment is translated by applying the transformation *equation 3.3* to each of the line endpoints and redrawing the line between the new endpoint positions. Polygons are translated by adding the translation vector to the coordinate position of each vertex and regenerating the polygon using the new set of vertex coordinates and the current attribute settings. *Figure 3.1* illustrates the application of a specified translation vector to move an object from one position to another.

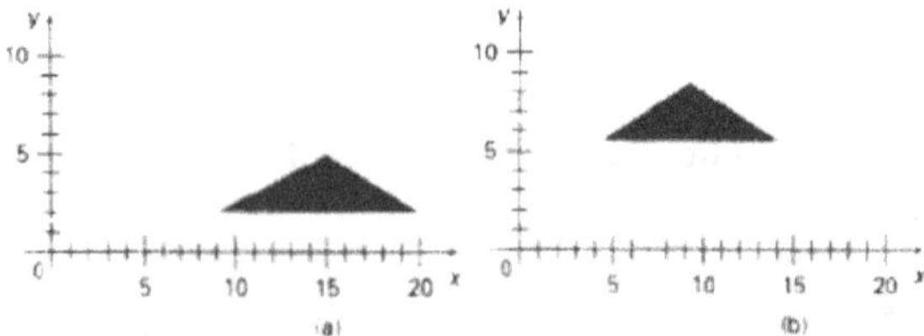

Figure 3.1: Moving a Polygon from Position (a) to Position (b) with the Translation Vector

3.1.2. Rotation

A two-dimensional rotation is applied to an object by repositioning it along a circular path in the xy plane. To generate a rotation, we specify a rotation angle θ and the position (x_r, y_r) of the rotation point (or pivot point) about which the object is to be rotated (Fig. 3.2). Positive values for the rotation angle define counter-clockwise rotations about the pivot point, as in Fig. 3.2, and negative values rotate objects in the clockwise direction. This transformation can also be described as a rotation about a rotation axis that is perpendicular to the xy plane and passes through the pivot point.

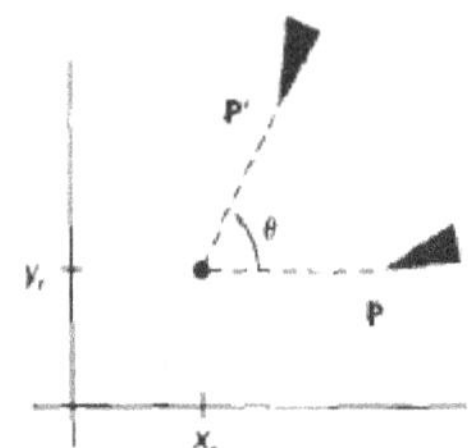

Figure 3.2: Rotation of an object through angle θ about the pivot point (x_r, y_r).

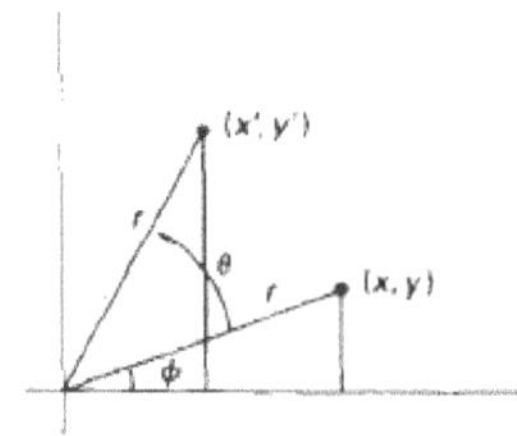

Figure 3.3: Rotation of a point from position (x, y) to position (x', y ') through an angle θ relative to the coordinate origin. The original angular displacement of the point from the x axis is ø

47

We first determine the transformation equations for rotation of a point position P when the pivot point is at the coordinate origin. The angular and coordinate relationships of the original and transformed point positions are shown in Fig. 3.3. In this figure, r is the constant distance of the point from the origin, angle ϕ is the original angular position of the point from the horizontal, and θ is the rotation angle. Using standard trigonometric identities, we can express the transformed coordinates in terms of angles θ and ϕ as

$$x' = r\cos(\phi + \theta) = r\cos\phi\cos\theta - r\sin\phi\sin\theta$$

$$(3.4)$$

$$y' = r\sin(\phi + \theta) = r\cos\phi\sin\theta + r\sin\phi\cos\theta$$

The original coordinates of the point in polar coordinates are,

$$x = r\cos\phi, \quad y = r\sin\phi \qquad (3.5)$$

Substituting expressions 3.5 into 3.4, we obtain the transformation equations for rotating a point at position (x, y) through an angle θ about the origin:

$$x' = x\cos\theta - y\sin\theta$$

$$(3.6)$$

$$y' = x\sin\theta + y\cos\theta$$

With the column-vector representations 3.2 for coordinate positions, we can write the rotation equations in the matrix form:

$$P' = R \cdot P \qquad (3.7)$$

where the rotation matrix is

$$R = \begin{bmatrix} \cos\theta & -\sin\theta \\ \sin\theta & \cos\theta \end{bmatrix} \qquad (3.8)$$

When coordinate positions are represented as row vectors instead of column vectors, the matrix product in rotation equation 3.7 is transposed so that the transformed row coordinate vector $[x', y']$ is calculated as

$$P'^T = (R \cdot P)^T$$

Where $P^T = (x\ y)$, and the transpose R^T of matrix R is obtained by interchanging rows and columns. For a rotation matrix, the transpose is obtained by simply changing the sign of the sine terms.

Rotation of a point about an arbitrary pivot position is illustrated in Fig. 3.5. Using the trigonometric relationships in this figure, we can generalize Eqs. 3.6 to obtain the transformation equations for rotation of a point about any specified rotation position (x_r, y_r).

$$x' = x_r + (x - x_r) \cos \theta - (y - y_r) \sin \theta$$

$$(3.9)$$

$$y' = y_r + (x - x_r) \sin \theta + (y - y_r) \cos \theta$$

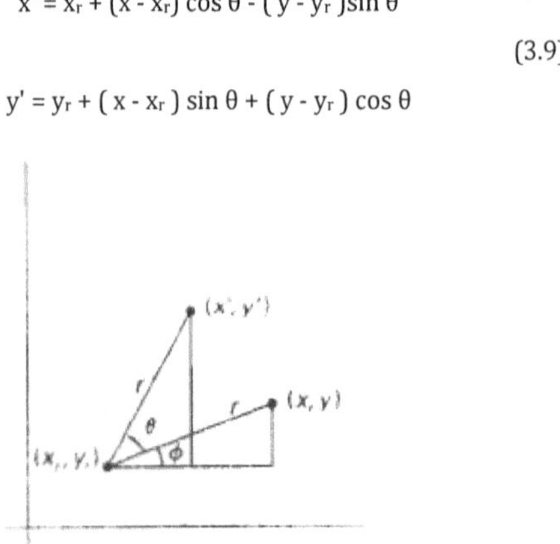

Figure 3.4 Rotating a Point from Position (x, y) to Position (x,y) through an Angle θ about Rotation Point (x_r, y_r)

3.1.3. Scaling

A scaling transformation alters the size of an object. This operation can be carried out for polygons by multiplying the coordinate values *(x, y)* of each vertex by scaling factors s_x and s_y to produce the transformed coordinates *(x', y')*:

$$x' = x \cdot s_x, \qquad y' = y \cdot s_y \qquad (3.10)$$

Scaling factor s_x scales objects in the *x* direction, while s_y scales in the *y* direction. The transformation equations 3.10 can also be written in the matrix form:

$$\begin{bmatrix} x' \\ y' \end{bmatrix} = \begin{bmatrix} s_x & 0 \\ 0 & s_y \end{bmatrix} \cdot \begin{bmatrix} x \\ y \end{bmatrix} \qquad (3.11)$$

Or

$$P' = S \cdot P \qquad (3.12)$$

Where *S* is the 2 by 2 scaling matrix in *Eq. 5.11*.

Any positive numeric values can be assigned to the scaling factors s_x and s_y. Values less than 1 reduce the size of objects; values greater than *1* produce an enlargement. Specifying a value of *1* for both s_x and s_y leaves the size of objects unchanged. When s_x and s_y are assigned the same value, a uniform scaling is produced that maintains relative object proportions.

Objects transformed with Eq. 3.11 are both scaled and repositioned. Scaling factors with values less than *1* move objects closer to the coordinate origin, while values greater than *1* move coordinate positions farther from the origin. *Figure 3.5* illustrates scaling a line by assigning the value *0.5* to both s_x and s_y in Eq. 3.11. Both the line length and the distance from the origin are reduced by a factor of *1/2*.

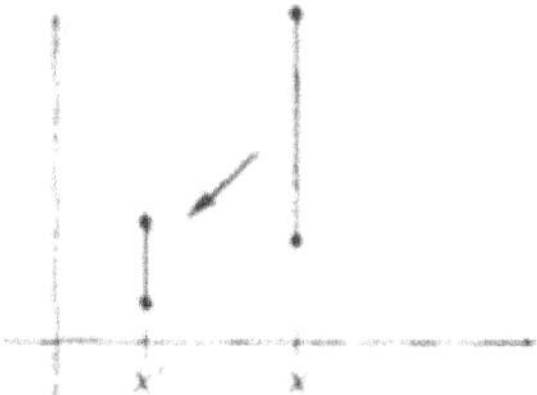

Figure 3.5: A Line Scaled with Eq 3-12 Using $s_x = s_y = 0.5$

We can control the location of a scaled object by choosing a position, called the fixed point, that is to remain unchanged after the scaling transformation. Coordinates for the fixed point *(x_f, y_f)* can be chosen as one of the vertices, the object centroid, or any other position (Fig. 3.6). A polygon is then scaled relative to the fixed point by scaling the distance from each vertex to the fixed point. For a vertex with coordinates *(x_f, y_f)* the scaled coordinates *(x', y')* are calculated as

$$x' = x_f + (x - x_f)s_x, \quad y' = y_f + (y - y_f)s_y \qquad (3.13)$$

We can rewrite these scaling transformations to separate the multiplicative and additive terms:

$$x' = x \cdot s_x + x_f (1 - s_x)$$

$$(3.14)$$

$$y' = y \cdot s_y + y_f (1 - s_y)$$

where the additive terms $x_f(1 - s_x)$ and $y_f(1 - s_y)$ are constant for all points in the object.

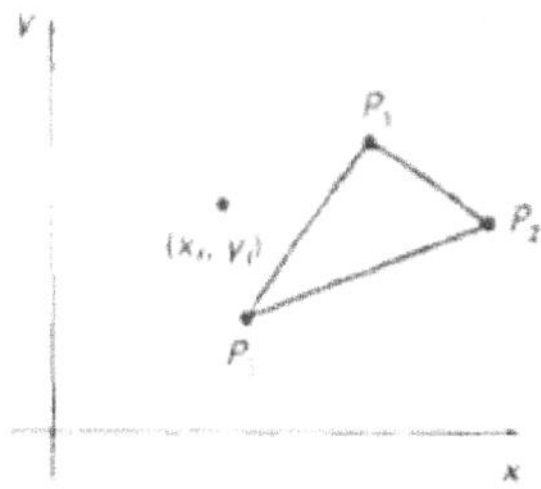

Figure 3.6: Scaling Relative to a Chosen Fixed Point (x_f, y_f)

3.2.   Matrix Representations and Homogeneous Coordinates

Many graphics applications involve sequences of geometric transformations. An animation, for example, might require an object to be translated and rotated at each increment of the motion. In design and picture construction applications, we perform translations, rotations, and scalings to fit the picture components into their proper positions each of the basic transformations can be expressed in the general matrix form,

$$P' = M_1 . P + M_2 \qquad (3.15)$$

with coordinate positions P and P' represented as column vectors. Matrix M_1 is a 2 by 2 array containing multiplicative factors, and M_2 is a two-element column matrix containing translational terms. For translation, M_1 is the identity matrix.

For rotation or scaling, M_2 contains the translational terms associated with the pivot point or scaling fixed point. To produce a sequence of transformations with these equations, such as scaling followed by rotation then translation, we must calculate the transformed coordinates one step at a time.

We can combine the multiplicative and translational terms for two-dimensional geometric transformations into a single matrix representation by expanding the 2 by 2 matrix representations to 3 by 3 matrices. This allows us to express all transformation equations as matrix multiplications, providing that we also expand the matrix representations for coordinate positions. To express any two-dimensional transformation as a matrix multiplication, we represent each Cartesian coordinate position (x, y) with the homogeneous coordinate triple (x_h, y_h, h),

Where,

$$x = \frac{x_h}{h}, \qquad y = \frac{y_h}{h} \qquad (3.16)$$

Thus, a general homogeneous coordinate representation can also be written as $(h.x, h.y, h)$. For two-dimensional geometric transformations, we can choose the homogeneous parameter h to be any nonzero value. Thus, there is an infinite number of equivalent homogeneous representations for each coordinate point (x, y). A convenient choice is simply to set $h = 1$. Each two-dimensional position is then represented with homogeneous coordinates $(x, y, 1)$. Other values for parameter h are needed, for example, in matrix formulations of three-dimensional viewing transformations.

Expressing positions in homogeneous coordinates allows us to represent all geometric transformation equations as matrix multiplications. Coordinates are represented with three-element column vectors, and transformation operations are written as 3 bv 3 matrices. For translation. we have,

$$\begin{bmatrix} x' \\ y' \\ 1 \end{bmatrix} = \begin{bmatrix} 1 & 0 & t_x \\ 0 & 1 & t_y \\ 0 & 0 & 1 \end{bmatrix} \cdot \begin{bmatrix} x \\ y \\ 1 \end{bmatrix} \qquad\qquad (3.17)$$

which we can write in the abbreviated form,

$$P' = T(t_x, t_y) \cdot P \qquad\qquad (3.18)$$

with $T(t_x, t_y)$ as the 3 by 3 translation matrix in *Eq. 3.17*. The inverse of the translation matrix is obtained by replacing the translation parameters t_x, and t_y, with their negatives: - t_x, and $-t_y$.

Similarly, rotation transformation equations about the coordinate origin are now written as

$$\begin{bmatrix} x' \\ y' \\ 1 \end{bmatrix} = \begin{bmatrix} cos\theta & -sin\theta & 0 \\ sin\theta & cos\theta & 0 \\ 0 & 0 & 1 \end{bmatrix} \cdot \begin{bmatrix} x \\ y \\ 1 \end{bmatrix} \qquad\qquad (3.19)$$

Or as

$$P' = R(\theta) \cdot P \qquad\qquad (3.20)$$

The rotation transformation operator $R(\theta)$ is the 3 by 3 matrix in *Eq. 3-19* with rotation parameter θ. We get the inverse rotation matrix when θ is replaced with $-\theta$.

Finally, a scaling transformation relative to the coordinate origin is now expressed as the matrix multiplication

$$\begin{bmatrix} x' \\ y' \\ 1 \end{bmatrix} = \begin{bmatrix} s_x & 0 & 0 \\ 0 & s_y & 0 \\ 0 & 0 & 1 \end{bmatrix} \cdot \begin{bmatrix} x \\ y \\ 1 \end{bmatrix} \qquad\qquad (3.21)$$

Or

$$P' = S(s_x, s_y) \cdot P \qquad\qquad (3.22)$$

where $S(s_x, s_y)$ is the 3 by 3 matrix in Eq. 3.21 with parameters s_x and s_y. Replacing these parameters with their multiplicative inverses $(1/s_x \text{ and } 1/s_y)$ yields the inverse scaling matrix.

3.3. Composite Transformations

A matrix for any sequence of transformations as a composite transformation matrix by calculating the matrix product of the individual transformations. Forming products of transformation matrices is often referred to as a concatenation, or composition, of matrices. For column-matrix representation of coordinate positions, we form composite transformations by multiplying matrices in order from right to left. That is, each successive transformation matrix pre-multiplies the product of the preceding transformation matrices.

3.3.1. Translations

If two successive translation vectors *(t_{x1}, t_{y1})* and *(t_{x2}, t_{y2})* are applied to a coordinate position P, the final transformed location P' is calculated as,

$$P' = T(t_{x2}, t_{y2}) . \{T(t_{x1}, t_{y1}) . P\}$$

$$(3.23)$$

$$= \{T(t_{x2}, t_{y2}) . T(t_{x1}, t_{y1}) . P\}$$

where P and P are represented as homogeneous-coordinate column vectors. We can verify this result by calculating the matrix product for the two associative groupings Also, the composite transformation matrix for this sequence of translations is

$$\begin{bmatrix} 1 & 0 & t_{x2} \\ 0 & 1 & t_{y2} \\ 0 & 0 & 1 \end{bmatrix} . \begin{bmatrix} 1 & 0 & t_{x1} \\ 0 & 1 & t_{y1} \\ 0 & 0 & 1 \end{bmatrix} = \begin{bmatrix} 1 & 0 & t_{x1} + t_{x2} \\ 0 & 1 & t_{y1} + t_{y2} \\ 0 & 0 & 1 \end{bmatrix} \qquad (3.24)$$

Or

$$T(t_{x2}, t_{y2}) . T(t_{x1}, t_{y1}) = T(t_{x1} + t_{x2}, t_{y1} + t_{y2}) \quad (3.25)$$

which demonstrates that two successive translations are additive.

3.3.2. Rotations

Two successive rotations applied to point P produce the transformed position

$$P' = R(\theta_2) . \{R(\theta_1) . P\}$$

$$= \{R(\theta_2) . R(\theta_1)\} . P \qquad (3.26)$$

By multiplying the two rotation matrices, we can verify that two successive rotations are additive:

$$R(\theta_2) . R(\theta_1) = R(\theta_1 + \theta_2) \qquad (3.27)$$

so that the final rotated coordinates can be calculated with the composite rotation matrix as

$$P' = R(\theta_1 + \theta_2) . P \qquad (3.28)$$

3.3.3. Scaling

Concatenating transformation matrices for two successive scaling operations produces the following composite scaling matrix:

$$
\begin{bmatrix} S_{x2} & 0 & 0 \\ 0 & S_{y2} & 0 \\ 0 & 0 & 1 \end{bmatrix} \cdot \begin{bmatrix} S_{x1} & 0 & 0 \\ 0 & S_{y1} & 0 \\ 0 & 0 & 1 \end{bmatrix} = \begin{bmatrix} S_{x1}.S_{x2} & 0 & 0 \\ 0 & S_{y1}.S_{y2} & 0 \\ 0 & 0 & 1 \end{bmatrix} \quad (3.29)
$$

Or

$$S(S_{x2}, S_{y2}) . S(S_{x1}, S_{y1}) = S(S_{x1} . S_{x2}, S_{y1} . S_{y2})$$

The resulting matrix in this case indicates that successive scaling operations are multiplicative. That is, if we were to triple the size of an object twice in succession, the final size would be nine times that of the original.

3.3.4. General Pivot-Point Rotation

With a graphics package that only provides a rotate function for revolving objects about the coordinate origin, we can generate rotations about any selected pivot point (x, y,) by performing the following sequence of translate-rotate-translate operations:

1. Translate the object so that the pivot-point position is moved to the coordinate origin.
2. Rotate the object about the coordinate origin.
3. Translate the object so that the pivot point is returned to its original position.

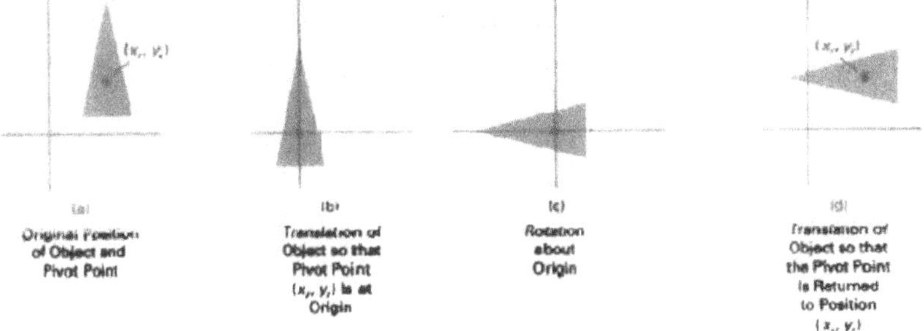

Figure 3.7: A Transformation Sequence for Rotating an Object about a Specified Pivot Mint Using the Rotation Matrix R(θ) of Transformation

This transformation sequence is illustrated in *Fig. 3.7*. The composite transformation matrix or this sequence is obtained with the concatenation.

$$
\begin{bmatrix} 1 & 0 & x_r \\ 0 & 1 & y_r \\ 0 & 0 & 1 \end{bmatrix} \cdot \begin{bmatrix} cos\theta & -sin\theta & 0 \\ sin\theta & cos\theta & 0 \\ 0 & 0 & 1 \end{bmatrix} \cdot \begin{bmatrix} 1 & 0 & -x_r \\ 0 & 1 & -y_r \\ 0 & 0 & 1 \end{bmatrix} = \begin{bmatrix} cos\theta & -sin\theta & x_r(1-cos\theta) + y_r\,sin\theta \\ sin\theta & cos\theta & y_r(1-cos\theta) - x_r\,sin\theta \\ 0 & 0 & 1 \end{bmatrix} \quad (3.31)
$$

which can be expressed in the form

$$T(x_r, y_r) . R(\theta) . T(-x_r, -y_r) = R(x_r, y_r, \theta) \quad (3.32)$$

where $T(-x_r, -y_r) = T'(x_r, y_r)$. In general, a rotate function can be set up to accept parameters for pivot-point coordinates, as well as the rotation angle, and to generate automatically the rotation matrix of Eq. 3.31.

3.3.5. General Fixed-Point Scaling

Figure 3.8 illustrates a transformation sequence to produce scaling with respect to a selected fixed position (x_f, y_f) using a scaling function that can only scale relative to the coordinate origin.

1. Translate object so that the fixed point coincides with the coordinate origin.
2. Scale the object with respect to the coordinate origin.
3. Use the inverse translation of step 1 to return the object to its original position.

Concatenating the matrices for these three operations produces the required scaling matrix,

$$\begin{bmatrix} 1 & 0 & x_f \\ 0 & 1 & y_f \\ 0 & 0 & 1 \end{bmatrix} \cdot \begin{bmatrix} s_x & 0 & 0 \\ 0 & s_y & 0 \\ 0 & 0 & 1 \end{bmatrix} \cdot \begin{bmatrix} 1 & 0 & -x_f \\ 0 & 1 & -y_f \\ 0 & 0 & 1 \end{bmatrix} = \begin{bmatrix} s_x & 0 & x_f(1 - s_x) \\ 0 & s_x & y_f(1 - s_y) \\ 0 & 0 & 1 \end{bmatrix} \tag{3.33}$$

Or

$$T(x_f, y_f) \cdot S(s_x, s_y) \cdot T(-x_f, -y_f) = S(x_f, y_f, s_x, s_y) \tag{3.34}$$

Where $T(-x_f, -y_f) = T'(x_f, y_f)$. In general, a rotate function can be set up to accept parameters for pivot-point coordinates, as well as the rotation angle, and to generate automatically the rotation matrix of Eq. 3.31.

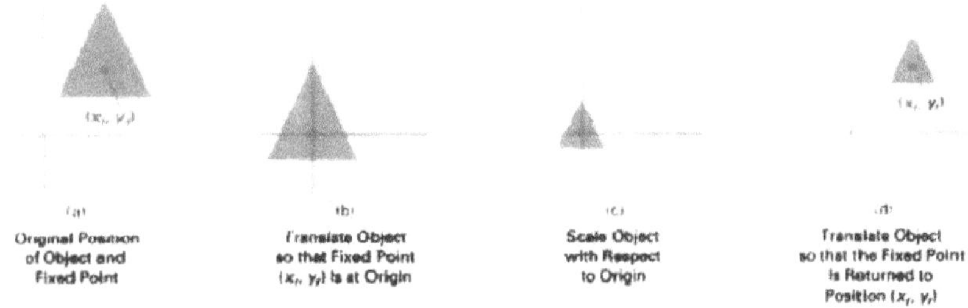

Figure 3.8: A transformation sequence for scaling an object with respect to a specified fixed position using the scaling matrix $S(s_x, s_y)$ of transformation

3.3.6. General Scaling Directions

Parameters (s_x, s_y) scale objects along the x and y directions. We can scale an object in other directions by rotating the object to align the desired scaling directions with the coordinate axes before applying the scaling transformation.

Suppose we want to apply scaling factors with values specified by parameters s_1 and $s2$ in the directions shown in Fig. 3.9. To accomplish the scaling without changing the orientation of the object, we first perform a rotation so that the directions for s_1 and $s2$ coincide with the x and y axes, respectively. Then the scaling transformation is applied, followed by an opposite rotation to return points to their original orientations. The composite matrix resulting from the product of these three transformations is given in eq. 3.35.

As an example of this scaling transformation, we turn a unit square into a parallelogram (Fig. 3.10) by stretching it along the diagonal from (0, 0) to (1, 1). We rotate the diagonal onto the y axis and double its length with the transformation parameters $\theta = 45^0$, $s_1 = 1$, and $s_2 = 2$.

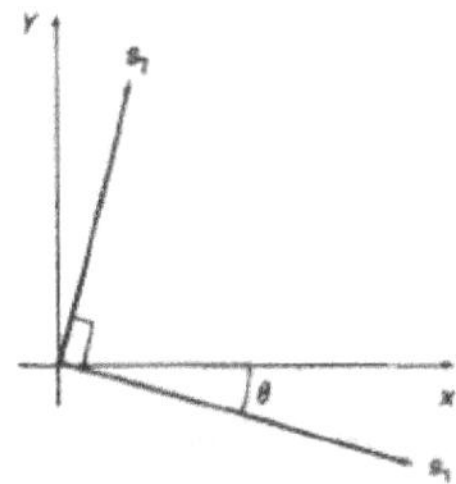

Figure 3.9 Scaling parameters s_1 and s_2 are to be applied in orthogonal directions.

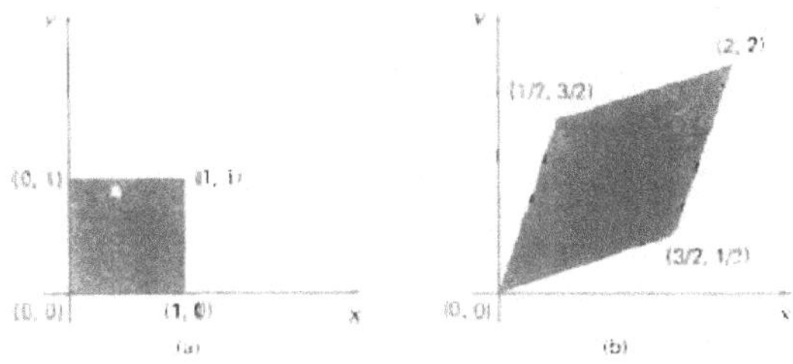

Figure 3.10 A square (a) is converted to a parallelogram (b) using the composite transformation matrix 3-35, with $s_1 = 1$, $s_2 = 2$, and $\theta = 45^0$

3.3.7. *Concatenation Properties*

Matrix multiplication is associative. For any three matrices, A B, and C, the matrix product $A . B . C$ can be performed by first multiplying A and B or by first multiplying B and C:

$$A . B . C = (A . B) . C = A . (B . C) \qquad (3.35)$$

Therefore, we can evaluate matrix products using either a left-to-right or a right to left associative grouping.

On the other hand, transformation products may not be commutative: The matrix product A. B is not equal to B. A, in general. This means that if we want to translate and rotate an object, we must be careful about the order in which the composite matrix is evaluated (Fig. 3.11). For some special cases, such as a sequence of transformations all of the same kind, the multiplication of transformation matrices is commutative. As an example, two successive rotations could be performed in either order and the final position would be the same. This commutative property holds also for two successive translations or two successive scaling's. Another commutative pair of operations is rotation and uniform scaling (s_x, s_y).

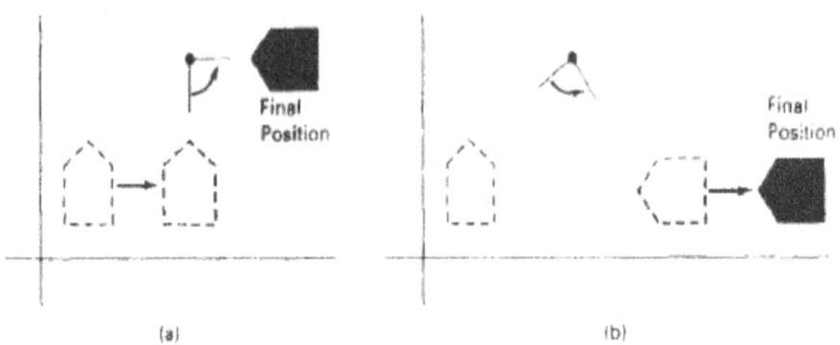

Figure 3.11: (a), An Object is First Translated, then Rotated (b), The Object is Rotated First, then Translated

3.4.   Other Transformations

Basic transformations such as translation, rotation, and scaling are included in most graphics packages. Some packages provide a few additional transformations that are useful in certain applications. Two such transformations are reflection and shear.

3.4.1. Reflection

A reflection is a transformation that produces a mirror image of an object. The mirror image for a two-dimensional reflection is generated relative to an axis of reflection by rotating the object 180^0 about the reflection axis. We can choose an axis of reflection in the xy plane or perpendicular to the xy plane. When the reflection axis is a line in the xy plane, the rotation path about this axis is in a plane perpendicular to the xy plane. For reflection axes that are perpendicular to the xy plane, the rotation path is in the xy plane.

Reflection about the line y = 0, the x axis, is accomplished with the transformation matrix

$$\begin{bmatrix} 1 & 0 & 0 \\ 0 & -1 & 0 \\ 0 & 0 & 1 \end{bmatrix} \qquad (3.36)$$

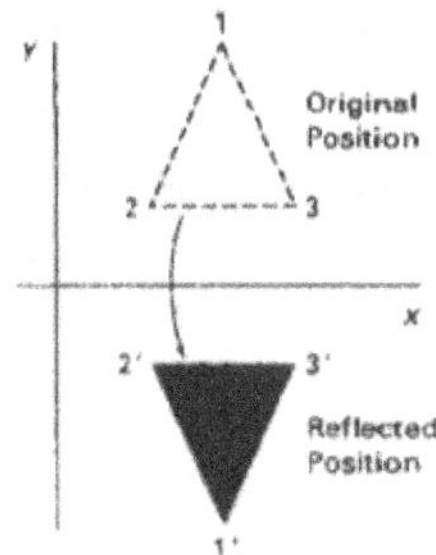

Figure 3.12: Reflection of an Object about the x Axis

This transformation keeps x values the same, but "flips" the y values of coordinate positions. The resulting orientation of an object after it has been reflected about the x axis is shown in Fig. 3.12.

A reflection about the y axis flips x coordinates while keeping y coordinates the same. The matrix for this transformation is

$$\begin{bmatrix} -1 & 0 & 0 \\ 0 & 1 & 0 \\ 0 & 0 & 1 \end{bmatrix} \qquad (3.37)$$

Figure 3.13 illustrates the change in position of an object that has been reflected about the line x = 0. The equivalent rotation in this case is 180^0 through three dimensional space about the y axis.

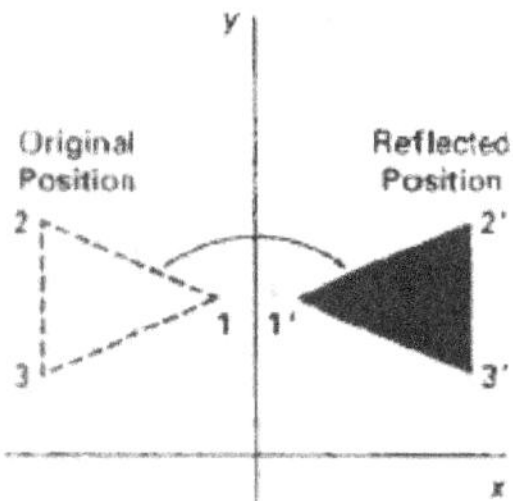

Figure 3.13: Reflection of an Object about the y Axis

We flip both the x and y coordinates of a point by reflecting relative to an axis that is perpendicular to the xy plane and that passes through the coordinate origin. This transformation, referred to as a reflection relative to the coordinate origin, has the matrix representation.

$$\begin{bmatrix} -1 & 0 & 0 \\ 0 & -1 & 0 \\ 0 & 0 & 1 \end{bmatrix} \qquad\qquad (3.38)$$

An example of reflection about the origin is shown in Fig. 3.18. The reflection matrix 3.38 is the rotation matrix $R(\theta)$ with $\theta = 180^0$. We are simply rotating the object in the xy plane half a revolution about the origin.

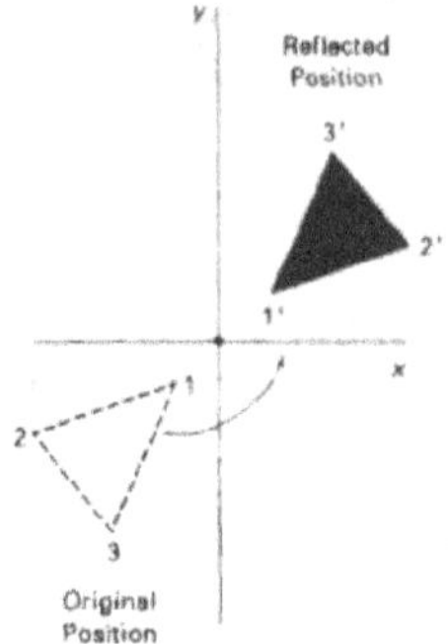

Figure 3.14: Reflection of an Object Relative to the xy Plane

If we chose the reflection axis as the diagonal line y = x (Fig. 3.15), the reflection matrix is

$$\begin{bmatrix} 0 & 1 & 0 \\ 1 & 0 & 0 \\ 0 & 0 & 1 \end{bmatrix} \qquad\qquad (3.39)$$

We can derive this matrix by concatenating a sequence of rotation and coordinate-axis reflection matrices. One possible sequence is shown In *Fig. 3.16*. Here, we first perform a clockwise rotation through a 45^0 angle, which rotates the line $y= x$ onto the x axis. Next, we perform a reflection with respect to the x axis. The final step is to rotate the line $y = x$ back to its original position with a counter clockwise rotation through 45^0.

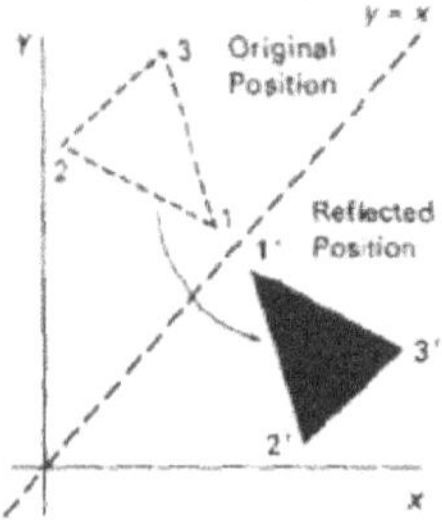

Figure 3.15: Reflection of an Object with Respect to the Line y = x

To obtain a transformation matrix for reflection about the diagonal $y = -x$, we could concatenate matrices for the transformation sequence: (1) clockwise rotation by 45^0, (2) reflection about the y axis, and (3) counter clockwise rotation by 45^0. The resulting transformation matrix is,

$$\begin{bmatrix} 0 & -1 & 0 \\ -1 & 0 & 0 \\ 0 & 0 & 1 \end{bmatrix} \qquad (3.40)$$

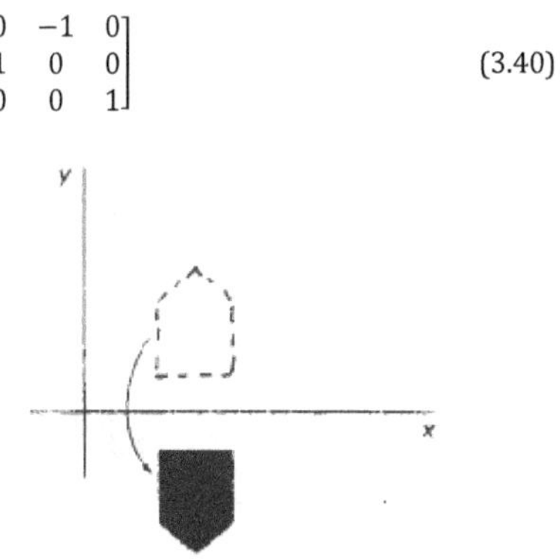

Figure 3.16: Reflection about the x axis

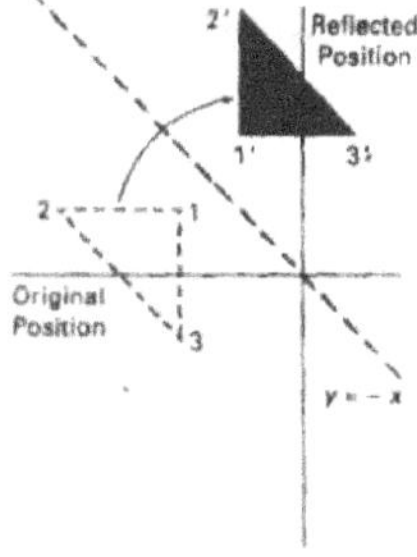

Figure 3.17: Reflection with Respect to the Line y = - x

3.4.2. Shear

A transformation that distorts the shape of an object such that the transformed shape appears as if the object were composed of internal layers that had been caused to slide over each other is called a *shear*. Two common shearing transformations are those that shift coordinate x values and those that shift y values.

An x-direction shear relative to the *x axis* is produced with the transformation matrix

$$\begin{bmatrix} 1 & sh_x & 0 \\ 0 & 1 & 0 \\ 0 & 0 & 1 \end{bmatrix} \qquad (3.41)$$

which transforms coordinate positions as

$$x' = x + sh_x \cdot y \,, y' = y \qquad (3.42)$$

Any real number can be assigned to the shear parameter sh_x. A coordinate position (x, y) is then shifted horizontally by an amount proportional to its distance (y value) from the x axis $(y = 0)$. Setting sh_x, to 2, for example, changes the square in *Fig. 3.18* into a parallelogram. Negative values for sh_x shift coordinate positions to the left.

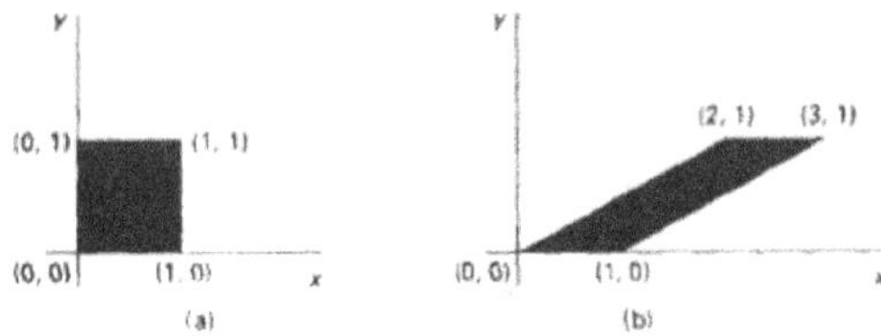

Figure 3.18: A Unit Square (a) is Converted to a Parallelogram (b) Using the x-direction Shear Matrix 3.41 with shx = 2

We can generate x-direction shears relative to other reference lines with

$$\begin{bmatrix} 1 & sh_x & sh_x \cdot y_{ref} \\ 0 & 1 & 0 \\ 0 & 0 & 1 \end{bmatrix} \qquad (3.43)$$

with coordinate positions transformed as

$$x' = x + sh_x (y - y_{ref}) \,, y' = y \qquad (3.44)$$

An example of this shearing transformation is given In Fig. 3.19 for a shear parameter value of *1 /2* relative to the line $y_{ref} = -1$.

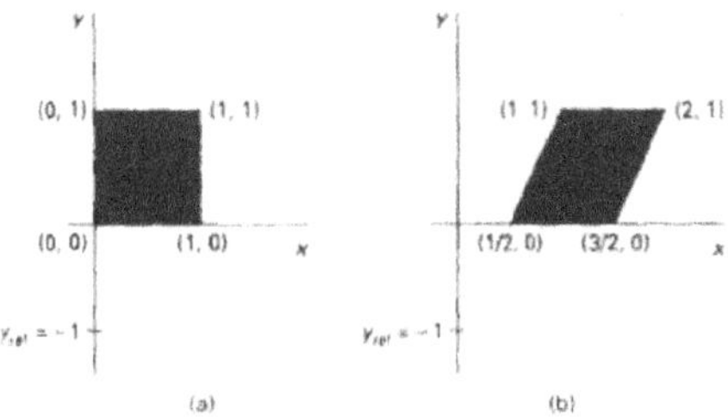

Figure 3.19: A Unit Square (a) is Transformed to a Shifted Parallelogram (b) with $sh_x = 1/2$ and $y_{ref} = -1$ in the Shear Matrix 3.43

A y-direction shear relative to the line x = x_{ref} is generated with the transformation matrix,

$$\begin{bmatrix} 1 & 0 & 0 \\ sh_y & 1 & -sh_y \cdot x_{ref} \\ 0 & 0 & 1 \end{bmatrix} \tag{3.45}$$

which generates transformed coordinate positions.

$$y' = y + sh_y (x - x_{ref}), x' = x \tag{3.46}$$

This transformation shifts coordinate position vertically by an amount proportional to its distance from the reference line $x = x_{ref}$. Fig 3.20 illustrates the conversion of a square into a parallelogram with $sh_y = 1/2$ and $x_{ref} = -1$.

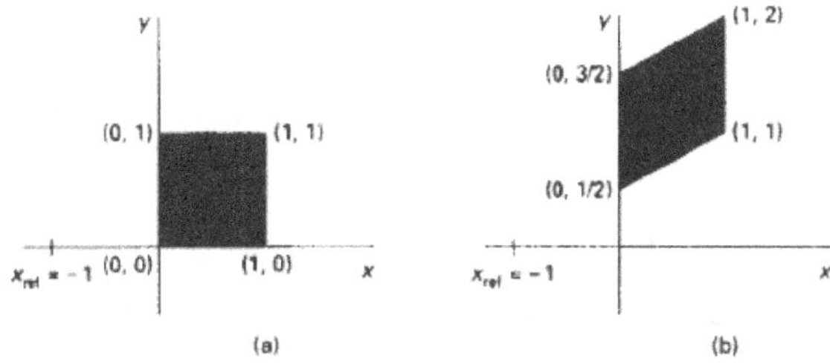

Figure 3.20: A Unit Square (a) is Turned into a Shifted Parallelogram (b) with Parameter Values $sh_y = 1/2$ and $x_{ref} = -1$ in the y Direction

3.5. Transformations between Coordinate Systems

Graphics applications often require the transformation of object descriptions from one coordinate system to another. Sometimes object are described in non-Cartesian reference frames that take advantage of object symmetries. Coordinate descriptions in these systems must then be converted to Cartesian device coordinates for display. Some examples of two-dimensional non-Cartesian systems are polar coordinates, elliptical coordinates, and parabolic coordinates. In other cases, we need to transform between two Cartesian systems. For modelling and design applications, individual objects may be defined in their own local Cartesian references, and the local coordinates must then be transformed to position the objects within the overall scene coordinate system.

Figure 3.21 shows two Cartesian systems, with the coordinate origins at *(0, 0)* and *(x₀, y₀)* and with an orientation angle θ between the x and x' axes. To transform object descriptions from xy coordinates to $x'y'$ coordinates, we need to set up a transformation that superimposes the $x'y'$ axes onto the xy axes. This is done in two steps:

1. Translate so that the origin *(x₀, y₀)* of the *x'y'* system is moved to the origin of the *xy* system.

2. Rotate the *x'* axis onto the *x* axis.

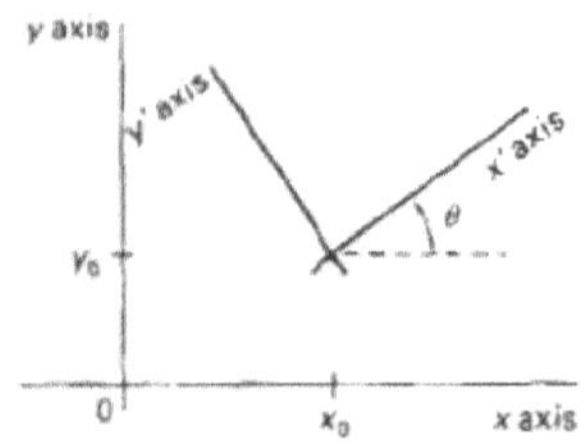

Figure 3.21: A Cartesian x' y' System Positioned at (x₀, y₀) with Orientation θ in an x Cartesian System

Translation of the coordinate origin is expressed with the matrix operation

$$T(-x_0,-y_0) = \begin{bmatrix} 1 & 0 & -x_0 \\ 0 & 1 & -y_0 \\ 0 & 0 & 1 \end{bmatrix} \qquad (3.47)$$

and the orientation of the two systems after the translation operation would appear as in Fig. 3.22. To get the axes of the two systems into coincidence, we then perform the clockwise rotation

$$R(-\theta) = \begin{bmatrix} \cos\theta & \sin\theta & 0 \\ -\sin\theta & \cos\theta & 0 \\ 0 & 0 & 1 \end{bmatrix} \qquad (3.48)$$

Concatenating these two transformations matrices gives us the complete composite matrix for transforming object descriptions from the *xy* system to the *x'y'* system:

$$M_{xy,x'y'} = R(\theta).T(-x_0,-y_0) \qquad (3.49)$$

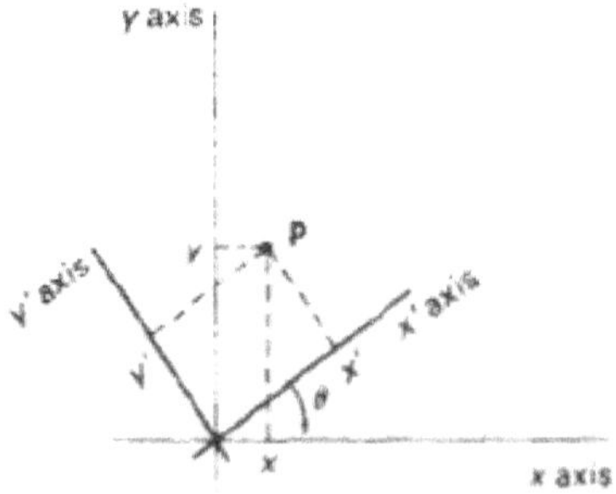

Figure 3.22: Position of the Reference Frames shown in Fig. 3.21 after Translating the Origin of the x'y' System to the Coordinate Origin of the xy System

CHAPTER IV

4. Two – Dimensional Viewing

4.1.   The Viewing Pipeline

A world-coordinate area selected for display is called a window. An area on a display device to which a window is mapped is called a viewport. The window defines *what* is to be viewed; the viewport defines *where* it is to be displayed. Often, windows and viewports are rectangles in standard position, with the rectangle edges parallel to the coordinate axes. Other window or viewport geometries, such as general polygon shapes and circles, are used in some applications, but these shapes take longer to process. In general, the mapping of a part of a world-coordinate scene to device coordinates is referred to as a viewing transformation. Sometimes the two-dimensional viewing transformation is simply referred to as the *window-to-viewport transformation* or the *windowing transformation.* Figure 4.1 illustrates the mapping of a picture section that falls within a rectangular window onto a designated rectangular viewport.

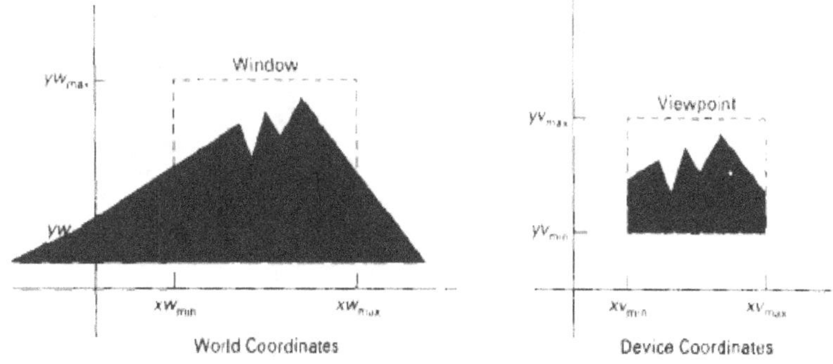

Figure 4.1: A Viewing Transformation Sing Standard Rectangles for the Window and Viewport

Some graphics packages that provide window and viewport operations allow only standard rectangles, but a more general approach is to allow the rectangular window to haw any orientation. In this case, we carry out the viewing transformation in several steps, as indicated in Fig. 4.2. First, we construct the scene in world coordinates using the output primitives and attributes. Next to obtain a particular orientation for the window, we can set up a two-dimensional viewing-coordinate system in the world-coordinate plane, and define a window in the viewing-coordinate system. The viewing coordinate reference frame is used to provide a method for setting up arbitrary orientations for rectangular windows. Once the viewing reference frame is established, we can transform descriptions in world coordinates to viewing coordinates. We then define a viewport in normalized coordinates in the range from (0 to 1) and map the viewing-coordinate description of the scene to normalized coordinates. At the final step, all parts of the picture that he outside the viewport are clipped, and the contents of the viewport are transferred to device coordinates.

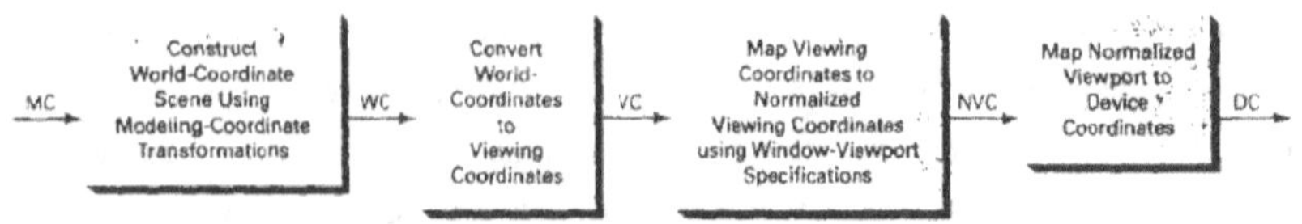

Figure 4.2: The two-dimensional Viewing-transformation Pipeline

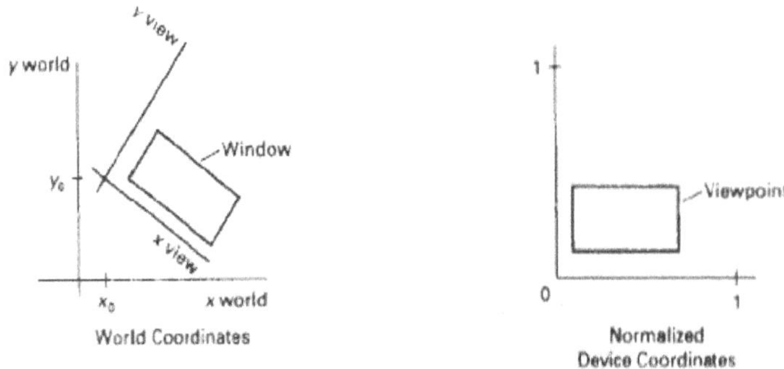

Figure 4.3: Setting up a Rotated World Window in Viewing Coordinates and the Corresponding Normalized-coordinate Viewport

Figure 4.3 illustrates a rotated viewing-coordinate reference frame and the mapping to normalized coordinates. By changing the position of the viewport, we can view objects at different positions on the display area of an output device. Also, by varying the size of viewports, we can change the size and proportions of displayed objects.

4.2. Viewing Coordinate Reference Frame

This coordinate system provides the reference frame for specifying the world coordinate Window. First, a viewing-coordinate origin is selected at some world position: $P_0 = (x_0, y_0)$. Then we need to establish the orientation, or rotation, of this reference frame. One way to do this is to specify a world vector V that defines the viewing, direction. Vector V is called the *view up vector.*

Given V, we can calculate the components of unit vectors $v = (v_x, v_y)$ and $u = (u_x, u_y)$ for the viewing y_v and x_v axes, respectively. These unit vectors are used to form the first and second rows of the rotation matrix R that aligns the viewing x_t, y_t, axes with the world x_w, y_w axes.

We obtain the matrix for converting world coordinate positions to viewing coordinates as a two-step composite transformation: First, we translate the viewing origin to the world origin, then we rotate to align the two coordinate reference frames. The composite two-dimensional transformation to convert world coordinates to viewing coordinate is

$$M_{WC, VC} = R \cdot T \qquad (4.1)$$

where T is the translation matrix that takes the viewing origin point P_0 to the world origin, and R is the rotation matrix that aligns the axes of the two reference frames. Figure 4.4 illustrates the steps in this coordinate transformation.

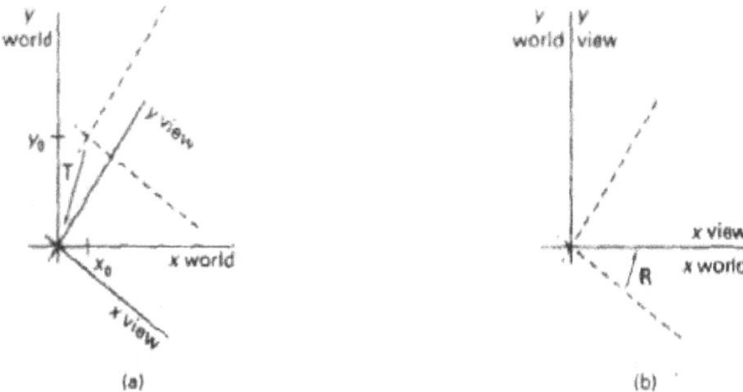

Figure 4.4: (a) Translate the Viewing Origin to the World Origin, then (b) Rotate to Align the Axes of the Two Systems

4.3. Window-to-viewport Coordinate Transformation

Figure 4.5 illustrates the window-to-viewport mapping. A point at position (x_w, y_w) in the window is mapped into position (x_v, y_v) in the associated viewport. To maintain the same relative placement in the viewport as in the window, we require that,

$$\frac{x_v - xv_{min}}{xv_{max} - xv_{min}} = \frac{x_w - xw_{min}}{xw_{max} - xw_{min}}$$

$$\frac{y_v - yv_{min}}{yv_{max} - yv_{min}} = \frac{y_w - yw_{min}}{yw_{max} - yw_{min}}$$

$$(4.2)$$

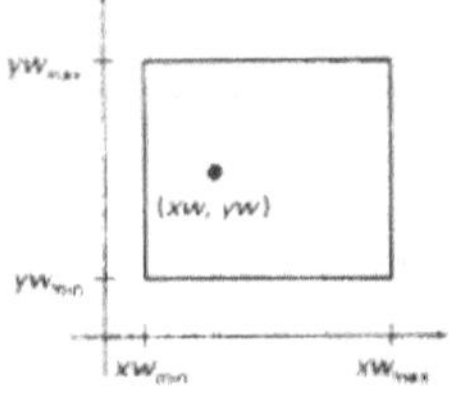
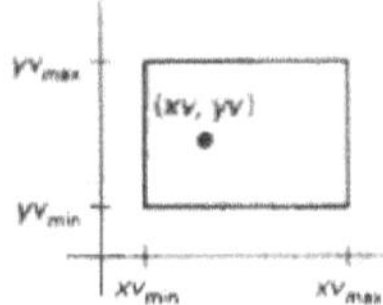

Figure 4.5: A Point at Position (x$_w$, y$_w$) in a Designated Window is Mapped to Viewport Coordinates (x$_v$, y$_v$) so that Relative Positions in the Two Areas are the same

Solving these expressions for the viewport position *(x$_v$, y$_v$)* we have,

$$xv = xv_{min} + (xw - xw_{min})s_x$$

(4.3)

$$yv = yv_{min} + (yw - yw_{min})s_y$$

where the scaling factors are

$$s_x = \frac{xv_{max} - xv_{min}}{xw_{max} - xw_{min}}$$

(4.4)

$$s_y = \frac{yv_{max} - yv_{min}}{yw_{max} - yw_{min}}$$

Equations 4.3 can also be derived with a set of transformations that converts the window area into the viewport area. This conversion is performed with the following sequence of transformations:

1. Perform a scaling transformation using a fixed-point position of *(xw$_{min}$ yw$_{min}$)* that scales the window area to the size of the viewport.
2. Translate the scaled window area to the position of the viewport.

Relative proportions of objects are maintained if the scaling factors are the same *(s$_x$ = s$_y$)*. Otherwise, world objects will be stretched or contracted in either the *x* or *y* direction when displayed on the output device.

Any number of output devices can be open in a particular application, and another window-to-viewport transformation can be performed for each open output device. This mapping, called the workstation transformation, is accomplished by selecting a window area in normalized space and a viewport area in the coordinates of the display device. As illustrated in Fig. 4.6, we can use workstation transformations to partition a view so that different parts of normalized space can be displayed on different output devices.

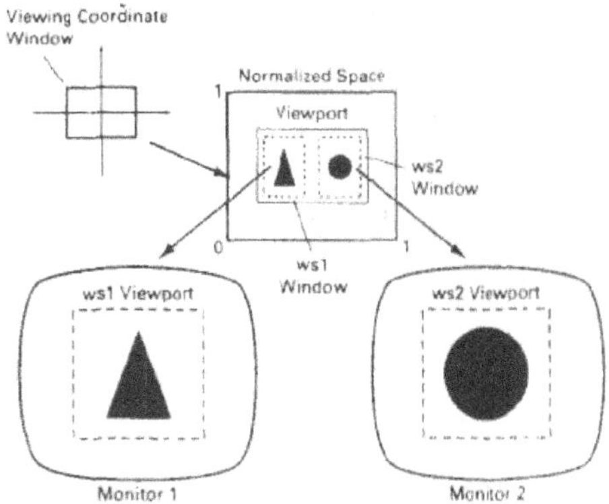

Figure 4.6: Mapping Selected Parts of a Scene in Normalized Coordinates to different Video Monitors with Workstation Transformations

4.4. Two-dimensional Viewing Functions

We define a viewing reference system in a PHIGS application program with the following function:

EvaluateViewOrientationMatrix (x0, y0, xV, yv, error, viewMatrix)

where parameters $x0$ and $y0$ are the coordinates of the viewing origin, and parameters xV and yV are the world coordinate positions for the view up vector. An integer *error* code is generated if the input parameters are in error; otherwise, the *viewMatrix* for the world-to-viewing transformation is calculated. Any number of viewing transformation matrices can be defined in an application.

To set up the elements of a window-to-viewport mapping matrix, we invoke the function

evaluateViewMappingMatrix (xwmin, wxmax , ywmin , ywmax. xvmin, xvmax, yvmin, yvmax, error, viewmappingmatrix)

Here, the window limits in viewing coordinates are chosen with parameters *xwmin, wxmax, ywmin, ywmax. xvmin, xvmax, yvmin, yvmax* and the viewport limits are set with the normalized coordinate *xwmin, wxmax, ywmin, ywmax. xvmin, xvmax, yvmin, yvmax* with the viewing-transformation matrix, we can construct several window-viewport pairs and use them for projecting various parts of the scene to different areas of the unit square.

Next, we can store combinations of viewing and window-viewport mappings for various workstations in a viewing table with *setViewRepresentation (ws, viewIndex, viewMatrlx, viewMappingMatrix, xclipmin, xclipmax,*

yclipmin, yclipmax, clipxy)

where parameter *ws* designates the output device (workstation), and parameter *viewIndex* sets an integer identifier for this particular window-viewport pair. The matrices *viewMatrix* and *viewMappingWatrix* can be concatenated and referenced by the *viewIndex*. Additional clipping limits can also be specified here, but they are usually set to coincide with the viewport boundaries. And parameter *clipxy* is assigned either the value *noclip* or the value *clip*.

The function

setViewndex(viewIndex)

selects a particular set of options from the viewing table. This view-index selection is then applied to subsequently specified output primitives and associated attributes and generates a display on each of the active workstations. At the find stage, we apply a workstation transformation by selecting a workstation window-viewport pair:

setWorkstationWindow (WS, xwswindmin, xwswindmax, ywswindmin. ywswindmax)

setWorksrationViewport (ws xwsVPortmin, xwsVPortmax, ywsVPortmin, ywsVPortmax)

where parameter *ws* gives the workstation number. Window coordinate extents are specified in the range from 0 to 1 (normalized space), and viewport limits are in integer device coordinates.

If a workstation viewport is not specified, the unit square *xy* of the normalized reference frame is mapped onto the largest square area possible on an output device. The coordinate origin of normalized space is mapped to the origin of device coordinates, and the aspect ratio is retained by transforming the unit square onto a square area on the output device.

4.5.   Point Clipping

Assuming that the clip window is a rectangle in standard position, we save a point $P = (x, y)$ for display if the following inequalities are satisfied:

$$xw_{min} \leq x \leq xw_{max}$$

$$yw_{min} \leq y \leq yw_{max}$$

(4.5)

where the edges of the clip window $(xw_{min}, xw_{max}, yw_{min}, yw_{max})$ can be either the world-coordinate window boundaries or viewport boundaries. If any one of these four inequalities is not satisfied, the point is clipped (not saved for display). Although point clipping is applied less often than line or polygon clipping, some applications may require a point clipping procedure. For example, point clipping can be applied to scenes involving explosions or sea foam that are modelled with particles (points) distributed in some region of the scene.

4.6. Line Clipping

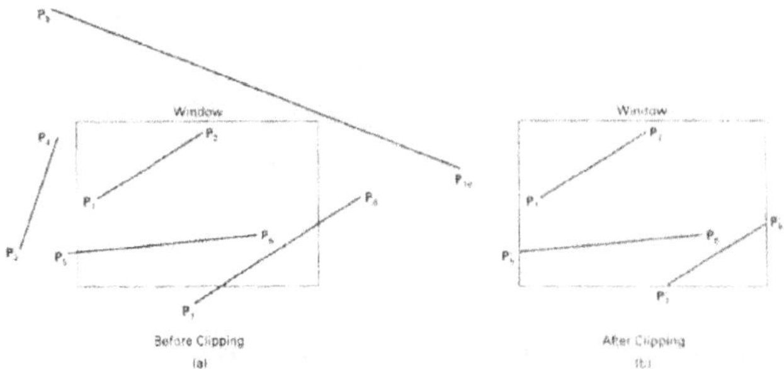

Figure 4.7: Line Clipping against a Rectangular Clip Window

Figure 4.7 illustrates possible relationships between line positions and a standard rectangular clipping region. A line clipping procedure involves several parts. First, we can test a given line segment to determine whether it lies completely inside the clipping window. If it does not, we try to determine whether it lies completely outside the window. Finally, if we cannot identify a line as completely inside or completely outside, we must perform intersection calculations with one or more clipping boundaries. We process lines through the "inside-outside" tests by checking the line endpoints. A line with both endpoints inside all clipping boundaries, such as the line from P_1 to P_2, is saved. A line with both endpoints outside any one of the clip boundaries (line P_3, P_4 in Fig. 4.7) is outside the window. All other lines cross one or more clipping boundaries, and may require calculation of multiple intersection points. To minimize calculations, we try to devise clipping algorithms that can efficiently identify outside lines and reduce intersection calculations.

For a line segment with endpoints (x_1, y_1) and $(x_2\ y_2)$ and one or both endpoints outside the clipping rectangle, the parametric representation,

$$x = x_1 + u(x_2 - x_1)$$

$$y = y_1 + u(y_2 - y_1)\ 0 \le u \le 1$$

(4.6)

could be used to determine values of parameter u for intersections with the clipping boundary coordinates. If the value of u for an intersection with a rectangle boundary edge is outside the range *0* to *1*, the line does not enter the interior of the window at that boundary. If the value of u is within the range from *0* to *1*, the line segment does indeed cross into the clipping area.

4.6.1. Cohen – Sutherland Line Clipping Algorithm

This is one of the oldest and most popular line - clipping procedures. Generally, the method speeds up the processing of line segments by performing initial tests that reduce the number of intersections that must be calculated. Every line end point in a picture is assigned a four-digit binary code, called a region code that identifies the location of the point relative to the boundaries of the clipping rectangle. Regions are set up in reference to the boundaries as shown in Fig. 4.8. Each bit position in the region code is used to indicate one of the four relative coordinate positions of the point with respect to the clip window: to the left, right, top, or bottom. By numbering the bit positions in the region code as 1 through 4 from right to left, the coordinate regions can be correlated with the bit positions as

bit 1: left

bit 2: right

bit 3: below

bit 4: above

A value of 1 in any bit position indicates that the point is in that relative position; otherwise, the bit position is set to 0. If a point is within the clipping rectangle, the region code is 0000. A point that is below and to the left of the rectangle has a region code of 0101.

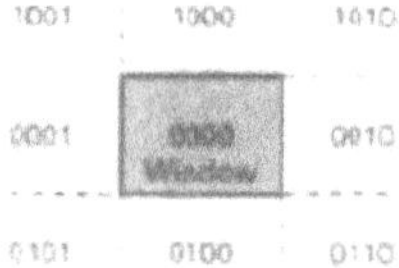

Figure 4.8: Binary Region Codes

Bit values in the region code are determined by comparing endpoint coordinate values *(x, y)* to the clip boundaries. Bit 1 is set to *1* if $x < xw_{min}$. The other three bit values can be determined using similar comparisons. For languages in which bit manipulation is possible, region-code bit values can be determined with the following two steps:

1. Calculate differences between endpoint coordinates and clipping boundaries.
2. Use the resultant sign bit of each difference.

Calculation to set the corresponding value in the region code. *Bit 1* is the sign bit of $x - xw_{min}$ bit *2* is the sign bit of $xw_{max} - x$; bit *3* is the sign bit of $y - yw_{min}$ and bit 4 is the sign bit of $yw_{max} - y$.

Once we have established region codes for all line endpoints, we can quickly determine which lines are completely inside the clip window and which are clearly outside. Any lines that are completely contained within the window boundaries have a region code of 0000 for both endpoints, and we trivially accept these lines. Any lines that have a 1 in the same bit position in the region codes for each endpoint are completely outside the clipping rectangle, and we trivially reject these lines. We would discard the line that has a region code of 1001 for one endpoint and a code of 0101 for the other endpoint. Both endpoints of this line are left of the clipping rectangle, as indicated by the 1 in the first bit position of each region code. A method that can be used to test lines for total clipping is to perform the logical and operation with both region codes. If the result is not 0000, the line is completely outside the clipping region.

Lines that cannot be identified as completely inside or completely outside a clip window by these tests are checked for intersection with the window boundaries. As shown in Fig. 4.9, such lines may or may not cross into the window interior. We begin the clipping process for a line by comparing an outside endpoint to a clipping boundary to determine how much of the line can be discarded. Then the remaining part of the Line is checked against the other boundaries, and we continue until either the line is totally discarded or a section is found inside the window. We set up our algorithm to check line endpoints against clipping boundaries in the order left, right, bottom, top.

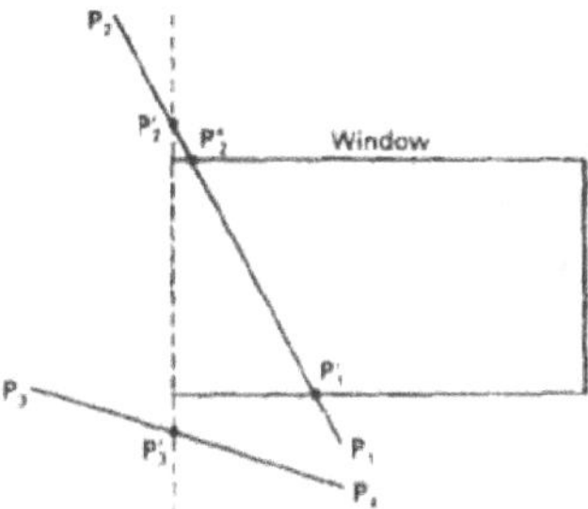

Figure 4.9: Line Intersect Clipping Boundaries without Entering the Window

To illustrate the specific steps in clipping lines against rectangular boundaries using the Cohen-Sutherland algorithm, we show how the lines in Fig. 4.9 could be processed. Starting with the bottom endpoint of the line from P_1 to P_2, we check P_1 against the left, right, and bottom boundaries in turn and find that this point is below the clipping rectangle. We then find the intersection point P_1 with the bottom boundary and discard the line section from P_1 to P_1'. The line now has been reduced to the section from P_1' to P_2. Since P_2 is outside the clip window, we check this endpoint against the boundaries and find that it is to the left of the window. Intersection point P_2' is calculated, but this point is above the window. So the final intersection calculation yields P_2'', and the line from P_1' to P_2'' is saved. This completes processing for this line, so we save this part and go on to the next line. Point P_3 in the next line is to the left of the clipping rectangle, so we determine the intersection P_3' and eliminate the line section from P_3 to $P3'$. By checking region codes for the line section from $P_{3'}$ to P_4 we find that the remainder of the line is below the clip window and can be discarded also.

Intersection points with a clipping boundary can be calculated using the slope-intercept form of the line equation. For a line with endpoint coordinates *(x₁, y₁)* and *(x₂, y₂)* they coordinate of the intersection point with a vertical boundary can be obtained with the calculation

$$y = y_1 + m(x - x_1) \qquad (4.7)$$

where the *x* value is set either to *xw$_{min}$* or to *xw$_{max}$* and the slope of the line is calculated as *m = (y₂ – y₁) / (x₂ – x₁)*. Similarly, if we are looking for the intersection with a horizontal boundary, the *x* coordinate can be calculated as

$$x = x_1 + \frac{y - y_1}{m} \qquad (4.8)$$

with y set either to *yw$_{min}$* or to *yw$_{max}$*.

4.7. Polygon Clipping

To clip polygons, we need to modify the line-clipping procedures discussed in the previous section. A polygon boundary processed with a line clipper may be displayed as a series of unconnected line segments (Fig. 4.10), depending on the orientation of the polygon to the clipping window. What we really want to display is a bounded area after clipping, as in Fig. 4.11. For polygon clipping, we require an algorithm that will generate one or more closed areas that are then scan converted for the appropriate area fill. The output of a polygon clipper should be a sequence of vertices that defines the clipped polygon boundaries.

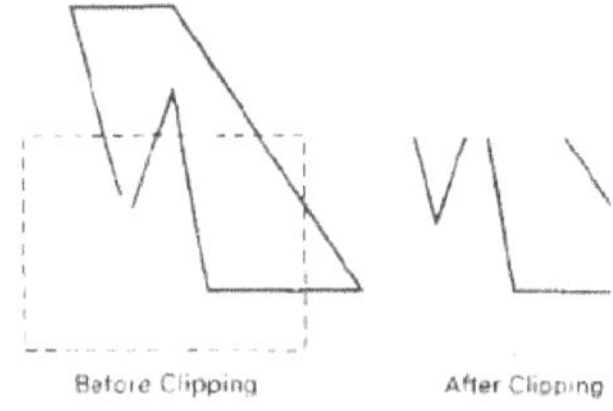

Figure 4.10: Display of a Polygon Processed by a Line-clipping Algorithm

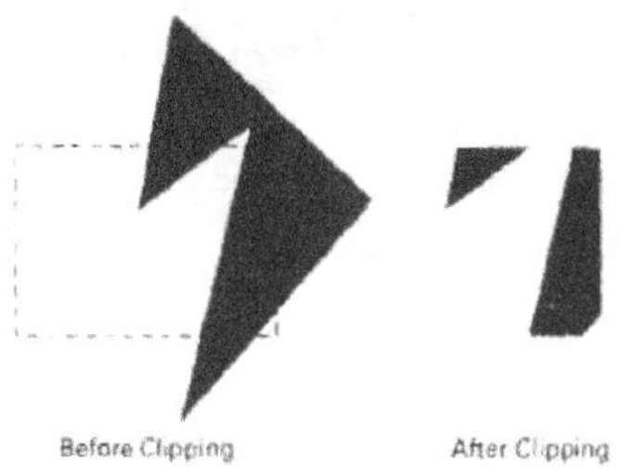

Figure 4.11: Display of Correctly Clipped Polygon

4.7.1. *Sutherland-Hodgeman Polygon Clipping*

We can correctly clip a polygon by processing the polygon boundary as a whole against each window edge. This could be accomplished by processing all polygon vertices against each clip rectangle boundary in turn. Beginning with the initial set of polygon vertices, we could first clip the polygon against the left rectangle boundary to produce a new sequence of vertices. The new set of vertices could then be successively passed to a right boundary clipper, a bottom boundary clipper, and a top boundary clipper, as in Fig. 4.12. At each step, a new sequence of output vertices is generated and passed to the next window boundary clipper.

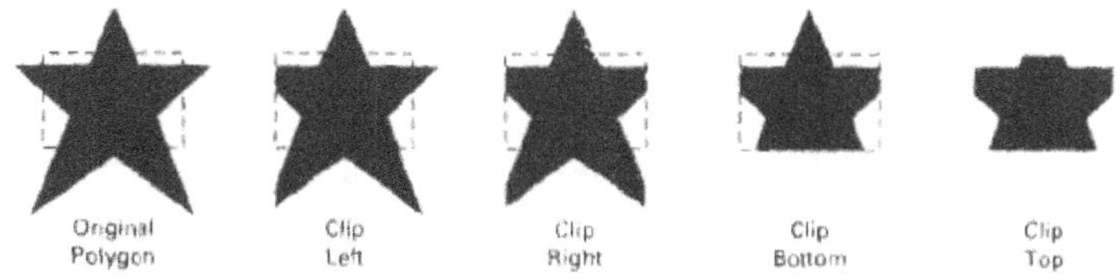

Figure 4.12: Clipping a Polygon against Successive Window Boundaries

There are four possible cases when processing vertices in sequence around the perimeter of a polygon. As each pair of adjacent polygon vertices is passed to a window boundary clipper, we make the following tests:

(1) If the first vertex is outside the window boundary and the second vertex is inside, both the intersection point of the polygon edge with the window boundary and the second vertex are added to the output vertex list.

(2) If both input vertices are inside the window boundary, only the second vertex is added to the output vertex list.

(3) If the first vertex is inside the window boundary and the second vertex is outside, only the edge intersection with the window boundary is added to the output vertex list.

(4) If both input vertices are outside the window boundary, nothing is added to the output list.

These four cases are illustrated in Fig. 4.13 for successive pairs of polygon vertices. Once all vertices have been processed for one clip window boundary, the output list of vertices is clipped against the next window boundary.

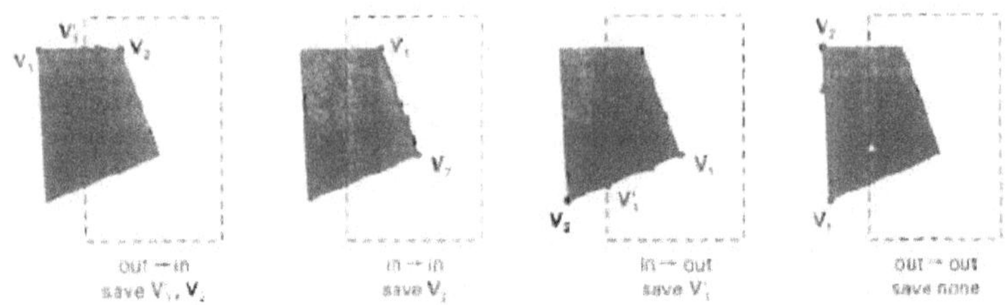

Figure 4.13: Successive Processing of Pairs of Polygon Vertices against the Left Widow Boundary

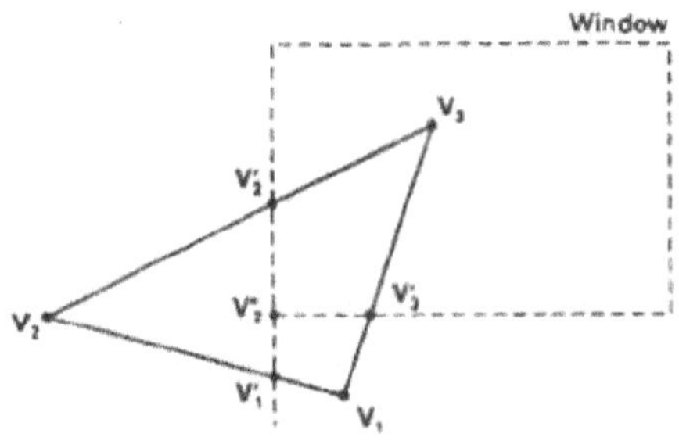

Figure 4.14: A Polygon Overlapping a Rectangular Clip Window

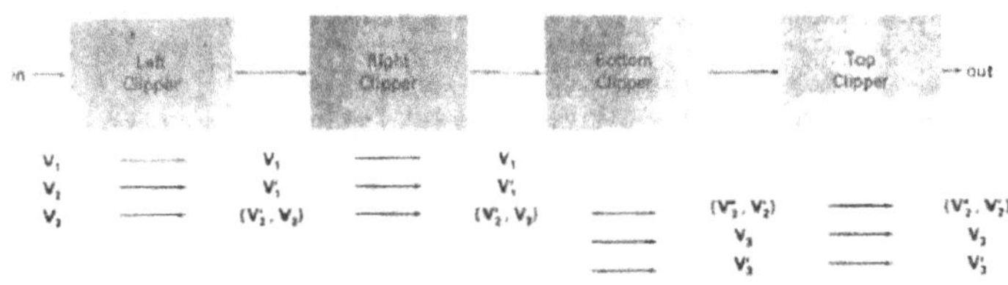

Figure 4.15: Processing the Vertices of the Polygon in Fig. 4.14 through a Boundary-clipping Pipeline. After all Vertices are Processed through the Pipeline, the Vertex List for the Clipped Polygon is (v2'', v2', v3, v3')

5. 3D Object Representations

5.1. Polygon Surfaces

The most commonly used boundary representation for a three-dimensional graphics object is a set of surface polygons that enclose the object interior. Many graphics systems store all object descriptions as sets of surface polygons. This simplifies and speeds up the surface rendering and display of objects, since all surfaces are described with linear equations.

5.1.1. Polygon Tables

Polygon data tables can be organized into two groups: *geometric tables* and *attribute tables*. Geometric data tables contain vertex coordinates and parameters to identify the spatial orientation of the polygon surfaces. Attribute information for an object includes parameters specifying the degree of transparency of the object and its surface reflectivity and texture characteristics.

A convenient organization for storing geometric data is to create three lists: a vertex table, an edge table, and a polygon table. Coordinate values for each vertex in the object are stored in the vertex table. The edge table contains pointers back into the vertex table to identify the vertices for each polygon edge. And the polygon table contains pointers back into the edge table to identify the edges for each polygon. This scheme is illustrated in Fig. 5.1 for two adjacent polygons on an object surface. In addition, individual objects and their component polygon faces can be assigned object and facet identifiers for easy reference.

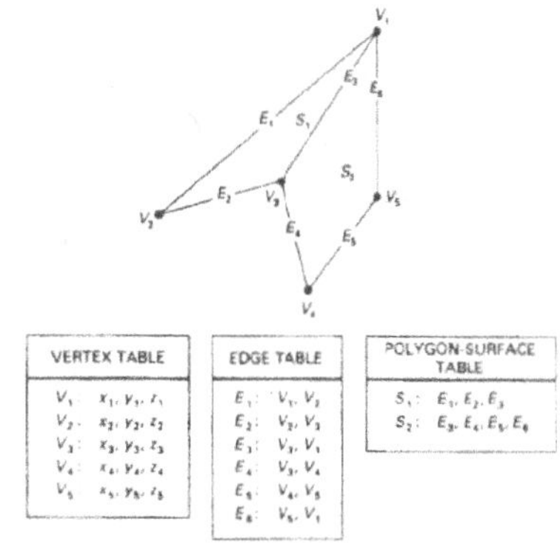

Figure 5.1: Geometric Data Table Representation

Listing the geometric data in three tables, as in Fig. 5.1, provides a convenient reference to the individual components (vertices, edges, and polygons) of each object. Also, the object can be displayed efficiently by using data from the edge table to draw the component lines. An alternative arrangement is to use just two tables: a vertex table and a polygon table. But this scheme is less convenient, and some edges could get drawn twice. Another possibility is to use only a polygon table, but this duplicates coordinate information, since explicit coordinate values are listed for each vertex in each polygon. Also edge Information would have to be reconstructed from the vertex listings in the polygon table.

We can add extra information to the data tables of Fig. 5.1 for faster information extraction. For instance. We could expand the edge table to include forward pointers into the polygon table so that common edges between polygons could be identified mow rapidly (Fig. 5.2). This is particularly useful for the rendering procedures that must vary surface shading smoothly across the edges from one polygon to the next. Similarly, the vertex table could be expanded so that vertices are cross-referenced to corresponding edge.

$$
\begin{aligned}
E_1 &: \quad V_1,\ V_2,\ S_1 \\
E_2 &: \quad V_2,\ V_3,\ S_1 \\
E_3 &: \quad V_3,\ V_1,\ S_1,\ S_2 \\
E_4 &: \quad V_3,\ V_4,\ S_2 \\
E_5 &: \quad V_4,\ V_5,\ S_2 \\
E_6 &: \quad V_5,\ V_1,\ S_2
\end{aligned}
$$

Figure 5.2: Edge Table for the Surfaces of Fig. 5.1 Expanded to Include Pointers to the Polygon Table

Since the geometric data tables may contain extensive listings of vertices and edges for complex objects, it is important that the data be checked for consistency and completeness. When vertex, edge, and polygon definitions are specified, it is possible, particularly in interactive applications, that certain input errors could be made that would distort the display of the object. The more information included in the data tables, the easier it is to check for errors. Therefore, error checking is easier when three data tables (vertex, edge, and polygon) are used, since this scheme provides the most information. Some of the tests that could be performed by a graphics package are (1) that every vertex is listed as an endpoint for at least two edges, (2) that every edge is part of at least one polygon, (3) that every polygon is closed, (4) that each polygon has at least one shared edge, and (5) that if the edge table contains pointers to polygons, every edge referenced by a polygon pointer has a reciprocal pointer back to the polygon.

5.1.2. *Plane Equations*

To produce a display of a three-dimensional object, we must process the input data representation for the object through several procedures. These processing steps include transformation of the modeling and world-coordinate descriptions to viewing coordinates, then to device coordinates; identification of visible surfaces; and the application of surface-rendering procedures This information is obtained from the vertex coordinate values and the equations that describe the polygon planes.

The equation for aplane surface can be expressed in the form,

$$Ax + By + Cz + D = 0 \tag{5.1}$$

where (x, y, z) is any point the plane, and the coefficients A, B, C, and D are constants describing the, spatial properties of the plane. We can obtain the values of A, B, C, and D by solving a set of three plane equations using the coordinate values for three non-collinear points in the plane. For this purpose, we can select three successive polygon vertices, (x_1, y_1, z_1), (x_2, y_2, z_2), and (x_3, y_3, z_3), and solve the following set of simultaneous linear plane equations for the ratios A/D, B/D, and C/D:

$$(A / D)x_k + (B / D)y_k + (C / D)z_k = -1 \qquad k = 1, 2, 3 \tag{5.2}$$

The solution for this set of equations can be obtained in determinant form, using Cramer's rule, as

$$A = \begin{vmatrix} 1 & y_1 & z_1 \\ 1 & y_2 & z_2 \\ 1 & y_3 & z_3 \end{vmatrix} \qquad B = \begin{vmatrix} x_1 & 1 & z_1 \\ x_2 & 1 & z_2 \\ x_3 & 1 & z_3 \end{vmatrix}$$

$$C = \begin{vmatrix} x_1 & y_1 & 1 \\ x_2 & y_2 & 1 \\ x_3 & y_3 & 1 \end{vmatrix} \qquad D = - \begin{vmatrix} x_1 & y_1 & z_1 \\ x_2 & y_2 & z_2 \\ x_3 & y_3 & z_3 \end{vmatrix} \tag{5.3}$$

Expanding the determinants, we can write the calculations for the plane coefficients in the form,

$$A = y_1(z_2 - z_3) + y_2(z_3 - z_1) + y_3(z_1 - z_2)$$
$$B = z_1(x_2 - x_3) + z_2(x_3 - x_1) + z_3(x_1 - x_2)$$
$$C = x_1(y_2 - y_3) + x_2(y_3 - y_1) + x_3(y_1 - y_2)$$
$$D = -x_1(y_2 z_3 - y_3 z_2) - x_2(y_3 z_1 - y_1 z_3) - x_3(y_1 z_2 - y_2 z_1) \tag{5.4}$$

As vertex values and other information are entered into the polygon data structure, values tor A, B, C, and D are computed for each polygon and stored with the other polygon data.

Plane equations are used also to identify the position of spatial points relative to the plane surfaces of an object. For any point *(x, y, z)* not on a plane with parameters *A, B, C, D*, we have

$$Ax + By + Cz + D \neq 0$$

We can identify the point as either inside or outside the plane surface according to the sign (negative or positive) of *Ax + By + Cz + D:*

if $Ax + By + Cz + D < 0$, the point (x, y, z) is inside the surface

if $Ax + By + Cz + D > 0$, the point (x, y, z) is outside the surface

These inequality tests are valid in a right-handed Cartesian system, provided the plane parameters A, *B,* C, and D were calculated using vertices selected in a counter clockwise order when viewing the surface in an outside-to-inside direction.

5.1.3. *Polygon Meshes*

Some graphics packages (for example, PHIGS) provide several polygon functions for modeling objects. A single plane surface can be specified with a function such as *fill Area*. But when object surfaces are to be tiled, it is more convenient to specify the surface facets with a mesh function. One type of polygon mesh is the triangle strip. This function produces n - 2 connected triangles, as shown in Fig. 5.3, given the coordinates for n vertices. Another similar function is the quadrilateral mesh, which generates a mesh of (n - 1) by (m - 1) quadrilaterals, given, the coordinates for an n by m array of vertices. Figure 5.4 shows 20 vertices forming a mesh of 12 quadrilaterals.

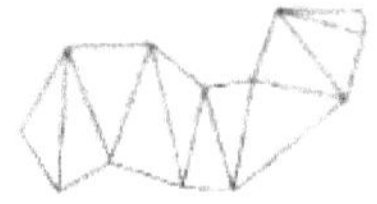

Figure 5.3

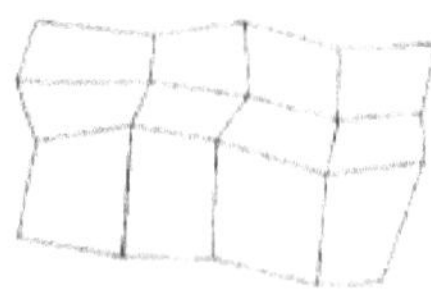

Figure 5.4

5.2. Quadric Surfaces

A frequently used class of objects are the quadric surfaces, which are described with second-degree equations (quadratics). They include spheres, ellipsoids, tori, parabolics, and hyperboloids. Quadric surfaces, particularly spheres and ellipsoids, are common elements of graphics scenes, and they are often available in graphics packages as primitives horn which more complex objects can be constructed.

Sphere

In Cartesian coordinates, a spherical surface with radius r centred on the coordinate origin is defined as the set of points (x, y, z) that satisfy the equation

$$x^2 + y^2 + z^2 = r^2 \tag{5.5}$$

We can also describe the spherical surface in parametric form, using latitude and longitude angles (Fig. 5.5):

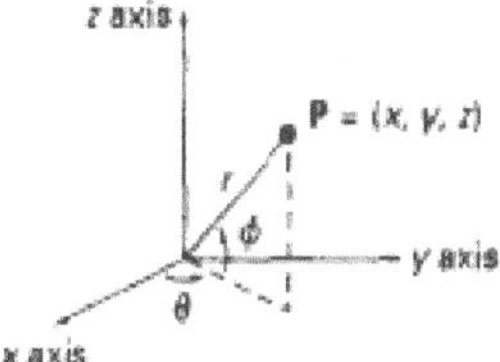

Figure 5.5: Parametric Coordinate Position (r, θ, φ) on the Surface of a Sphere with Radius r

$$x = r \cos\phi \cos\theta, \qquad -\pi/2 \leq \phi \leq \pi/2$$
$$y = r \cos\phi \sin\theta, \qquad -\pi \leq \theta \leq \pi$$
$$z = r \sin\phi \tag{5.6}$$

The parametric representation in Eqs. 5.6 provides a symmetric range for the angular parameters θ and ϕ.

Ellipsoid

An ellipsoidal surface can be described as an extension of a spherical surface, where the radii in three mutually perpendicular directions can have different values (Fig. 5.6). The Cartesian representation for points over the surface of an ellipsoid centered on the origin is,

$$\left(\frac{x}{r_x}\right)^2 + \left(\frac{y}{r_y}\right)^2 + \left(\frac{z}{r_z}\right)^2 = 1 \tag{5.7}$$

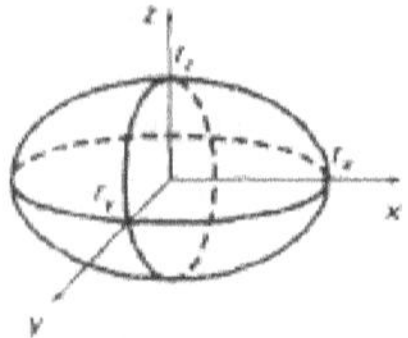

Figure 5.6: An Ellipsoid

and a parametric representation for the ellipsoid in terms of the latitude angle ϕ and the longitude angle θ in Fig 5.5 is,

$$
\begin{aligned}
x &= r_x \cos\phi \cos\theta, & -\pi/2 \leq \phi \leq \pi/2 \\
y &= r_y \cos\phi \sin\theta, & -\pi \leq \theta \leq \pi \\
z &= r_z \sin\phi
\end{aligned}
\tag{5.8}
$$

Torus

A torus is a doughnut-shaped object, as shown in Fig. 5.7. It can be generated by rotating a circle or other conic about a specified axis. The Cartesian representation for points over the surface of a torus can be written in the form.

$$
\left[r - \sqrt{\left(\frac{x}{r_x}\right)^2 + \left(\frac{y}{r_y}\right)^2} \right]^2 + \left(\frac{z}{r_z}\right)^2 = 1
\tag{5.9}
$$

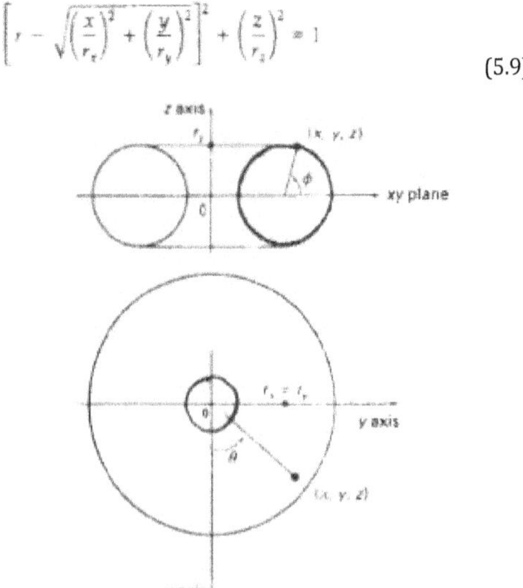

Figure 5.7: A Torus with a Circular Cross Section Centered on the Coordinate Origin

where r is any given offset value. Parametric representations for a torus are similar to those for an ellipse, except that angle d extends over 360^0. Using latitude and longitude angles θ and ϕ, we can describe the torus surface as the set of points that satisfy,

$$x = r_1(r + \cos\phi)\cos\theta, \qquad -\pi \leq \phi \leq \pi$$
$$y = r_2(r + \cos\phi)\sin\theta, \qquad -\pi \leq \theta \leq \pi$$
$$z = r_z \sin\phi$$

$$(5.10)$$

5.3.   Spline Representation

In drafting terminology, a spline is a flexible strip used to produce a smooth curve through a designated set of points. Several small weights are distributed along the length of the strip to hold it in position on the drafting table as the curve is drawn. The term spline curve originally referred to a curve drawn in this manner. We can mathematically describe such a curve with a piecewise cubicpolynomial function whose first and second derivatives are continuous across the various curve sections. In computer graphics, the term spline curve now refers to any composite curve formed with polynomial sections satisfying specified continuity conditions at the boundary of the pieces. A spline surface can be described with two sets of orthogonal spline curves. There are several different kinds of spline specifications that are used in graphics applications. Each individual specification simply refers to a particular type of polynomial with certain specified boundary conditions.

Splines are used in graphics applications to design curve and surface shapes, to digitize drawings for computer storage, and to specify animation paths for the objects or the camera in a scene.

Interpolation and Approximation Splines

We specify a spline curve by giving a set of coordinate positions, called control points, which indicates the general shape of the curve. These control points are then fitted with piecewise continuous pararneteric polynomial functions in one of two ways. When polynomial sections are fitted so that the curve passes through each control point, as in Fig. 5.8, the resulting curve is said to interpolate the set of control points. On the other hand, when the polynomials are fitted to the general control-point path without necessarily passing through any control point, the resulting curve is said to approximate the set of control points (Fig. 5.9)

The convex polygon boundary that encloses a set of control points is called the *convex hull*. One way to envision the shape of a convex hull is to imagine a rubber band stretched around the positions of the control points so that each control point is either on the perimeter of the hull or inside it (Fig. 5.10). Convex hulls provide a measure for the deviation of a curve or surface from the region bounding the control points.

A polyline connecting the sequence of control points for an approximation spline is usually displayed to remind a designer of the control-point ordering. This set of connected line segments is often referred to as the control graph of the curve. Other names for the series of straight-line sections connecting the control points in the order specified are control polygon and characteristic polygon. Figure 5.11 show the shape of the control graph for the control-point sequences in Fig. 5.10.

Figure 5.8: Interpolation

Figure 5.9: Approximation

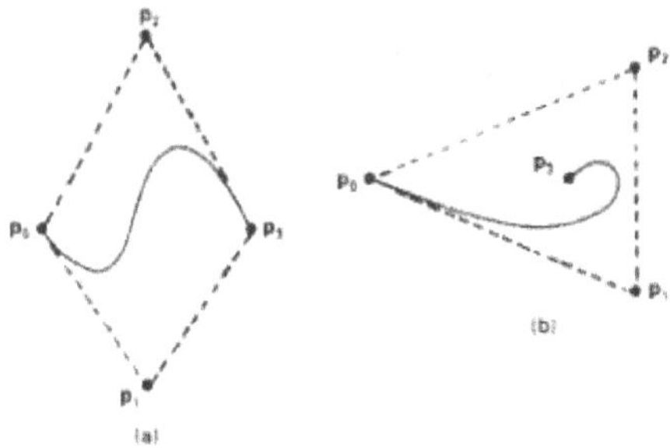

Figure 5.10: Convex-hull Shapes (Dashed Lines) for Two Sets of Control Points

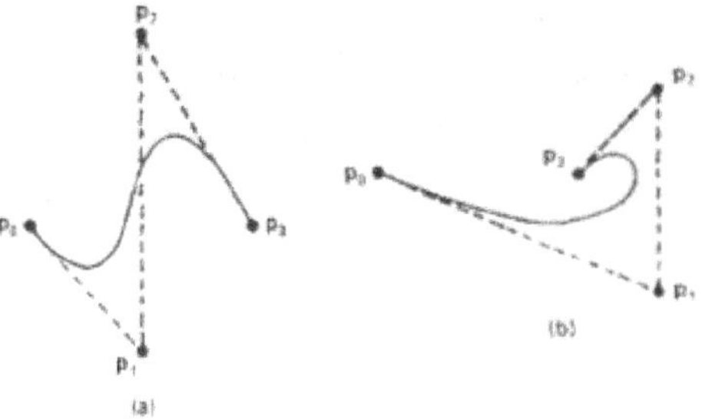

Figure 5.11: Control-graph Shapes (Dashed Lines) for Two different Sets of Control Points

Parametric Continuity Conditions

To ensure a smooth transition from one section of a piecewise parametric curve to the next, we can impose various continuity conditions at the connection points. If each section of a spline is described with a set of parametric coordinate functions of the form

$$x = x(u), y = y(u), z = z(u) \qquad u_1 \leq u \leq u_2 \qquad (5.11)$$

we set parametric continuity by matching the parametric derivatives of adjoining curve sections at their common boundary.

Zero-order parametric continuity, described as C^0 continuity, means simply that the curves meet. That is, the values of x, y, and z evaluated at u_2 for the first curve section are equal, respectively, to the values of x, y, and z evaluated at u_1 for the next curve section. *First-order parametric continuity*, referred to as C^1 continuity, means that the first parametric derivatives (tangent lines) of the coordinate functions in Eq. 5.11 for two successive curve sections are equal at their joining point. *Second-order parametric continuity*, or C^2 continuity, means that both the first and second parametric derivatives of the two curve sections are the same at the intersection, Higher-order parametric continuity conditions are defined similarly. Figure 5.12 shows examples of C^0, C^1, and C^2 continuity.

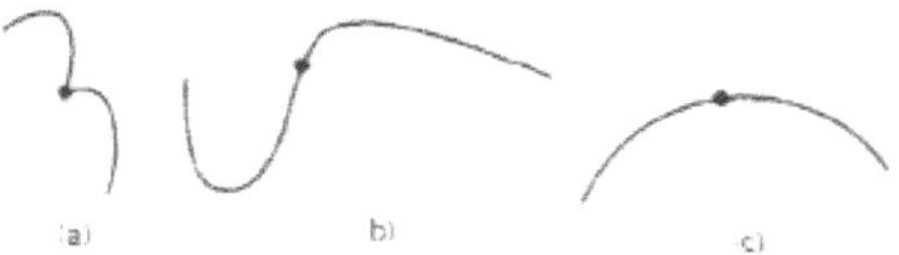

Figure 5.12: Piecewise Construction of a Curve by Joining Two Curve Segments Using different Orders of Continuity: (a) Zero-order Continuity only, (b) First-order Continuity, and (c) Second-order Continuity

Geometric Continuity Condition

An alternate method for joining two successive curve sections is to specify conditions for geometric continuity. In this case, we only require parametric derivatives of the two sections to be proportional to each other at their common boundary instead of equal to each other.

Zero-order geometric continuity, described as G^0 continuity is the same as zero-order parametric continuity. That is, the two curves sections must have the same coordinate position at the boundary point. *First-order geometric continuity*, or G^1 continuity, means that the parametric first derivatives are proportional at the intersection of two successive sections. If we denote the parametric position on the curve as $P(u)$, the direction of the tangent vector $P'(u)$, but not necessarily its magnitude, will be the same for two successive curve sections at their joining point under G^1 continuity. *Second-order geometric continuity*, or G^2 continuity means that both the first and second parametric derivatives of the two curve sections are proportional at their boundary. Under G^2 continuity, curvatures of two curve sections will match at the joining position.

A curve generated with geometric continuity conditions is similar to one generated with parametric continuity, but with slight differences in curve shape. Figure 5.13 provides a comparison of geometric and parametric continuity. With geometric continuity, the curve is pulled toward the section with the greater tangent vector.

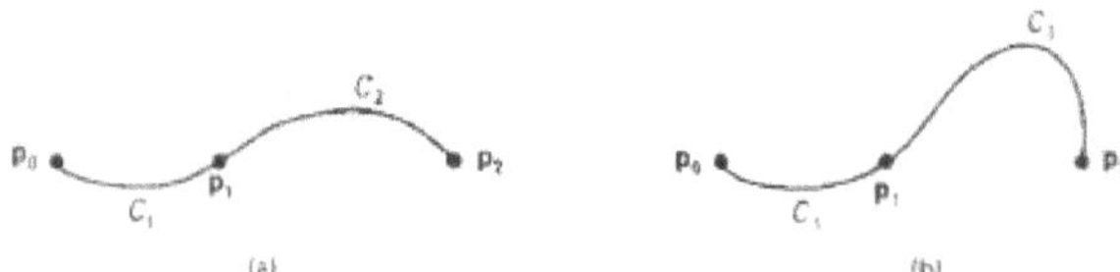

Figure 5.13: Three Control Points Fitted with Two Curve Sections Joined with (a) Parametric Continuity and (b) Geometric Continuity, where the Tangent Vector of Curve C_3 at Point p_1 has a Greater Magnitude than the Tangent Vector of Curve C_1 at p_1

Spline Specification

There are three equivalent methods for specifying a particular spline representation:

(1) We can state the set of boundary conditions that are imposed on the spline; or (2) we can state the matrix that characterizes the spline; or (3) we can state the set of blending functions (or basis functions) that determine how specified geometric constraints on the curve are combined to calculate positions along the curve path.

To illustrate these three equivalent specifications, suppose we have the following parametric cubic polynomial representation for the x coordinate along the path of a spline section:

$$x(u) = a_x u^3 + b_x u^2 + c_x u + d_x \qquad 0 \leq u \leq 1 \qquad (5.12)$$

Boundary conditions for this curve might be set, for example, on the endpoint coordinates $x(0)$ and $x(1)$ and on the parametric first derivatives at the endpoints $x'(0)$ and $x'(1)$. These four boundary conditions are sufficient to determine the values of the four coefficients a_x, b_x, c_x, and d_x

From the boundary conditions, we can obtain the matrix that characterizes this spline curve by first rewriting Eq. 5.12 as the matrix product

$$x(u) = [u^3 \ u^2 \ u \ 1] \begin{bmatrix} a_x \\ b_x \\ c_x \\ d_x \end{bmatrix}$$

$$(5.13)$$

$$= U \cdot C$$

where U is the row matrix of powers of parameter u, and C is the coefficient column matrix. Using

Eq. 5.13, we can write the boundary conditions in matrix form and solve for the coefficient matrix C as

$$C = M_{spline} \cdot M_{geom} \qquad (5.14)$$

Where M_{geom} is a four-element column matrix containing the geometric constraint values (boundary conditions) on the spline; and M_{spline} is the 4-by-4 matrix that transforms the geometric constraint values to the polynomial coefficients and provides a characterization for the spline curve. Matrix M_{geom} contains control point coordinate values and other geometric constraints that have been specified. Thus, we can substitute the matrix representation for C into Eq. 5.13 to obtain

$$x(u) = U \cdot M_{spline} \cdot M_{geom} \qquad (5.15)$$

The matrix, M_{spline} characterizing a spline representation, sometimes called the basis matrix, is particularly useful for transforming from one spline representation to another.

Finally, we can expand Eq. 5.15 to obtain a polynomial representation for coordinate x in terms of the geometric constraint parameters

$$x(u) = \sum_{k=0}^{3} g_k \cdot BF_k(u)$$

$$(5.16)$$

where g_k are the constraint parameters, such as the control-point coordinates and slope of the curve at the control points, and $BF_k(u)$ are the polynomial blending functions. In the following sections, we discuss some commonly used splines and their matrix and blending-function specifications.

CHAPTER VI

6. 3D Geometric Transformations

6.1. Translation

In a three-dimensional homogeneous coordinate representation, a point is translated (Fig. 6.1) from position

P = (x, y, z) to position P' = (x', y', z') with the matrix operation,

$$\begin{bmatrix} x' \\ y' \\ z' \\ 1 \end{bmatrix} = \begin{bmatrix} 1 & 0 & 0 & t_x \\ 0 & 1 & 0 & t_y \\ 0 & 0 & 1 & t_z \\ 0 & 0 & 0 & 1 \end{bmatrix} \cdot \begin{bmatrix} x \\ y \\ z \\ 1 \end{bmatrix}$$

(6.1)

Or

$$P' = T . P$$

(6.2)

Parameters t_x, t_y, and t_z, specifying translation distances for the coordinate directions x, y, and z, are assigned any real values. The matrix representation in Eq. 6.1 is equivalent to the three equation,

$$x' = x + t_x$$
$$y' = y + t_y$$
$$z' = z + t_z$$

(6.3)

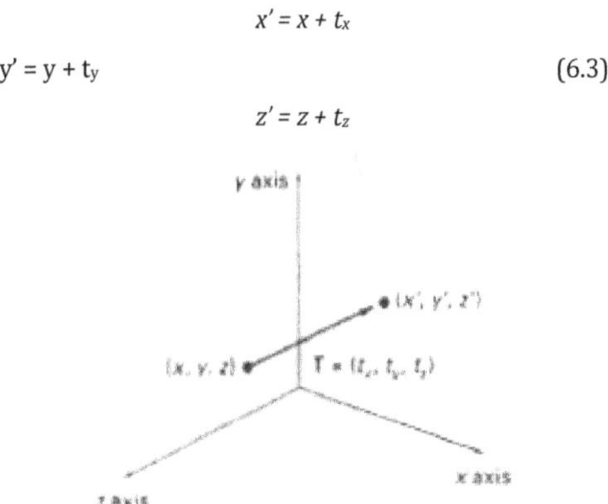

Figure 6.1: Translating a Point

An object is translated in three dimensions by transforming each of the defining points of the object. For an object represented as a set of polygon surfaces, we translate each vertex of each surface and redraw the polygon facets in the new position.

We obtain the inverse of the translation matrix in Eq. 6.1 by negating the translation distances t_x, t_y, and t_z. This produces a translation in the opposite direction, and the product of a translation matrix and its inverse produces the identity matrix.

6.2. Rotation

To generate a rotation transformation for an object, we must designate an axis of rotation (about which the object is to be rotated) and the amount of angular rotation. Unlike two-dimensional applications, where all transformations are carried out in the xy plane, a three-dimensional rotation can be specified around any line in space. The easiest rotation axes to handle are those that are parallel to the coordinate axes. Also, we can use combinations of coordinate axis rotations (along with appropriate translations) to specify any general rotation.

By convention, positive rotation angles produce counter clockwise rotations about a coordinate axis, if we are looking along the positive half of the axis toward the coordinate origin. This agrees with our earlier discussion of rotation in two dimensions, where positive rotations in the *xy* plane are counterclockwise about axes parallel to the z axis.

Coordinate-Axes Rotations

The two-dimensional z-axis rotation equations are easily extended to three dimensions:

$$x' = x \cos \theta - y \sin \theta$$
$$y' = x \sin \theta + y \cos \theta \tag{6.4}$$
$$z' = z$$

Parameter θ specifies the rotation angle. In homogeneous coordinate form, the three-dimensional *z*-axis rotation equations are expressed as,

$$\begin{bmatrix} x' \\ y' \\ z' \\ 1 \end{bmatrix} = \begin{bmatrix} \cos \theta & -\sin \theta & 0 & 0 \\ \sin \theta & \cos \theta & 0 & 0 \\ 0 & 0 & 1 & 0 \\ 0 & 0 & 0 & 1 \end{bmatrix} \begin{bmatrix} x \\ y \\ z \\ 1 \end{bmatrix} \tag{6.5}$$

which we can write more compactly as

$$P' = R_z(\theta) \cdot P \tag{6.6}$$

Transformation equations for rotations about the other two coordinate axes can be obtained with a cyclic permutation of the coordinate parameters x, y, and z in Eqs. 6.4. That is, we use the replacements

$$x \to y \to z \to x \tag{6.7}$$

Substituting permutations *6.7* in *Eqs. 6.4*, we get the equations for an *x-axis* rotation:

$$y' = y \cos \theta - z \sin \theta$$

$$z' = y \sin \theta + z \cos \theta \qquad (6.8)$$

$$x' = x$$

which can be written in the homogeneous coordinate form,

$$\begin{bmatrix} x' \\ y' \\ z' \\ 1 \end{bmatrix} = \begin{bmatrix} 1 & 0 & 0 & 0 \\ 0 & \cos \theta & -\sin \theta & 0 \\ 0 & \sin \theta & \cos \theta & 0 \\ 0 & 0 & 0 & 1 \end{bmatrix} \cdot \begin{bmatrix} x \\ y \\ z \\ 1 \end{bmatrix} \qquad (6.9)$$

Or

$$P' = R_x(\theta) \cdot P \qquad (6.10)$$

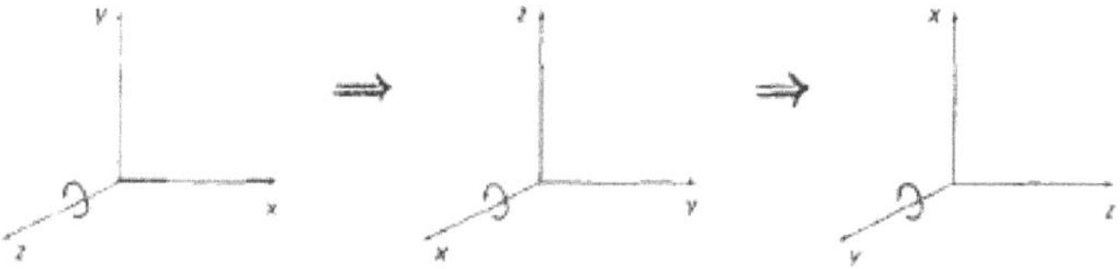

Figure 6.2: Cyclic Permutation of the Cartesian – Coordinate Axes to Produce the Rotation Equations

Cyclically permuting coordinates in Eqs. 6.8 give us the transformation equations for a y-axis rotation

$$z' = z\cos \theta - x \sin \theta$$

$$x' = z \sin \theta + x\cos \theta \qquad (6.11)$$

$$y' = y$$

The matrix representation for *y-axis* rotation is

$$\begin{bmatrix} x' \\ y' \\ z' \\ 1 \end{bmatrix} = \begin{bmatrix} \cos \theta & 0 & \sin \theta & 0 \\ 0 & 1 & 0 & 0 \\ -\sin \theta & 0 & \cos \theta & 0 \\ 0 & 0 & 0 & 1 \end{bmatrix} \cdot \begin{bmatrix} x \\ y \\ z \\ 1 \end{bmatrix} \qquad (6.12)$$

Or

$$P' = R_y(\theta) \cdot P \qquad (6.13)$$

General Three-Dimensional Rotations

A rotation matrix for any axis that does not coincide with a coordinate axis can be set up as a composite transformation involving combinations of translation and the coordinate-axes rotations. We obtain the required composite matrix by first setting up the transformation sequence that moves the selected rotation axis onto one of the coordinate axes. Then we set up the rotation matrix about that coordinate axis for the specified rotation angle. The last step is to obtain the inverse transformation sequence that returns the rotation axis to its original position.

In the special case where an object is to be rotated about an axis that is parallel to one of the coordinate axes, we can attain the desired rotation with the following transformation sequence.

- Translate the object so that the rotation axis coincides with the parallel coordinate axis.
- Perform the specified rotation about that axis.
- Translate the object so that the rotation axis is moved back to its original position.

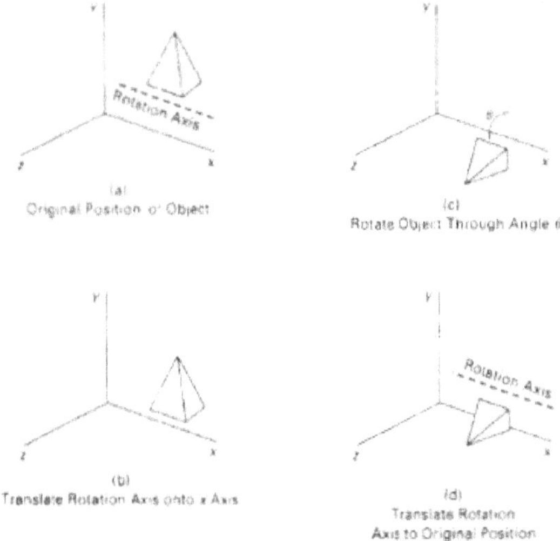

Figure 6.3: Sequence of Transformations for Rotating an Object about an Axis that is Parallel to the x Axis

The steps in this sequence are illustrated in *Fig. 6.3*. Any coordinate position P on the object in this figure is transformed with the sequence shown as,

$$T' = T^{-1} . R_x(\theta) . T . P$$

Where the composite matrix for the transformation is,

$$R(\theta) = T^{-1} . R_x(\theta) . T$$

which is of the same form as the two-dimensional transformation sequence for rotation about an arbitrary pivot point.

When an object is to be rotated about an axis that is not parallel to one of the coordinate axes, we need to perform some additional transformations. In this case, we also need rotations to align the axis with a selected coordinate axis and to bring the axis hack to its original orientation. Given the specifications for the rotation axis and the rotation angle, we can accomplish the required rotation in five step

- Translate the object so that the rotation axis passes through the coordinate origin.
- Rotate the object so that the axis of rotation coincides with one of the coordinate axes.
- Perform the specified rotation about that coordinate axis.
- Apply inverse rotations to bring the rotation axis back to its original orientation.
- Apply the inverse translation to bring the rotation axis back to its original position.

We can transform the rotation axis onto any of the three coordinate axes. The z axis is a reasonable choice and the following discussion shows how to set up the transformation matrices for getting the rotation axis onto the z axis and returning the rotation axis to its original position (*Fig. 6.4*).

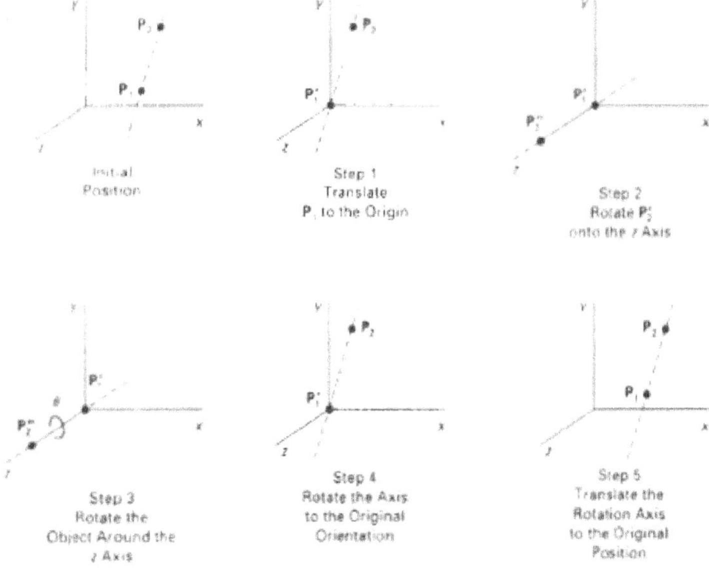

Figure 6.4: Five Transformation Steps for Obtaining a Composite Matrix for Rotation about an Arbitrary Axis, with the Rotation Axis Projected onto the z Axis

6.3.   Scaling

The matrix expression tor the scaling transformation of a position $P = (x, y, z)$ relative to the coordinate origin can be written as,

$$\begin{bmatrix} x' \\ y' \\ z' \\ 1 \end{bmatrix} = \begin{bmatrix} s_x & 0 & 0 & 0 \\ 0 & s_y & 0 & 0 \\ 0 & 0 & s_z & 0 \\ 0 & 0 & 0 & 1 \end{bmatrix} \cdot \begin{bmatrix} x \\ y \\ z \\ 1 \end{bmatrix} \tag{6.14}$$

Or

$$P' = S . P \tag{6.15}$$

where scaling parameters s_x, s_y, and s_z are assigned any positive values. Explicit expressions for the coordinate transformations for scaling relative to the origin are

$$x' = x . s_x, \qquad y' = y . s_y \qquad z' = z . s_z \tag{6.16}$$

Scaling an object with transformation eqn 6.14 changes the size of the object and repositions the object relative to the coordinate origin. Also, if the transformation parameters are not all equal, relative dimensions in the object are changed: We preserve the original shape of an object with a uniform scaling $(s_x = s_y = s_z)$. The result of scaling an object uniformly with each scaling parameter set to 2 is shown in Fig. 6.5.

Scaling with respect to a selected fixed position (x_f, y_f, z_f) can be represented with the following transformation sequence:

1. Translate the fixed point to the origin.

2. Scale the object relative to the coordinate origin using Eq. 6.14.

3. Translate the fixed point back to its original position.

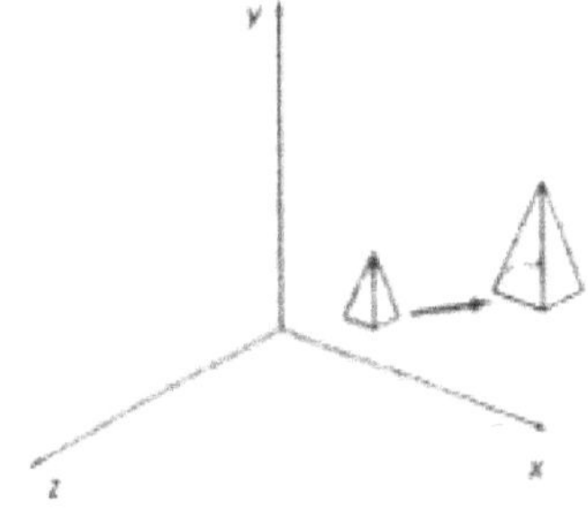

Figure 6.5: Scaling the Object

This sequence of transformations is demonstrated in *Fig. 6.6*. The matrix representation for an arbitrary fixed-point scaling can then be expressed as the concatenation of these translate-scale-translate transformations as

$$T(x_f, y_f, z_f) \cdot S(s_x, s_y, s_z) \cdot T(-x_f, -y_f, -z_f) = \begin{bmatrix} s_x & 0 & 0 & (1-s_x)x_f \\ 0 & s_y & 0 & (1-s_y)y_f \\ 0 & 0 & s_z & (1-s_z)z_f \\ 0 & 0 & 0 & 1 \end{bmatrix} \tag{6.17}$$

We form the inverse scaling matrix for either *Eq. 6.14* or *Eq. 6.17* by replacing the scaling parameters s_x, s_y, and s_z with their reciprocals. The inverse matrix generates an opposite scaling transformation, so the concatenation of any scaling matrix and its inverse produces the identity matrix.

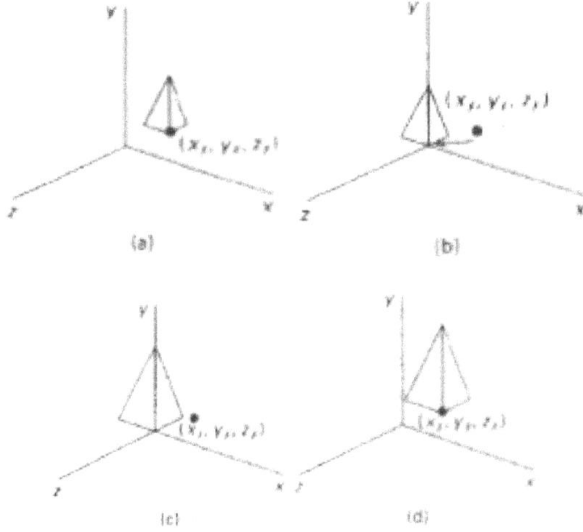

Figure 6.6: Scaling an Object Relative to a Selected Fixed Point is Equivalent to the Sequence of Transformations

6.4. Reflections

A three-dimensional reflection can be performed relative to a selected reflection axis or with respect to a selected repection plane. In general, three-dimensional refledion matrices are set up similarly to those for two dimensions. Reflections relative to a given axis are equivalent to 180° rotations about that axis. Reflections with respect to a plane are equivalent to 180° rotations in four-dimensional space. When the reflection plane is a coordinate plane (either xy, xz, or yz), we can think of the transformation as a conversion between Left-handed and right-handed systems.

An example of a reflection that converts coordinate specifications from aright-handed system to a left-handed system (or vice versa) is shown in Fig. 6.7. This transformation changes the sign of the z coordinates, leaving the x and y-coordinate values unchanged. The matrix representation for this reflection of points relative to the xy plane is

$$RF_z = \begin{bmatrix} 1 & 0 & 0 & 0 \\ 0 & 1 & 0 & 0 \\ 0 & 0 & -1 & 0 \\ 0 & 0 & 0 & 1 \end{bmatrix} \tag{6.18}$$

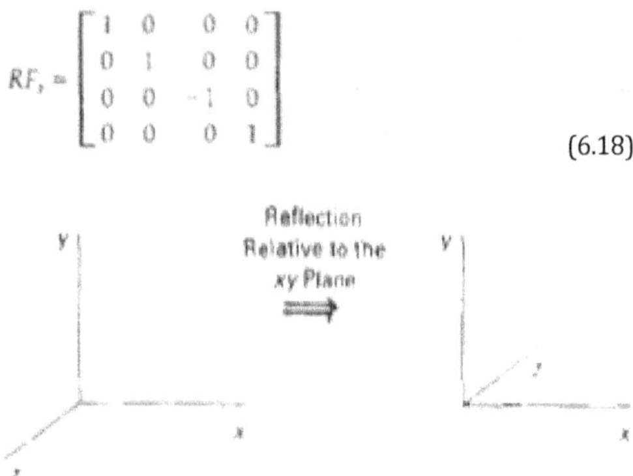

Figure 6.7: Conversion of Coordinate Specifications from a Right handed to a Left-handed System can be Carried Out with the Reflection Transformation

6.5. Shears

Shearing transformations can he used to modify object shapes. They are also useful in three-dimensional viewing for obtainuig grneral projection transformations. In two dimensions, we discussed tranformations relative to the x or y axes to produce distortions in the shapes of objects. In three dimensions, we can also generate shears relative to the z axis.

As an example of three-dimensional shearing the following transformation produces a $z\text{-}axis$ shear:

$$SH_z = \begin{bmatrix} 1 & 0 & a & 0 \\ 0 & 1 & b & 0 \\ 0 & 0 & 1 & 0 \\ 0 & 0 & 0 & 1 \end{bmatrix} \tag{6.19}$$

Parameters a and b can be assigned any real values. The effect of this transformation matrix is to alter x- and y coordinate values by an amount that is proportional to the z value, while leaving the z coordinate unchanged. Boundaries of planes that are perpendicular to the z axis are thus shifted by an amount proportional to z. An example of the effect of this shearing matrix on a unit cube is shown in Fig. 6.8, for shearing values a = b = 1. Shearing matrices for the x axis and y axis are defined similarly.

6.6.   Composite Transformations

As with two-dimensional transforrnations. we form a composite three-dimensional transformation by multiplying the matrix representations for the individual operations in the transformation sequence. The concatenation is carried outfrom right to left, where the right most matrix is the first transformation to be applied to an object and the leftmost matrix is the last transformation. A sequence of basic, three-dimensional geometric transformations are combined to produce a single composite transformation, which is then applied to the coordinate definition of an object.

6.7.   3D Viewing

In two-dimensional graphics applications, viewing operations transfer positions from the world-coordinate plane to pixel positions in the plane of the output device. Using the rectangular boundaries for the world-coordinate window and the device viewport, a two-dimensional package maps the world sceneto device coordinates and clips the scene against the four boundaries of the viewport. For three-dimensional graphics applications, the situation is a bit more involved, since we now have more choices as to how views are to be generated. First of all, we can view an object from any spatial position: from the front, from above, or from the back. Or we could generate a view of what we would see if we were standing in the middle of a group of objects or inside a single object, such asa building. Additionally, three-dimensional descriptions of objects must be projected onto the flat viewing surface of the output device. And the clipping boundaries now enclose a volume of space, whose shape depends on the type of projection we select. In this chapter, we explore the general operations needed to produce views of a three-dimensional scene, and we also discuss specific viewing procedures provided in packages such as PHIGS and GL.

6.8.   Viewing Pipeline

The steps for computer generation of a view of a three-dimensional scene are somewhat analogous to the processes involved in taking a photograph. To take asnapshot, we first need to position the camera at a particular point in space. Thenwe need to decide on the camera orientation *(Fig. 6.8):* Which way do we point the camera and how should we rotate it around the line of sight to set the up direction for the picture? Finally, when we snap the shutter, the scene is cropped to the size of the "window" of the camera, and light from the visible surfaces is projected onto the camera film. We need to keep in mind, however, that the camera analogy can be carried only so far, since we have more flexibility and many more options for generating views of a scene with a graphics package thanwe do with a camera.

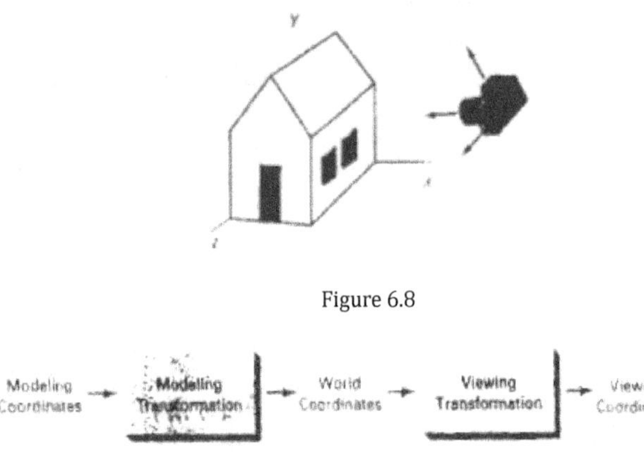

Figure 6.8

Figure 6.9

Figure 6.9 shows the general processing steps for modeling and converting a world-coordinate description of a scene to device coordinates. Once the scene has been modeled, world-coordinate positions are converted to viewing coordinates. The viewing-coordinate system is used in graphics packages as a reference for specifying the observer viewing position and the position of the projection plane, which we can think of in analogy with the camera film plane. Next, projection operations are performed to convert the viewing-coordinate description of the scene to coordinate positions on the projection plane, which will then be mapped to the output device. Objects outside the specified viewing limits are clipped h m further consideration, and the remaining objects are processed through visible-surface identification and surface-rendering procedures to produce the display within the device viewport.

6.9.   Viewing Coordinates

Generating a view of an object in three dimensions is similar to photographing the object. We can walk around and take its picture from any angle, at various distances, and with varying camera orientations. Whatever appears in the view finder is projected onto the flat film surface. The type and size of the camera lens determines which parts of the scene appear in the final picture. These ideas are incorporated into three dimensional graphics packages so that views of ascene can be generated, given the spatial position, orientation, and aperture size of the "camera".

Specifyingthe View Plane

We choose a particular view for a scene by first establishing the viewing-coordinate system, also called the view reference coordinate system, as shown in *Fig. 6.10*. A view plane, or projection plane, is then set up perpendicular to the viewing z_v axis. We can think of the view plane as the film plane in a camera that has been positioned and oriented for a particular shot of the scene. World-coordinate positions in the scene are transformed to viewing coordinates, then viewing coordinates are projected onto the view plane.

To establish the viewing-coordinate reference frame, we first pick a world coordinate position called the *view reference point*. This point is the origin ofour viewing-coordinate system. The view reference point is often chosen to beclose to or on the surface of some object in a scene. But we could also choose a point that is at the cent4.r of an object, or at the center of a group of objects, or somewhere out rn front of the scene to be displayed. If we choose a point that isnear to or on some object, we tan think of this point as the position where we might want to aim a camera to take a picture of the object. Alternatively, if we choose a point that is at some distance from a scene, we could think of this as the camera position.

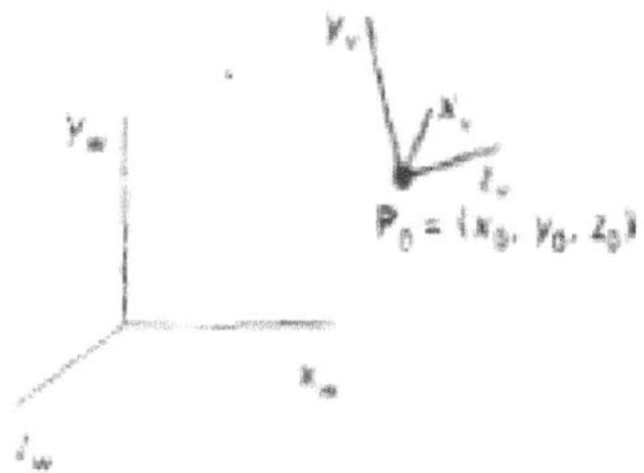

Figure 6.10: A Right Handed Viewing

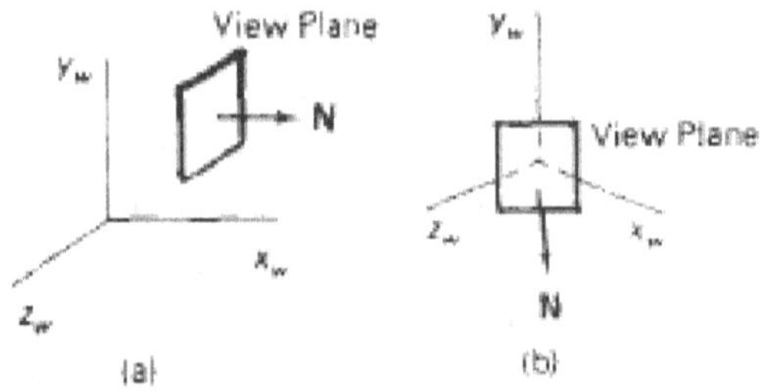

Figure 6.11: Orientations of the Viewplane for Specified Normal Vector Coordinates Relative to the World Origin, Position (1,0,0) Orients the View Plane as in (a), While (1,0,1) gives the Orientation in (b)

Next, we select the positive direction for the viewing z_v axis, and the orientation of the view plane, by specifying the view-plane normal vector, N. We choose a world-coordinate position, and this point establishes the direction for N relative either to the world orign or to the viewing-coordinate origin. Graphics packages such as GKS and PHIGS, for example, orient N relative to the world coordinate origin, as shown in Fig. 6.11. The view-plane normal N is then the directed line segment from the world origin to the selected coordinate position. Inother words, N is simply specified as a world-coordinate vector. Some other packages establish the direction for Nusing the selected coordinate position as a look-at point relative to the view reference point. Figure 6.12 illustrates this method for defining the direction of N, which is from the look-at point to the view reference point. Another possibility is to set up a left-handed viewing system and take N and the positive z_v axis from the viewing origin to the look-at point. Only the direction of N is needed to establish the z_v direction the magnitude is irrelevant, because N will be normalized to a unit vector by the viewing calculations.

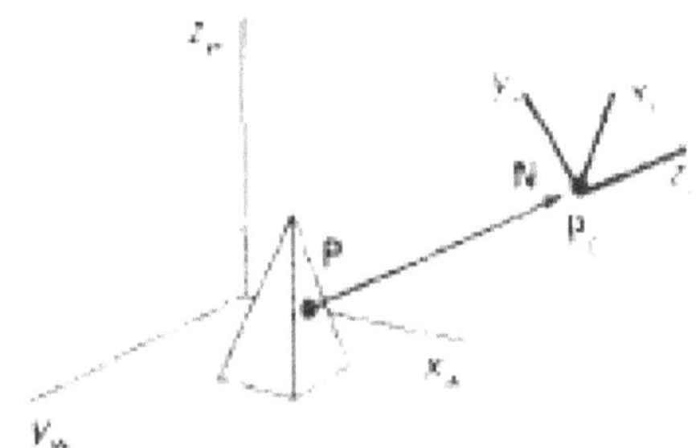

Figure 6.12: Orientation of View Plane

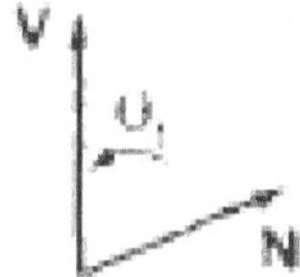

Figure 6.13: Specifying View up Vector with Angle θ

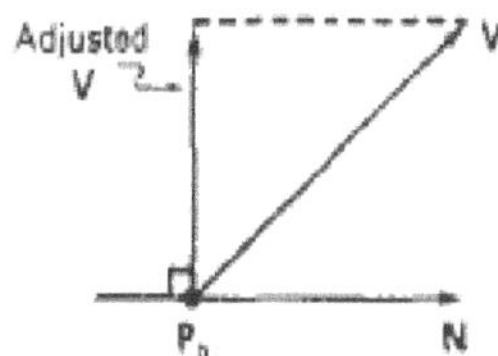

Figure 6.14: Adjusting the Input Position of the View-up Vector V to a Position Perpendicular to the Normal Vector N

Finally we choose thc up direction for the view by specifving a vector *V*, called the vierv-up vector This vector is used to establish the positive direction for the y_v axis. vector *V* also can be defined as a world-coordinate vector, or in some packages, it is specified with a twist angle θ about thc z_v, axis, as shown in Fig. 6.13. For a general orientation of the normal vector, it can be difficult to determine the direction for V that is precisely perpendicular to *N* Therefore, viewing procedure typically adjust the user-defined orientation of vector *V*, as shown in Fig. 6.14, so that *V* is projected into a plane that is perpendicular to the normal vector. We can choose the view.up vector *V* to be in any convenient direction along as it is not parallel to *N*.

Transformation from World to Viewing Coordinates

Before object descriptions can be projected to the view plane, they must be transferred to viewing coordinates. Conversion of object descriptions from world to viewing coordinates is equivalent to a transformation that super imposes the viewing reference frame onto the world frame using the basic geometric translate-rotate operations. This transformation sequence is

1. Translate the view reference point to the origin of the world-coordinate system.
2. Apply rotations to align the x_v, y_v, and z_v axes with the world xu, y, and z, axes, respectively.

If the view reference point is specified at world position (xo yo, zo), this point istranslated to the world origin with the matrix transformation,

$$T = \begin{bmatrix} 1 & 0 & 0 & -x_0 \\ 0 & 1 & 0 & -y_0 \\ 0 & 0 & 1 & -z_0 \\ 0 & 0 & 0 & 1 \end{bmatrix}$$

(6.20)

The rotation sequence can require up to three coordinate-axis rotations, depending on the direction we choose for N. In general, if N is not aligned with an world-coordinate axis, we can super impose the viewing and world systems with the transformation sequence R_x, R_y, R_z. That is, we first rotate around the world x_w, axis to bring z_v into the $x_w z_v$, plane. Then, we rotate around the world y_w axis to align the z_w and z_v axes. The final rotation is about the z_w axis to align the y_w and y_v axes. Further if the view reference system is left-handed, a reflection of one of the viewing axes is also necessary. Figure 6.15 illustrates the general sequence of translate-rotate transformations the composite transformation matrix is then applied to world-coordinate descriptions to transfer them to viewing coordinates.

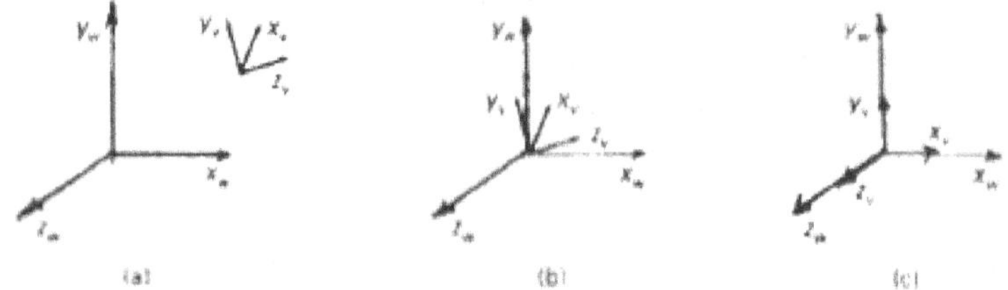

Figure 6.15: Aligning a Viewing System with the World Coordinate Axes Using a Sequence of Translate-rotate Transformations

Another method for generating the rotation-transformation matrix is to calculate unit uvn vectors and form the composite rotation matrix directly, Given vectors N and V, these unit vectors are calculated as,

$$\mathbf{n} = \frac{\mathbf{N}}{|\mathbf{N}|} = (n_1, n_2, n_3)$$

$$\mathbf{u} = \frac{\mathbf{V} \times \mathbf{N}}{|\mathbf{V} \times \mathbf{N}|} = (u_1, u_2, u_3)$$

$$\mathbf{v} = \mathbf{n} \times \mathbf{u} = (v_1, v_2, v_3)$$

(6.21)

This method also automatically adjusts the direction for V so that v is perpendicular to n. The composite rotation matrix for the viewing transformation is then,

$$
R = \begin{bmatrix} u_1 & u_2 & u_3 & 0 \\ v_1 & v_2 & v_3 & 0 \\ n_1 & n_2 & n_3 & 0 \\ 0 & 0 & 0 & 1 \end{bmatrix}
$$

(6.22)

which transforms u onto the world x_w axis, v onto the y_w axis, and n onto the z_w axis. In addition, this matrix automatically performs the reflection necessary to transform a left-handed viewing svstem onto the right-handed world system. The complete wrorld-to-viewing coordinate transformation matrix is obtained as the matrix product

$$M_{wc.vc} = R \cdot T$$

(6.23)

This transformation is then applied to coordinate descriptions of objects in thescene to transfer them to the viewing reference frame.

6.10. View Volumes and General Projection Transformations

In the camera analogy, the type of lens used on the camera is one factor that determines how much of the scene is caught on film. A wideangle lens takes in more of the scene than a regular lens. In three-dimensional viewing, a rectangul a rview window, or projection window, in the vlerv plane is used to the same effect. Edges of the view window are parallel to the $x_v y_v$ axes, and the window boundary positions are specified in viewing coordinates, as shown in Fig. 6.16. The view window can be placed anywhere on the view plane.

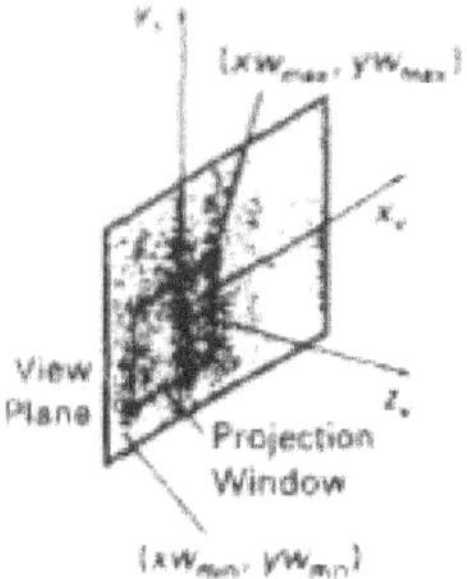

Figure 6.16: Window Specification on the View Plane, with Minimum and Maxlmum Coordinates given in the Viewing Reference System

Given the specification of the view window, we can set up a view volume using the window boundaries. Only those objects within the view volume will appear in the generated display on an output device all others are clipped from the display. The size of the view volume depends on the size of the window, while the shape of the view volume depends on the type of projection to be used to generate the display. In any case, four sides of the volume are planes that pass through the edges of the window. For a parallel projection, these four sides of theview volume form an infinite parallele piped, as in Fig. 6.17. For a perspective projection, the view volume is a pyramid with apex at the projection reference point (Fig. 6.18).

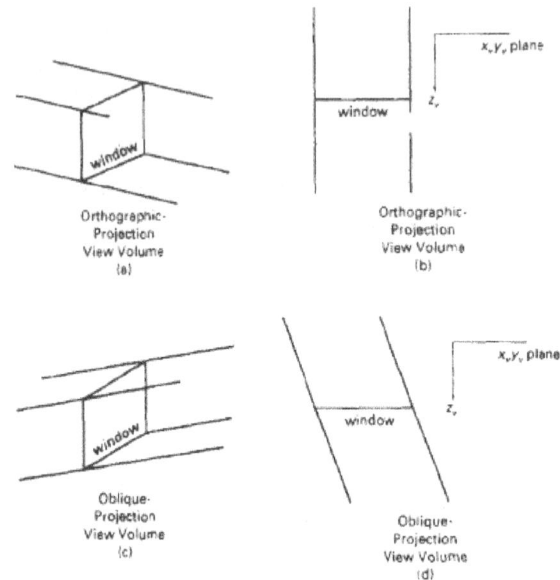

Figure 6.17: View Volume for a Parallel Projection. In (a) and (b), the Side and Topviews of the View Volume for an Orthographic Projection are Shown; and in (c) and (d), the Side and Top Views of an Oblique View Volume are Shown

Figure 6.18: Examples of a Perspective-projection view Volume for various Positions of the Projection Reference Point

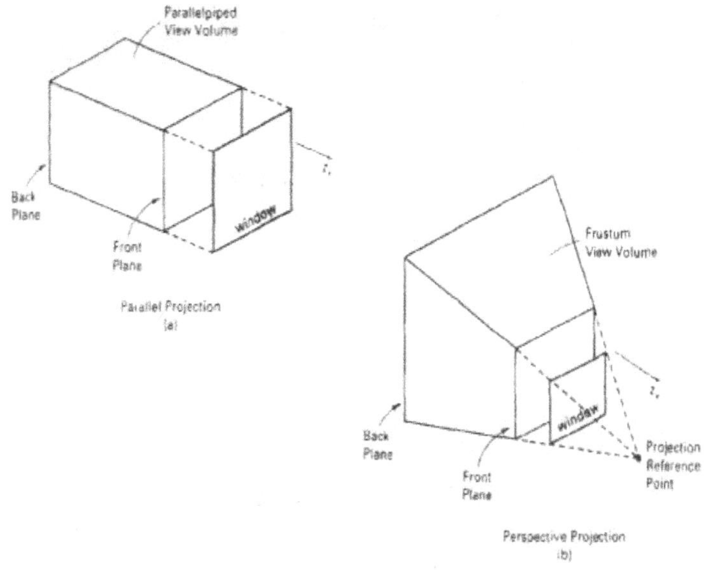

Figure 6.19: View Volumes Bounded by Front and Back Planes, and by Top, Bottom, and Side Planes

A finite view volume is obtained by limiting the extent of the volume in the z_v direction. This is done by specifying positions for one or two additional boundary planes. These z_v- boundary planes are referred to as the front plane and back plane, or the near plane and the far plane, of the viewing volume. The front and back planes are parallel to the view plane at specified-positions z_{front} and z_{back}. Both planes must be on the same side of the projection reference point, and the back plane must be farther from the projection point than the front plane. Including the front and back planes produces a view volume bounded by six planes, as shown in Fig. 6.19 With an orthographic parallel projection, the sixplanes form a rectangular parallele piped, while an oblique parallel projection produces an oblique parallele piped view volume. With a perspective projection, the front and back clipping planes truncate the infinite pyramidal view volume to form a frustum.

Oblique projections may be affected by view-plane positioning, depending on how the projection direction is to be specified. In PHIGS, the oblique projection direction is parallel to the line from the projection reference point to the center of the window.

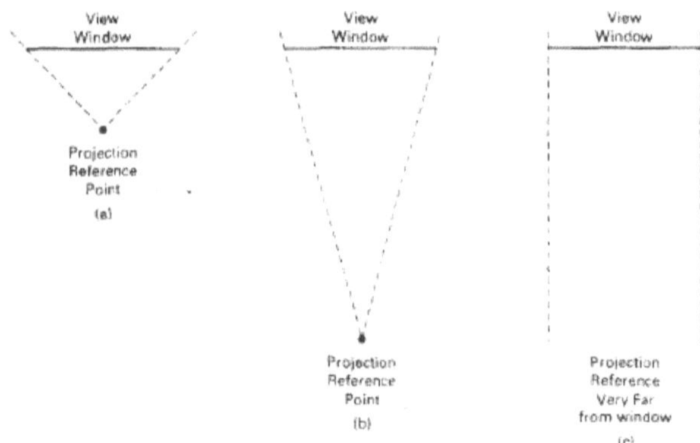

Figure 6.20: Changing Perspective Effects by Moving the Projection Reference Point awray from the View Plane

Perspective effects depend on the positioning of the projection reference point relative to the view plane, as shown in Figure 6.20 If we place the projection reference point close to the view plane, perspective effects are emphasized; that is, closer objects will appear much larger than more distant obpcts of the same size. Similarly, as we move the projection reference point farther from the view plane, the difference in the size of near and far objects decreases. In the limit, as we move the projection reference point infinitely far from the viewplane, a perspective projection approaches a parallel projection.

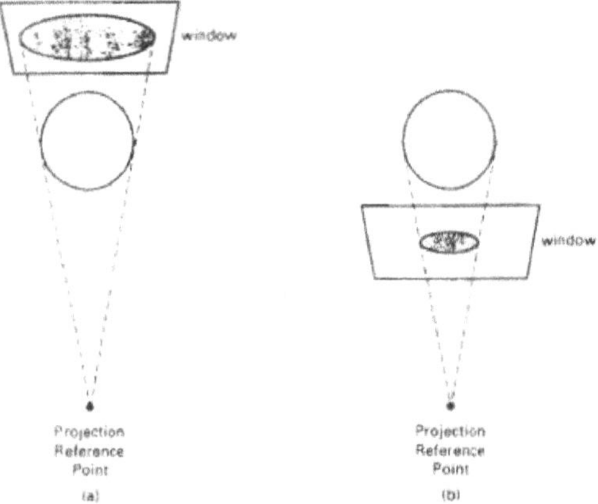

Figure 6.21: Projected Object Size depends on whether the View Plane is positioned in Front of the Object or behind it, Relative to the Position of the Projection Reference Point

The projected size of an object in a perspective view is also affected by the relative position of the object and the view plane (Fig. 6.21). If the view plane isin front of the object (nearer the projection reference point), the projected size is smaller. Conversely, object size is increased when we project onto a view plane in back of the object.

General Parallel-Projection Transformations

In PHIGS, the direction of a parallel projection is specified with a projection vector from the projection reference point to the center of the view window. Figure 6.22 shows the general shape of a finite view volume for a given projection vector and projection window in the view plane. We obtain the oblique projection transformation with a shear operation that converts the view volume in Fig. 6.22 to the regular parallele piped shown in Fig. 6.23.

The elements of the shearing transformation needed to generate the view volume shown in Fig. 6.24 are obtained by considering the shear transformation of the projection vector. If the projetion vector is specified in world coordinates, it must first be transformed to viewing coordinates using the rotation matrix.

Suppose the elements of the projection vector in viewing coordinates are,

$$V_p = (p_x,\ p_y,\ p_z) \qquad\qquad (6.24)$$

We need to determine the elements of a shear matrix that will align the projection vector V_p with the, view plane normal vector N. This transformation can be expressed as

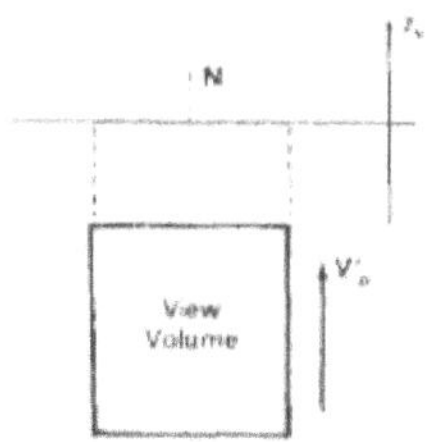

Figure 6.22: Regular Parallelepiped View Volume

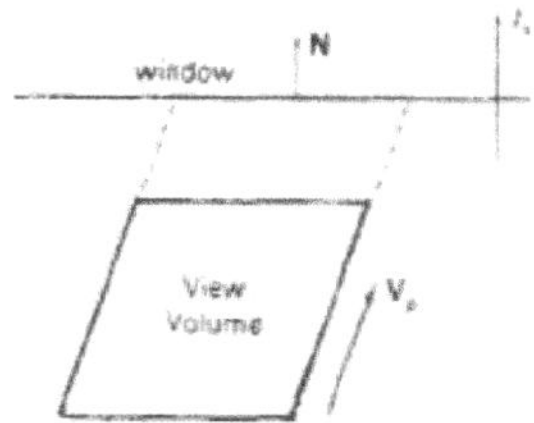

Figure 6.23: Oblique Projection Vector and Associated View Volume

$$V'_p = M_{parallel} \cdot V_p$$

$$= \begin{bmatrix} 0 \\ 0 \\ p_z \\ 0 \end{bmatrix}$$

(6.25)

where $M_{parallel}$ is equivalent to the parallel projection matrix *6.25* and represents a *z-axis* shear of the form

$$M_{parallel} = \begin{bmatrix} 1 & 0 & a & 0 \\ 0 & 1 & b & 0 \\ 0 & 0 & 1 & 0 \\ 0 & 0 & 0 & 1 \end{bmatrix}$$

(6.26)

The explicit transformation equations from *6.25* in terms of shear parameters a and b are

$$0 = p_x + a p_z$$
$$0 = p_y + b p_z$$

(6.27)

so that the values for the shear parameters are

$$a = -\frac{p_x}{p_z}, \qquad b = -\frac{p_y}{p_z}$$

(6.28)

Thus, we have the general parallel-projection matrix in terms of the elements of the projection vector as

$$M_{parallel} = \begin{bmatrix} 1 & 0 & -p_x/p_z & 0 \\ 0 & 1 & -p_y/p_z & 0 \\ 0 & 0 & 1 & 0 \\ 0 & 0 & 0 & 1 \end{bmatrix}$$

(6.29)

This matrix is then concatenated with transformation $R \cdot T$, to produce the transformation from world coordinates to parallel-projection coordinates.

General Perspective-Projection Transformations

With the PHIGS programming standard, the projection reference point can be located at any position in the viewing system, except on the view plane or between the front and back clipping planes. Figure 6.24 shows the shape of a fmite view volume for an arbitrary position of the projection reference point. We can obtain the general perspective-projection transformation with the following two operations:

1. Shear the view volume so that the centerliie of the frustum is perpendicular to the view plane.

2. Scale the view volume with a scaling factor that depends on $1 / z$.

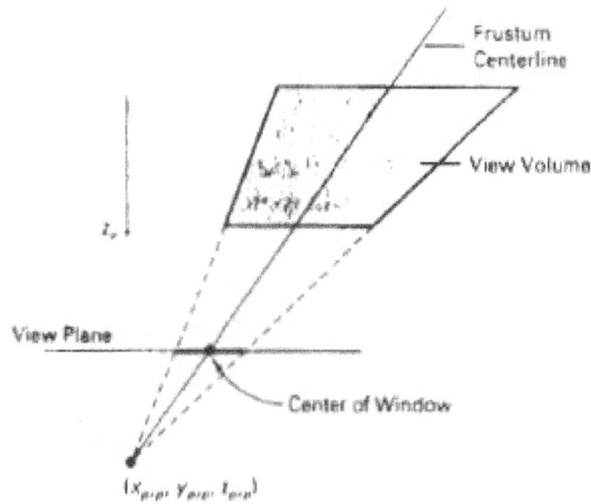

Figure 6.24: General Shape for the Perspective View Volume with a Projetion Reference Point that is not on the z - Axis

A shear operation to align a general perspective view volume with the projection window is shown in Fig. 6.25. This transformation has the effect of shifting all positions that lie along the frustum centerline, including the window center, to a line perpendicular to the view plane. With the projection reference pointat a general position $(x_{prp}, y_{prp}, z_{prp})$ the transformation involves a combination *z-axis* shear and a translation:

$$M_{shear} = \begin{bmatrix} 1 & 0 & a & -a z_{prp} \\ 0 & 1 & b & -b z_{prp} \\ 0 & 0 & 1 & 0 \\ 0 & 0 & 0 & 1 \end{bmatrix}$$

(6.30)

where the shear parameters are,

$$a = -\frac{x_{prp} - (xw_{min} + xw_{max})/2}{z_{prp}}$$

$$b = -\frac{y_{prp} - (yw_{min} + yw_{max})/2}{z_{prp}}$$

(6.31)

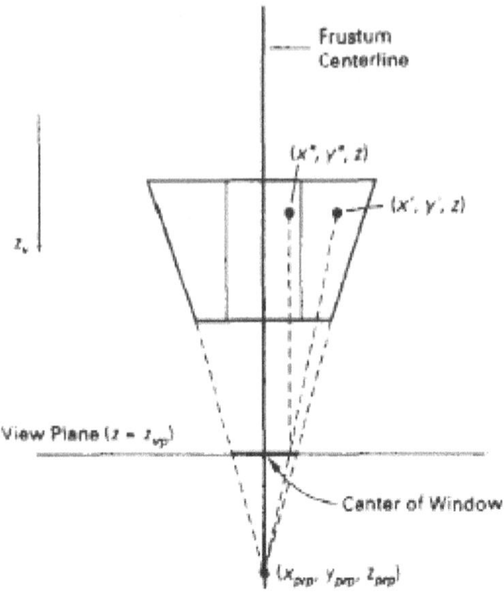

Figure 6.25: Shearing a General Perspective View Volume to Center it on the Projection Window

Points within the view volume are transformed by this operation as,

$$x' = x + a(z - z_{prp})$$
$$y' = y + b(z - z_{prp})$$
$$z' = z \qquad\qquad (6.32)$$

When the projection reference point is on the z_v axis, $x_{prp} = y_{prp} = 0$.

Once we have converted a position (x, y, z) in the onginal view volume to position (x', y', z') in the sheared frustum, we then apply a scaling transformation to produce a regular parallele piped. The transformation for this conversion is

$$x'' = x'\left(\frac{z_{prp} - z_{vp}}{z_{prp} - z}\right) + x_{prp}\left(\frac{z_{vp} - z}{z_{prp} - z}\right)$$

$$y'' = y'\left(\frac{z_{prp} - z_{vp}}{z_{prp} - z}\right) + y_{prp}\left(\frac{z_{vp} - z}{z_{prp} - z}\right) \qquad\qquad (6.33)$$

and the homogeneous matrix representation is

$$\mathbf{M}_{scale} = \begin{bmatrix} 1 & 0 & \dfrac{-x_{prp}}{z_{prp}-z_{vp}} & \dfrac{x_{prp}z_{vp}}{z_{prp}-z_{vp}} \\[2ex] 0 & 1 & \dfrac{-y_{prp}}{z_{prp}-z_{vp}} & \dfrac{y_{prp}z_{vp}}{z_{prp}-z_{vp}} \\[2ex] 0 & 0 & 1 & 0 \\[2ex] 0 & 0 & \dfrac{-1}{z_{prp}-z_{vp}} & \dfrac{z_{prp}}{z_{prp}-z_{vp}} \end{bmatrix} \qquad (6.34)$$

Therefore, the general perspective-projection transformation can be expressed in matrix form as

$$M_{perspective} = M_{Scale} \cdot M_{Shear} \qquad (6.35)$$

The complete transformation from world coordinates to perspective-projection coordinates is obtained by right concatenating $M_{perspective}$ with the composite viewing transformation $R \cdot T$.

6.11. Clipping

An algorithm for three-dimensional clipping identifies and saves all surface segments within the view volume for display on the output device. All parts ofobjects that are outside the view volume are discarded. Clipping in three dimensions can be accomplished using extensions of two-dimensional clipping methods. Instead of clipping against straight-line window boundaries, we now clip objects against the boundary planes of the view volume.

To clip a line segment against the view volume, we would need to test the relative position of the line using the view volume's boundary plane equations. By substituting the line endpoint coordinates into the plane equation of each boundary in turn, we could determine whether the endpoint is inside or outside that boundary. An endpoint (x, y, z) of a line segment is outside a boundary plane if $Ax + By + Cz + D > 0$, where $A, B, C,$ and D are the plane parameters for that boundary. Similarly, the point is inside the boundary if $Ax + By + Cz + D < 0$. Lines with both endpoints outside a boundary plane are discarded, and those with both endpoints inside all boundary planes are saved. The intersection of a line with a boundary is found using the line equations along with the plane equation. intersection coordinates (x_l, y_l, z_l) are values that are on the line and that satisfy the plane equation $Ax_l + By_l + Cz_l + D = 0$.

To clip a polygon surface, we can clip the individual polygon edges. First, we could test the coordinate extents against each boundary of the view volume to determine whether the object is completely inside or completely outs~deth at boundary. If the coordinate extents of the object are inside all boundaries, we save it. If the coordinate extents are outside all boundaries, we discard it. Otherwise, we need to apply the intersection calculations. We could do this by determining the polygon edge-intersection positions with the boundary planes of the view volume.

Normalized View Volumes

Figure 6.26 the expanded PHIGS transformation pipeline. At the first step, a scene is constructed by transforming object descriptions from modeling coordinates to world coordinates. Next, a view mapping convert: the world description to viewing coordinates. At the projection stage, the viewing coordinates are transformed to projection coordinates, which effectively converts the view volume into a rectangular parallelepiped. Then, the parallelepiped is mapped into the unit cube, a normalized view volume called the normalized projection coordinate system. The mapping to normalized projection coordinates is accomplished by transforming points within the rectangular parallelepiped into a position within a specified three-dimensional viewport, which occupies part or all of the unit cube. Finally, at the workstation stage, normalized projection coordinates are converted to device coordinates for display.

The normalized view volume is a region defined by the planes,

$$x = 0, \quad x = 1, \quad y = 0, \quad y = 1, \quad z = 0, \quad z = 1 \qquad (6.36)$$

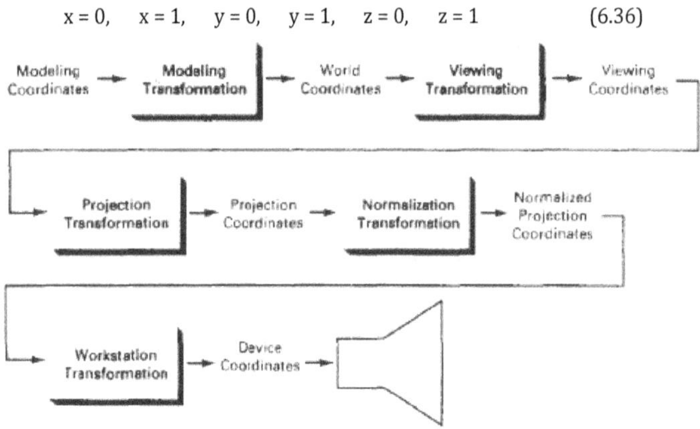

Figure 6.26: Expanded PHIGS Transformation Pipeline

Mapping positions within a rectangular view volume to a three-dimensional rectangular viewport is accomplished with a combination of scaling and translation, similar to the operations needed for a two-dimensional window-to-viewport mapping. We can express the three-dimensional hansformation matrix for these operations in the form,

$$
\begin{bmatrix}
D_x & 0 & 0 & K_x \\
0 & D_y & 0 & K_y \\
0 & 0 & D_z & K_z \\
0 & 0 & 0 & 1
\end{bmatrix}
\tag{6.37}
$$

Factors D_x, D_y, *and* D_z am the ratios of the dimensions of the viewport and regular parallelepiped view volume in the x, y and z directions Fig 6.27.

$$
D_x = \frac{xv_{max} - xv_{min}}{xw_{max} - xw_{min}}
$$

$$
D_y = \frac{yv_{max} - yv_{min}}{yw_{max} - yw_{min}}
$$

$$
D_z = \frac{zv_{max} - zv_{min}}{z_{back} - z_{front}}
\tag{6.38}
$$

$$
K_x = xv_{min} - xw_{min} D_x
$$

$$
K_y = yv_{min} - yw_{min} D_y
$$

$$
K_z = zv_{min} - z_{front} D_z
\tag{6.39}
$$

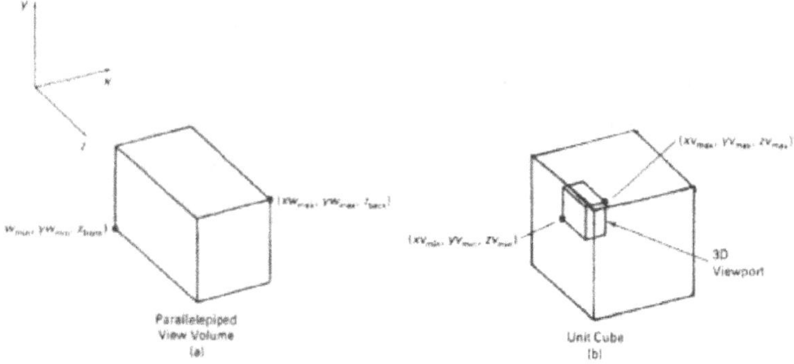

Figure 6.27: Dimensions of the View Volume and Three-dimensional Viewport

Viewport Clipping

The two-dimensional concept of region codes can be extended to three dimensions by considering positions in front and in back of the three-dimensional viewport, as well as positions that are left, right, below, or above the volume. For two dimensional clipping, we used a four digit binary region code to identify the position of a line endpoint relative to the viewport boundaries. For three dimensional points, we need to expand the region code to six bits. Each point in the description of a scene is then assigned a six-bit region code that identifies the relative position of the point with respect to the viewport. For a line endpoint at position (x, y, z) we assign the bit positions in the region code from right to left as

$$\text{bit } 1 = 1, \quad \text{if } x < xv_{min} \text{ (left)}$$
$$\text{bit } 2 = 1, \quad \text{if } x > xv_{max} \text{ (right)}$$
$$\text{bit } 3 = 1, \quad \text{if } y < yv_{min} \text{ (below)}$$
$$\text{bit } 4 = 1, \quad \text{if } y > yv_{max} \text{ (above)}$$
$$\text{bit } 5 = 1, \quad \text{if } z < zv_{min} \text{ (front)}$$
$$\text{bit } 6 = 1, \quad \text{if } z > zv_{max} \text{ (back)}$$

For example, a region code of *101000* identifies a point as above and behind the viewport, and the region code *000000* indicates a point within the volume. A line segment can immediately identified as completely within the viewport if both endpoints have a region code of *000000*. If either endpoint of a line segment does not have a regon code of *000000*, we perform the logical and operation on the two endpoint codes. The result of this and operation will be nonzero for any line segment that has both endpoints in one of the six outside regions. For example, a nonzero value will be generated if both endpoints are behind the viewport, or both endpoints are above the viewport. If we cannot identify a line segment as completely inside or completely outside the volume, we test for intersections with the bounding planes of the volume.

Equations for three-dimensional line segments are conveniently expressed in parametric form. The two-dimensional parametric clipping methods of Cyrus-Beck or Liang-Barsky can be extended to three-dimensional scenes. For a line segment with endpoints $P_1 = (x_1, y_1, z_1)$ and $P_2 = (x_2, y_2, z_2)$, we can write the parametric line equations as

$$x = x_1 + (x_2 - x_1)u, \quad 0 \leq u \leq 1$$
$$y = y_1 + (y_2 - y_1)u$$
$$z = z_1 + (z_2 - z_1)u \tag{6.40}$$

Coordinates (x, y, z) represent any point on the line between the two endpoints. At $u = 0$, we have the point P_1, and $u = 1$ puts us at P_2.

To find the intersection of a line with a plane of the viewport, we substitute the coordinate value for that plane into the appropriate parametric expression of *Eq. 6.40* and solve for u. For instance, suppose we are testing a line against the zv_{min} plane of the viewport. Then

$$u = \frac{zv_{min} - z_1}{z_2 - z_1} \tag{6.41}$$

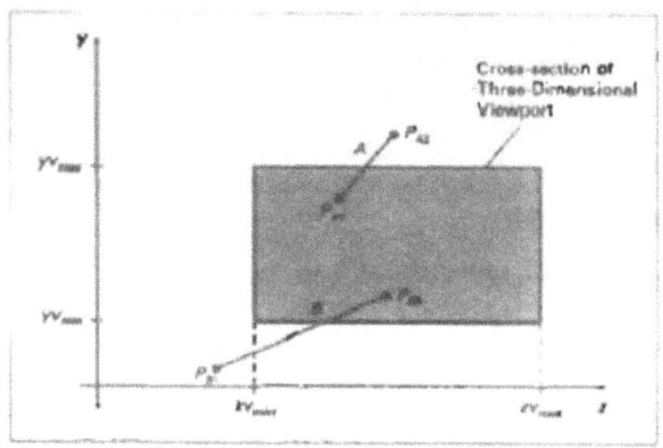

Figure 6.28: Line Clipping

When the calculated value for u is not in the range from 0 to 1, the line segment does not intersect the plane under consideration at any point between endpoints P_1 and P_2 (line A in Fig. 6.28). If the calculated value for u in *Eq. 6.41* is in the interval from 0 to 1, we calculate the intersection's x and y coordinates as

$$x_I = x_1 + (x_2 - x_1)\left(\frac{zv_{min} - z_1}{z_2 - z_1}\right)$$

$$y_I = y_1 + (y_2 - y_1)\left(\frac{zv_{min} - z_1}{z_2 - z_1}\right)$$

(6.42)

If either x_1 or y_1 is not in the range of the boundaries of the viewport, then this line intersects the front plane beyond the boundaries of the volume (*line B in Fig. 6.28*).

Clipping in Homogeneous Coordinates

The clipping procedures in terms of three-dimensional coordinates, PHIGS and other packages actually represent coordinate positions in homogeneous coordinates. This allows the various transformations to be represented as 4 by 4 matrices, which can be concatenated for efficiency. After all viewing and other transformations are complete, the homogeneous coordirtate positions are converted back to three-dimensional points. As each coordinate position enters the transfonnation pipeline, it is converted to a homogeneous-coordinate representation:

$$(x, y, z) \rightarrow (x, y, z, 1)$$

The various transformations are applied and we obtain the final homogeneous point:

$$\begin{bmatrix} x_h \\ y_h \\ z_h \\ h \end{bmatrix} = \begin{bmatrix} a_{11} & a_{12} & a_{13} & a_{14} \\ a_{21} & a_{22} & a_{23} & a_{24} \\ a_{31} & a_{32} & a_{33} & a_{34} \\ a_{41} & a_{42} & a_{43} & a_{44} \end{bmatrix} \cdot \begin{bmatrix} x \\ y \\ z \\ 1 \end{bmatrix}$$

$$(6.43)$$

where the homogeneous parameter h may not be *1*. In fact, h can have any real value. Clipping is then performed in homogeneous coordinates, and clipped homogeneous positions are converted to nonhomogeneous coordinates in three dimensional normalized-proption coordinates:

$$x' = \frac{x_h}{h}, \quad y' = \frac{y_h}{h}, \quad z' = \frac{z_h}{h}$$

$$(6.44)$$

To determine homogeneous viewport clipping boundaries, we note thatany homogeneous coordinate position (x_k, y_k, z_k, h) g inside the viewport if it satisfies the in equalities

$$xv_{min} \le \frac{x_h}{h} \le xv_{max}, \qquad yv_{min} \le \frac{y_h}{h} \le yv_{max}, \qquad zv_{min} < \frac{z_h}{h} \le zv_{max}$$

$$(6.45)$$

Thus, the homogeneous clipping limits are

$$h\,xv_{min} \le x_h \le h\,xv_{max}, \qquad h\,yv_{min} \le y_h \le h\,yv_{max}, \qquad h\,zv_{min} \le z_h \le h\,zv_{max}, \qquad \text{if } h > 0$$
$$h\,xv_{max} \le x_h \le h\,xv_{min}, \qquad h\,yv_{max} \le y_h \le h\,yv_{min}, \qquad h\,zv_{max} \le z_h \le h\,zv_{min}, \qquad \text{if } h < 0 \quad (6.46)$$

and clipping is carried out with procedures similar to those discussed in the previously. To avoid applying both sets of inequalities in *Eqn 6.46*, we can simply negate the coordinates for any point with $h < 0$ and use the clipping inequalities for $h > 0$.

CHAPTER VII

7. Visible Surface Detection Methods

7.1. Introduction

A major consideration in the generation of realistic graphics displays is identifying those parts of a scene that are visible from a chosen viewing position. There are many approaches we can take to solve this problem, and numerous algorithms have been devised for efficient identification of visible objects for different types of applications. Some methods require more memory, some involve more processing time, and some apply only to special types of objects. Deciding upon a method for a particular application can depend on such factors as the complexity of the scene, type of objects to be displayed, available equipment, and whether static or animated displays are to be generated. The various algorithms are referred to as visible-surface detection methods. Sometimes these methods are also referred to as hidden-surface elimination methods, although there can be subtle differences between identifying visible surfaces and eliminating hidden surfaces. For wireframe displays, for example, we may not want to actually eliminate the hidden surfaces, but rather to display them with dashed boundaries or in some other way to retain information about their shape.

7.2. Classification of Visible-surface Detection Algorithms

Visible-surface detection algorithms are broadly classified according to whether they deal with object definitions directly or with their projected images. These two approaches are called object-space methods and image-space methods, respectively. An object-space method compare objects and parts of objects to each other within the scene definition to determine which surfaces, as a whole, we should label as visible. In an image-space algorithm, visibility is decided point by point at each pixel position on the projection plane. Most visible-surface algorithms use image-space methods, although object space methods can be used effectively to locate visible surfaces in some cases. Line-display algorithms, on the other hand, generally use object-space methods to identify visible lines in wireframe displays, but many image-space visible-surface algorithms can be adapted easily to visible-line detection.

7.3. Back Face Detection

A fast and simple object-space method for identifying the back faces of a polyhedron is based on the "*inside-outside*" tests. A point *(x, y, z)* is "*inside*" a polygon surface with plane parameters A, B, C, and D if

$$Ax + By + Cz + D < 0 \qquad\qquad (7.1)$$

When an inside point is along the line of sight to the surface, the polygon must be a back face (we are inside that face and cannot see the front of it from our viewing position).

We can simplify this test by considering the normal vector N to a polygon surface, which has Cartesian components (A, B, C). In general, if V is a vector in the viewing direction from the eye (or "camera") position, as shown in *Fig. 7.1*, then this polygon is a back face if

$$V . N > 0 \qquad\qquad (7.2)$$

Furthermore, if object descriptions have been converted to projection coordinates and our viewing direction is parallel to the viewing z_z axis, then $V = (0, 0, V_z)$ and

$$V . N = V_z C$$

so that we only need to consider the sign of C, the ; component of the normal vector N.

In a right-handed viewing system with viewing direction along the negative z_v axis *(Fig. 7.2)*, the polygon is a back face if $C < 0$. Also, we cannot see any face whose normal has z component $C = 0$, since our viewing direction is grazing that polygon. Thus, in general, we can label any polygon as a back face if its normal vector has a z-component value:

$$C \leq 0 \qquad\qquad (7.3)$$

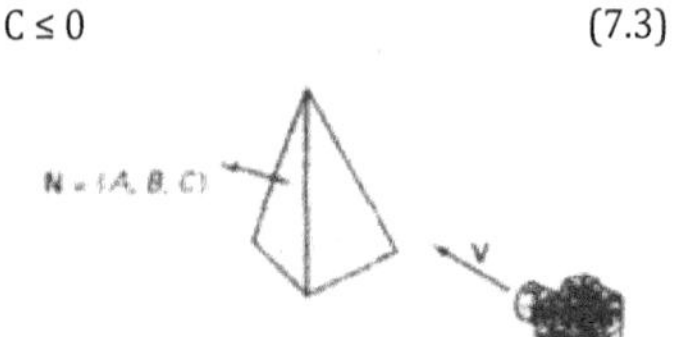

Figure 7.1: Vector V in the Viewing Direction and a Back-face Normal Vector N of a Polyhedron

Similar methods can be used in packages that employ a left-handed viewing system. In these packages, plane parameters $A, B, C, and D$ can be calculated from polygon vertex coordinates specified in a clockwise direction (instead of the counterclockwise direction used in a right-handed system). Also, back faces have normal vectors that point away from the viewing position and are identified by $C \geq 0$ when the viewing direction is along the positive z_v axis.

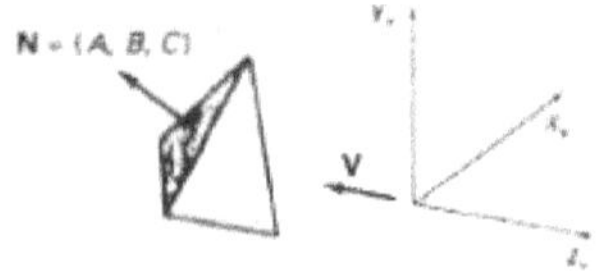

Figure 7.2: A Polygon Surface with Plane Parameter C < 0

7.4.   Depth-buffer Method

A commonly used image-space approach to detecting visible surfaces is the depth-buffer method, which compares surface depths at each pixel position on the projection plane. This procedure is also referred to as the z-buffer method, since object depth is usually measured from the view plane along the z axis of a viewing system. Each surface of a scene is processed separately, one point at a time across the surface. The method is usually applied to scenes containing only polygon surfaces, because depth values can be computed very quickly and the method is easy to implement. But the method can be applied to non-planar surfaces.

With object descriptions converted to projection coordinates, each (x, y, z) position on a polygon surface corresponds to the orthographic projection point (x, y) on the view plane. Therefore, for each pixel position (x, y) on the view plane, object depths can be compared by comparing z values. Figure 7.3 shows three surfaces at varying distances along the orthographic projection line from position (x, y) in a view plane taken as the x_v, y_v, plane. Surface S_1 is closest at this position, so its surface intensity value at (x, y) is saved.

We can implement the depth-buffer algorithm in normalized coordinates, so that z values range from 0 at the back clipping plane to z_{max} at the front clipping plane. The value of z, can be set either to 1 (for a unit cube) or to the largest value that can be stored on the system. As implied by the name of this method, two buffer areas are required. A depth buffer is used to store depth values for each (x, y) position as surfaces are processed, and the refresh buffer stores the intensity values for each position.

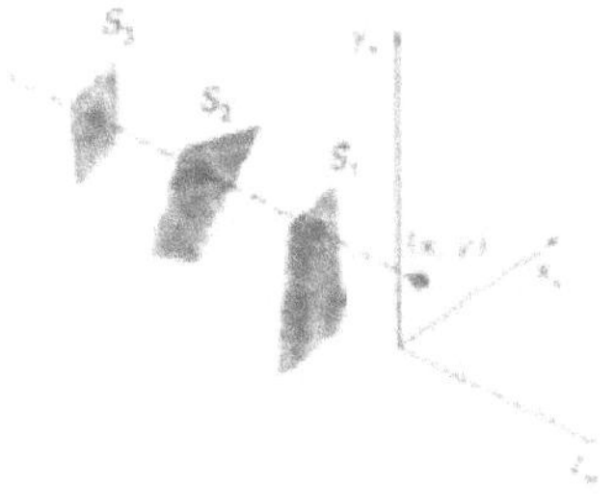

Figure 7.3: At View-plane Position (x, y), Surface S, has the Smallest Depth from the View Plane and so is Visible at that Position

We summarize the steps of a depth-buffer algorithm as follows:

1. Initialize the depth buffer and refresh buffer so that for all buffer positions (x, y),

$$\text{depth}(x, y) = 0, \qquad \text{refresh}(x, y) = I_{backgnd}$$

2. For each position on each polygon surface, compare depth values to previously stored values in the depth buffer to determine visibility.

- Calculate the depth z for each (x, y) position on the polygon.
- If $z > \text{depth}(x, y)$, then set

$$\text{depth}(x, y) = z, \qquad \text{refresh}(x, y) = I_{surf}(x,y)$$

where $I_{backgnd}$ is the value for the background intensity, and $I_{surf}(x,y)$ is the projected intensity value for the surface at pixel position (x,y). After all surfaces have been processed, the depth buffer contains depth values for the visible surfaces and the refresh buffer contains the corresponding intensity values for those surfaces.

Depth values for a surface position (x, y) are calculated from the plane equation for each surface:

$$z = \frac{-Ax - By - D}{C} \qquad (7.4)$$

For any scan line (Fig. 7.4), adjacent horizontal positions across the line differ by 1, and a vertical y value on an adjacent scan line differs by 1. If the depth of position (x, y) has been determined to be z, then the depth z' of the next position $(x + 1, y)$ along the scan line is obtained from Eq. 7.4 as

$$z' = \frac{-A(x+1) - By - D}{C} \qquad (7.5)$$

Or

$$z' = z - \frac{A}{C} \qquad (7.6)$$

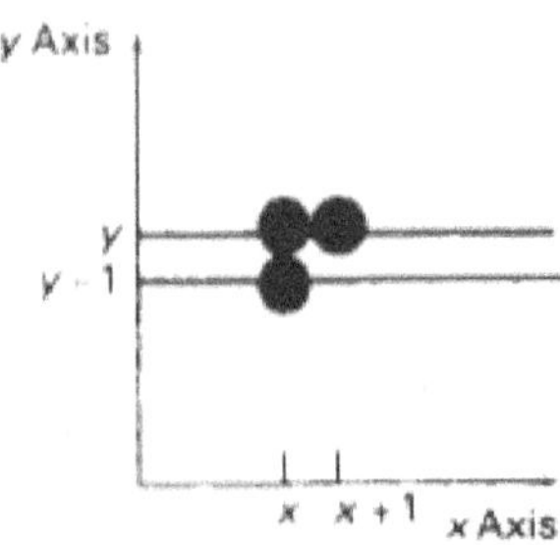

Figure 7.4: From Position (x, y) on a Scan Line

The ratio -A/C is constant for each surface, so succeeding depth values across a scan line are obtained from preceding values with a single addition.

We first determine the y-coordinate extents of each polygon, and process the surface from the topmost scan line to the bottom scan line, as shown in Fig. 7.5. Starting at a top vertex, we can recursively calculate x positions down a left edge of the polygon as $x' = x - l/m$, where rn is the slope of the edge (Fig. 7.5). Depth values down the edge are then obtained recursively as

$$z' = z + \frac{\frac{A}{m} + B}{C} \qquad (7.7)$$

If we are processing down a vertical edge, the slope is infinite and the recursive calculations reduce to

$$z' = z + \frac{B}{C}.$$

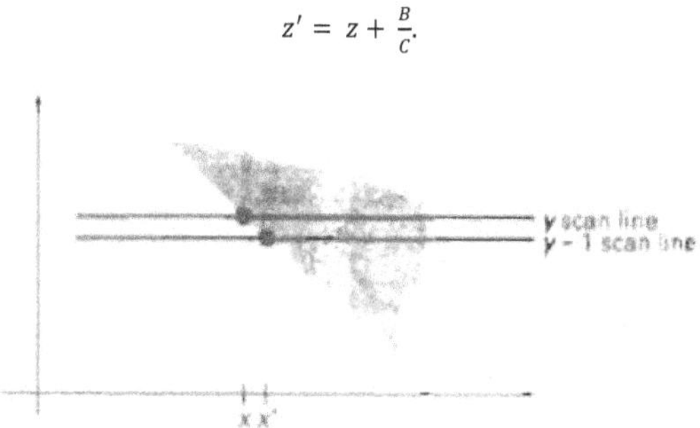

Figure 7.5: Intersection Positions on Successive Scan Lines along a Left Polygon Edge

7.5. A-buffer Method

An extension of the ideas in the depth-buffer method is the A-buffer method (at the other end of the alphabet from "z-buffer", where z represents depth). The A-buffer method represents an antaliased, area-averaged, accumulation-buffer method developed by Lucasfilm for implementation in the surface-rendering system called REYES (an acronym for "Renders Everything You Ever Saw").

A drawback of the depth-buffer method is that it can only find one visible surface at each pixel position. The A-buffer method expands the depth buffer so that each position in the buffer can reference a linked list of surfaces. Thus, more than one surface intensity can be taken into consideration at each pixel position, and object edges can be antialiased.

Each position in the A-buffer has two fields:

- **Depth field** - stores a positive or negative real number
- **Intensity field** - stores surface-intensity information or a pointer value.

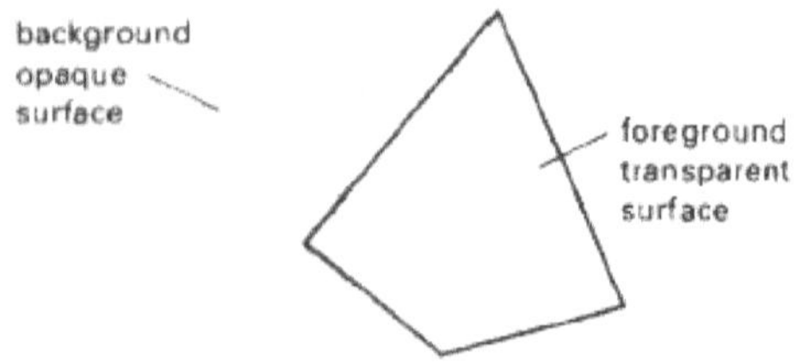

Figure 7.6: Viewing an Opaque Surface

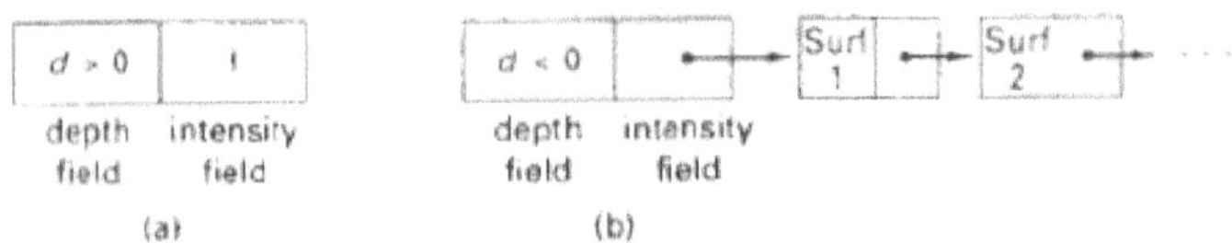

Figure 7.7: Organization of an A-buffer Pixel Position: (a) Single-surface Overlap of the Corresponding Pixel Area, and (b) Multiple Surface Overlap

If the depth field is positive, the number stored at that position is the depth of a single surface overlapping the corresponding pixel area. The intensity field then stores the RCB components of the surface color at that point and the percent of pixel coverage, as illustrated in *Fig. 7.7(a)*.

If the depth field is negative, this indicates multiple-surface contributions to the pixel intensity. The intensity field then stores a pointer to a linked list of surface data, as in *Fig. 7.7(b)*. Data for each surface in the linked list includes,

- RGB intensity components
- Opacity parameter (percent of transparency)
- Depth
- Percent of area coverage
- Surface identifier
- Other surface-rendering parameters
- Pointer to next surface

7.6. Scan-line Method

This image space method for removing hidden surface 5 is an extension of the scan-line algorithm for tilling polygon interiors. Instead of filling just one surface, we now deal with multiple surfaces. As each scan line is processed, all polygon surfaces intersecting that line are examined to determine which are visible. Across each scan line, depth calculations are made for each overlapping surface to determine which is nearest to the view plane. When the visible surface has been determined, the intensity value for that position is entered into the refresh buffer.

Figure 7.8 illustrates the scan-line method for locating visible portions of surfaces for pixel positions along the line. The active list for scan line 1 contains information from the edge table for edges AB, BC, EH, and FG. For positions along this scan line between edges AB and BC, only the flag for surface S_1 is on. Therefore no depth calculations are necessary, and intensity information for surface S_1 is entered from the polygon table into the refresh buffer. Similarly, between edges EH and FG, only the flag for surface S_2 is on. No other positions along scan line 1 intersect surfaces, so the intensity values in the other areas are set to the background intensity. The background intensity can be loaded throughout the buffer in an initialization routine.

For scan lines 2 and 3 in Fig. 7.8, the active edge list contains edges AD, EH, BC, and FG. Along scan line 2 from edge AD to edge EH, only the flag for surface S_1 is on. But between edges EH and BC, the flags for both surfaces are on. In this interval, depth calculations must be made using the plane coefficients for the two surfaces. For this example, the depth of surface S_1 is assumed to be less than that of S_2 so intensities for surface S_1 are loaded into the refresh buffer until boundary BC is encountered. Then the flag for surface S_1 goes off, and intensities for surface S_2 are stored until edge FG is passed.

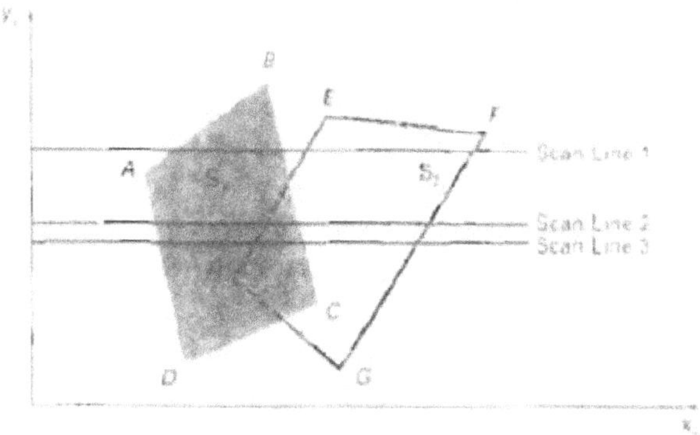

Figure 7.8: Scan Lines Crossing the Projection of Two Surfaces, S_1 and S_2 in the View Plane. Dashed Lines indicate the Boundaries of Hidden Surfaces

7.7.   Depth-sorting Method

Using both image-space and object-space operations, the depth-sorting method performs the following basic functions:

1.   Surfaces are sorted in order of decreasing depth.
2.   Surfaces are scan converted in order, starting with the surface of greatest depth.

Sorting operations are carried out in both image and object space, and the scan conversion of the polygon surfaces is performed in image space.

This method for solving the hidden-surface problem is often referred to as the *painter's algorithm*. In creating an oil painting, an artist first paints the background colors. Next, the most distant objects are added, then the nearer objects, and so forth. At the final step, the foreground objects are painted on the canvas over the background and other objects that have been painted on the canvas. Each layer of paint covers up the previous layer. Using a similar technique, we first sort surfaces according to their distance from the view plane. The intensity values for the farthest surface are then entered into the refresh buffer. Taking each succeeding surface in turn (in decreasing depth order), we "paint" the surface intensities onto the frame buffer over the intensities of the previously processed surfaces.

Painting polygon surfaces onto the frame buffer according to depth is carried out in several steps. Assuming we are viewing along the-z direction, surfaces are ordered on the first pass according to the smallest z value on each surface. Surface S with the greatest depth is then compared to the other surfaces in the list to determine whether there are any overlaps in depth. If no depth overlaps occur, S is scan converted.

Figure 7.9 shows two surfaces that overlap in the xy plane but have no depth overlap. This process is then repeated for the next surface in the list. As long as no overlaps occur, each surface is processed in depth order until all have been scan converted. If a depth overlap is detected at any point in the list, we need to make some additional comparisons to determine whether any of the surfaces should be reordered.

We make the following tests for each surface that overlaps with S. If any one of these tests is true, no reordering is necessary for that surface. The tests are listed in order of increasing difficulty.

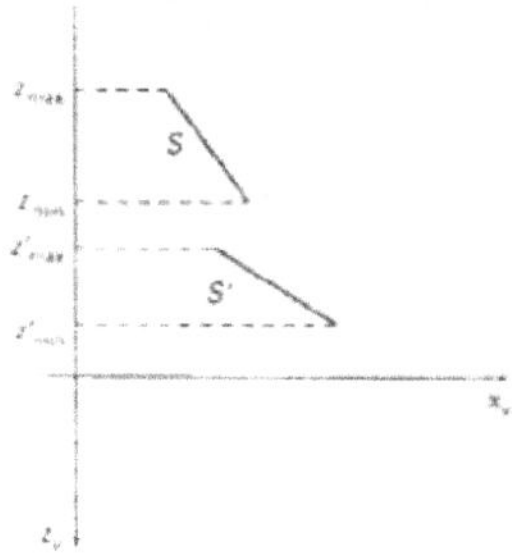

Figure 7.9: Two Surfaces with no Depth Overlap

1. The bounding rectangles in the xy plane for the two surfaces do not overlap
2. Surface S is completely behind the overlapping surface relative to the viewing position.
3. The overlapping surface is completely in front of 5 relative to the viewing position.
4. The projections of the two surfaces onto the view plane do not overlap.

Test 1 is performed in two parts. We first check for overlap in the x direction, then we check for overlap in the y direction. If either of these directions show no overlap, the two planes cannot obscure one other. An example of two surfaces that overlap in the z direction but not in the x direction is shown in Fig. 7.10.

We can perform tests 2 and 3 with an "inside-outside" polygon test. That is, we substitute the coordinates for all vertices of S into the plane equation for the overlapping surface and check the sign of the result. If the plane equations are set up so that the outside of the surface is toward the viewing position, then S is behind S' if all vertices of S are "inside" S' (fig. 7.11). Similarly, S' is completely in front of S if all vertices of S are "outside" of S'. Figure 7.12 shows an overlap ping surface S' that is completely in front of S, but surface S is not completely "inside" S' (test 2 is not true).

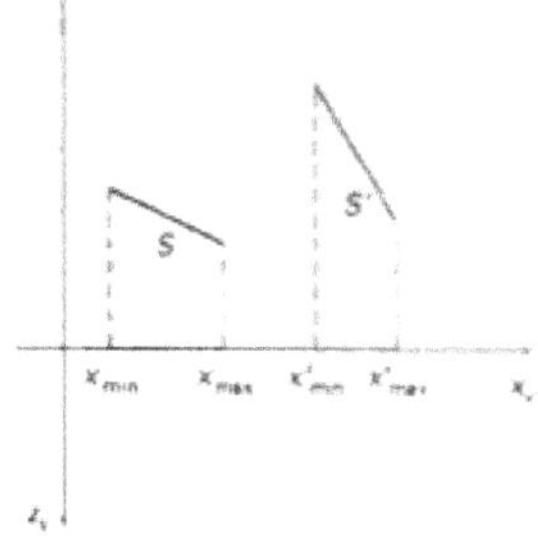

Figure 7.10: Two Surfaces with Depth Overlap but no Overlap in the x Direction

124

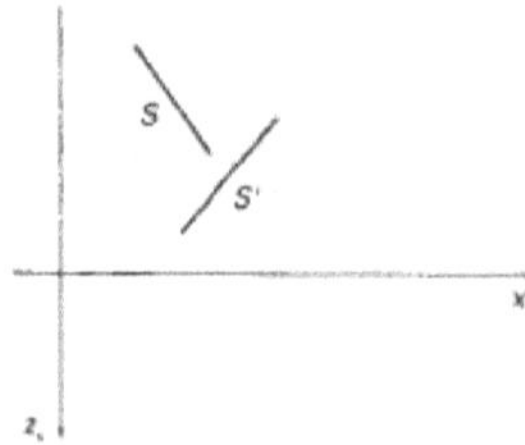

Figure 7.11: Surface S is Completely behind ("inside") the Overlapping Surface S

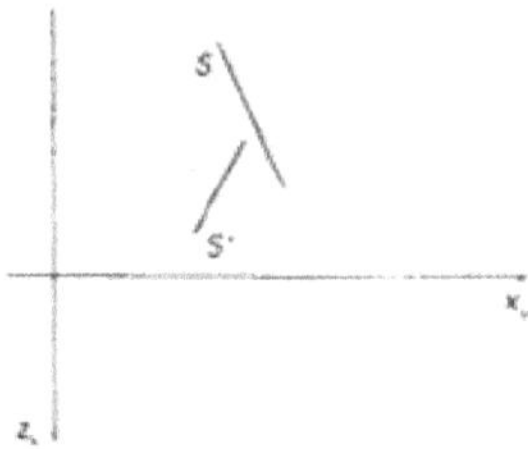

Figure 7.12: Overlapping Surface S' IS Completely in Front ("outside") of Surface S, but S is not Completely behind S'

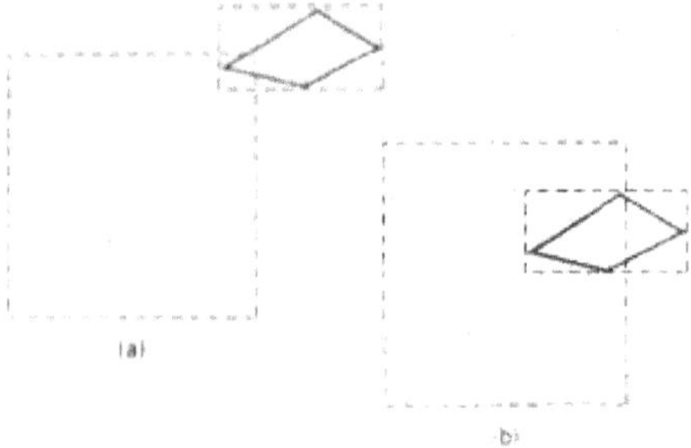

Figure 7.13: Two surfaces with Overlapping Bounding Rectangles in the xy Plane

If tests 1 through 3 have all failed, we try test 4 by checking for intersections between the bounding edges of the two surfaces using line equations in the xy plane. As demonstrated in Fig. 7.13, two surfaces may or may not intersect even though their coordinate extents overlap in the x, y, and z directions.

Should all four tests fail with a particular overlapping surface S', we interchange surfaces S and S' in the sorted lit. An example of two surfaces that would be reordered with this procedure is given in Fig. 7.14. At this point, we still do not know for certain that we have found the farthest

125

surface from the view plane. Figure 7.15 illustrates a situation in which we would first interchange S and S". But since S" obscures part of S', we need to interchange S" and S' to get the three surfaces into the correct depth order. Therefore, we need to repeat the testing process for each surface that is reordered in the list.

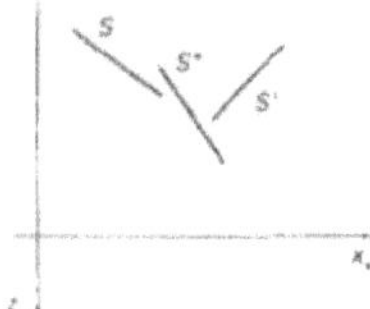

Figure 7.14: Surface S has Greater Depth but Obscures Surface S'.

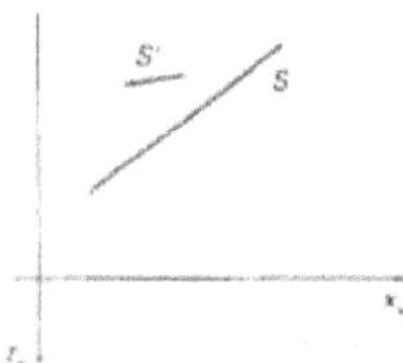

Figure 7.15: Three Surfaces Entered into the Sorted Surface List in the Order S, S', S" should be Reordered S', S", S

7.8.   BSP-tree Method

A binary space-partitioning (BSP) tree is an efficient method for determining object visibility by painting surfaces onto the screen from back to front, as in the painter's algorithm. The BSP tree is particularly useful when the view reference point changes, but the objects in a scene are at fwed positions.

Applying a BSP tree to visibility testing involves identifying surfaces that are "inside" and "outside" the partitioning plane at each step of the space subdivrsion, relative to the viewing direction. Figure 7.16 illustrates the basic concept in this algorithm. With plane P_1, we first partition the space into two sets of objects. One set of objects is behind, or in back of, plane P_1 relative to the viewing direction, and the other set is in front of P_1. Since one object is intersected by plane P_1, we divide that object into two separate objects, labeled A and B. Objects A and C are in front of P_1, and objects B and Dare behind P_1. We next partition the space again with plane P2 and construct the binary tree representation shown in Fig. 7.16(b). In this tree, the objects are represented as terminal nodes, with front objects as left branches and back objects as right branches.

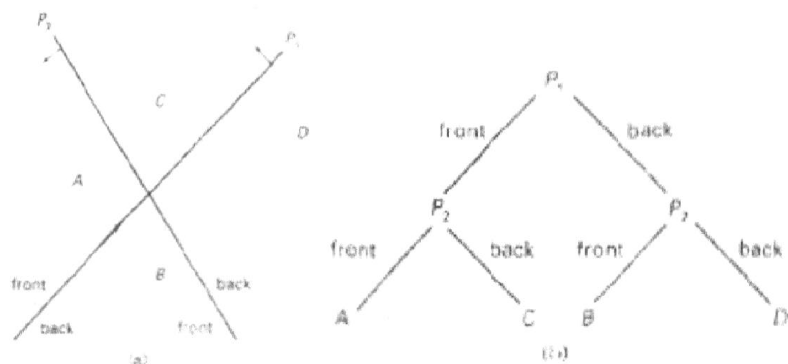

Figure 7.16: A Region of Space (a) is Partitioned with Two Planes P₁ and P₂ to form the BSP Tree Representation in (b)

7.9. Area-subdivision Method

This technique for hidden-surface removal is essentially an image-space method, but object-space operations can be used to accomplish depth ordering of surfaces. The area-subdivision method takes advantage of area coherence in a scene by locating those view areas that represent part of a single surface. We apply this method by successively dividing the total viewing area into smaller and smaller rectangles until each small area is the projection of part of n single visible surface or no surface at all.

To implement this method, we need to establish tests tnat can quickly identify the area as part of a single surface or tell us that the area is too complex to analyze easily. Starting with the total view, we apply the tests to determine whether we should subdivide the total area into smaller rectangles. If the tests indicate that the view is sufficiently complex, we subdivide it. Next. we apply the tests to each of the smaller areas, subdividing these if the tests indicate that visibility of a single surface is still uncertain. We continue this process until the subdivisions are easily analyzed as belonging to a single surface or until they are reduced to the size of a single pixel. An easy way to do this is to successively divide the area into four equal parts at each step, as shown in Fig. 7.17. This approach is similar to that used in constructing a quadtree. A viewing area with a resolution of 1024 by 1024 could be subdivided ten times in this way before a. subarea is reduced to a point.

Tests to determine the visibility of a single surface within a specified area are made by comparing surfaces to the boundary of the area. There are four possible relationships that a surface can have with a specified area boundary. We can describe these relative surface characteristics in the following way (Fig. 7.18):

- Surrounding surface-One that completely encloses the area.
- Overlapping surface-One that is partly inside and partly outside the area.
- Inside surface-One that is completely inside the area.
- Outside surface-One that is completely outside the area.

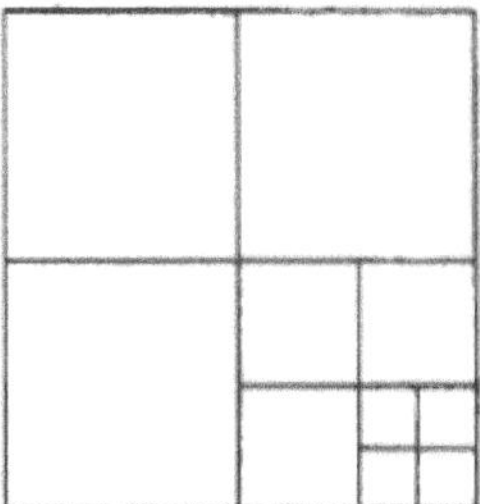

Figure 7.17: Dividing a Square Area into Equal-sized Quadrants at each Step

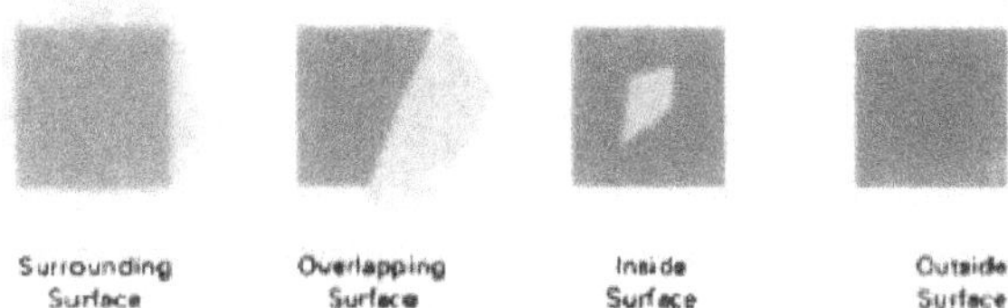

Figure 7.18: Possible Relationships between Polygon surfaces and a Rectangular Area

The tests for determining surface visibility within an area can be stated in terms of these four classifications. No further subdivisions of a specified area are needed if one of the following conditions is true:

1. All surfaces are outside surfaces with respect to the area.
2. Only one inside, overlapping, or surrounding surface is in the area.
3. A surrounding surface obscures all other surfaces within the area boundaries.

Test 1 can be camed out by checking the bounding rectangles of all surfaces against the area boundaries. Test 2 can also use the bounding rectangles in the xy plane to identify an inside surface. For other types of surfaces, the bounding mtangles can be used as an initial check. If a single bounding rectangle intersects the area in some way, additional checks are wd to determine whether the surface is surrounding, overlapping, or outside. Once a single inside, overlapping, or surrounding surface has been identified, its pixel intensities are transferred to the appropriate area within the frame buffer.

One method for implementing test 3 is to order surfaces according to their minimum depth from the view plane. For each surrounding surface, we then compute the maximum depth within the area under consideration. If the maximum depth of one of these surrounding surfaces is closer to the view plane than the minimum depth of all other surfaces within the area, test 3 is satisfied.

7.10. Octree Methods

When an octree representation is used for the viewing volume, hidden-surface elimination is accomplished by projecting octree nodes onto the viewing surface in a front-to-back order. In Fig. 7.19, the front face of a region of space (the side toward the viewer) is formed with octants 0, 1, 2, and 3. Surfaces in the front of these octants are visible to the viewer. Any surfaces toward the rear of the front octants or in the back octants (4, 5, 6, and 7) may be hidden by the front surfaces.

Back surfaces are eliminated, for the viewing direction given in Fig. 7.19, by proceesing data elements in the octree nodes in the order 0, 1, 2, 3, 4, 5, 6, 7. This results in a depth-first traversal of the octree, so that nodes representing octants 0, 1.2, and 3 for the entire region are visited before the nodes representing octants 4, 5, 6, and 7. Similarly, the nodes for the front four suboctants of octant 0 are visited before the nodes for the four back suboctants. The traversal of the octree continues in this order for each octant subdivision.

When a color value is encountered in an octree node, the pixel area in the frame buffer corresponding to this node is assigned that color value only if no values have previously been stored in this area. In this way, only the bont colors are loaded into the buffer. Nothing is loaded if an area is void. Any node that is found to be completely obscured is eliminated from further processing, so that its subtrees are not accessed. Different views of objects ripresented as octrees can be obtained by applying transformations to the octree representation that reorient the object according to the view selected. We assume that the octree representation is always set up so that octants 0, 1, 2, and 3 of a region form the front face, as in Fig. 7.19.

A method for displaying an octree is first to map the octree onto a quadtree of visible areas by traversing octree nodes from front to back in a recursive procedure. Then the quadtree representation for the visible surfaces is loaded into the frame buffer. Figure 7.20 depicts the octants in a region of space and the corresponding quadrants on the view plane. Contributions to quadrant 0 come from octants 0 and 4. Color values in quadrant 1 are obtained from surfaces in octants 1 and 5, and values in each of the other two quadrants are generated from the pair of octants aligned with each of these quadrants.

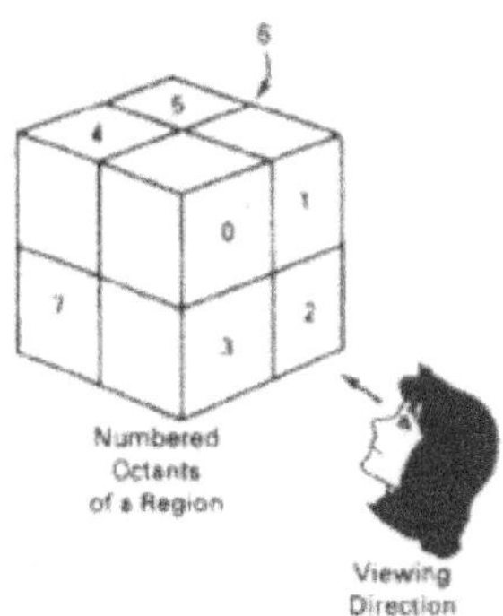

Figure 7.19: Objects in Octants 0, 1, 2, and 3 Obscure Objects in the Back Octants (4, 5, 6, 7) when the Viewing Direction is as shown

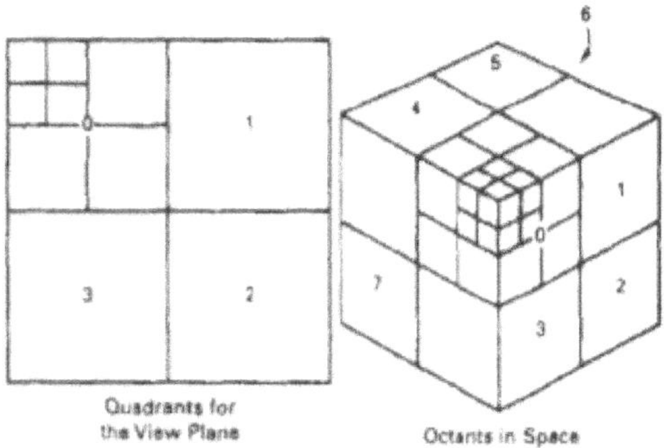

Figure 7.20: Octant Divisions for a Region of Space and the Corresponding Quadrant Plane

CHAPTER VIII

8. Illumination Models and Surface Rendering Methods

8.1. Basic Illumination Models

8.1.1. Ambient Light

A surface that is not exposed directly to a light source still will be visible it nearby objects are illuminated. In our basic illumination model, we can set a general level of brightness for a scene. This is a simple way to model the combination of light reflections from various surfaces to produce a uniform illumination called the ambient light, or background light. Ambient light has no spatial or directional characteristics. The amount of ambient light incident on each object is a constant for all surfaces and over all directions.

We can set the level for the ambient light in a scene with parameter I_a and each surface is then illuminated with this constant value. The resulting reflected light is a constant for each surface, independent of the viewing direction and the spatial orientation of the surface. But the intensity of the reflected light for each surface depends on the optical properties of the surface; that is, how much of the incident energy is to be reflected and how much absorbed.

8.1.2. Diffuse Reflection

Ambient-light reflection is an approximation of global diffuse lighting effects. Diffuse reflections are constant over each surface in a scene, independent of the viewing direction. The fractional amount of the incident light that is diffusely reflected can be set for each surface with parameter k_d, the diffuse-reflection coefficient, or diffuse reflectivity. Parameter k_d is assigned a constant value in the interval 0 to 1, according to the reflecting properties we want the surface to have. If we want a highly reflective surface, we set the value of k_d near 1. This produces a bright surface with the intensity of the reflected light near that of the incident light. To simulate a surface that absorbs most of the incident light, we set the reflectivity to a value near 0. Actually, parameter k_d is a function of surface color, but for the time being we will assume k_d is a constant.

$$Iambdiff = kd \ Ia$$

Since ambient light produces a flat uninteresting shading for each surface (Fig. 8.1), scenes are rarely rendered with ambient light alone. At least one light source is included in a scene, often as a point source at the viewing position.

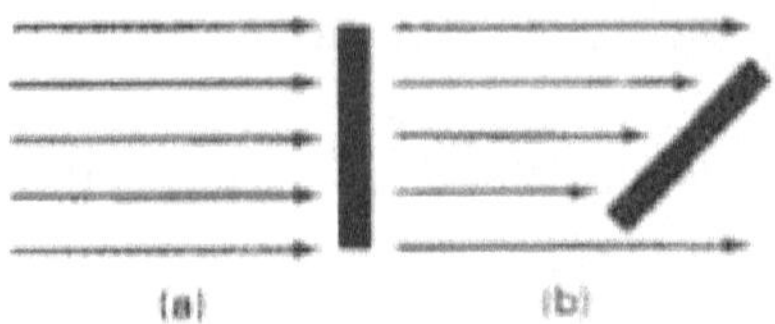

Figure 8.1: A surface Perpendicular to the Direction of the Incident Light (a) is more Illuminated than an Equal Sized surface at an Oblique Angle (b) to the Incoming Light Direction

8.1.3. *Specular Reflection and the Phong Model*

When we look at an illuminated shiny surface, such as polished metal, an apple, or a person's forehead, we see a highlight, or bright spot, at certain viewing directions. This phenomenon, called specular reflection, is the result of total, or near total, reflection of the incident light in a concentrated region around the specular reflection angle. Figure 8.2 shows the specular reflection direction at a point on the illuminated surface. The specular-reflection angle equals the angle of the incident light, with the two angles measured on opposite sides of the unit normal surface vector N. In this figure, we use R to represent the unit vector in the direction of ideal specular reflection; L to represent the unit vector directed toward the point light source; and V as the unit vector pointing to the viewer from the surface position. Angle ϕ is the viewing angle relative to the specular-reflection direction R. For an ideal reflector (perfect mirror), incident light is reflected only in the specular-reflection direction. In this case, we would only see reflected light when vectors V and R coincide ($\phi = 0$).

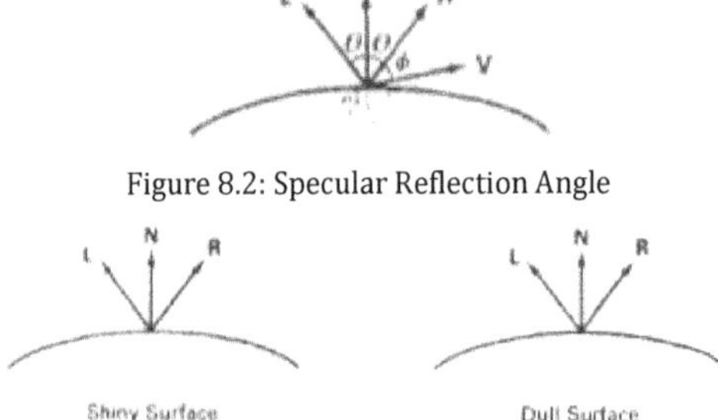

Figure 8.2: Specular Reflection Angle

Figure 8.3: Modeling Specular Reflections with Parameter n_s

Objects other than ideal reflectors exhibit specular reflections over a finite range of viewing positions around vector R. shiny surfaces have a narrow specular reflection range, and dull surfaces have a wider reflection range. An empirical model for calculating the specular-reflection range, developed by Phong Bui Tuong and called the Phong specular-reflection model, or simply the Phong model, sets the intensity of specular reflection proportional to $\cos^{ns} \phi$. Angle ϕ can be assigned values in the range 0^0 to 90^0 so that $\cos \phi$ varies from 0 to 1. The value assigned to specular-reflection parameter n, is determined by the type of surface that we want to display. A very shiny surface is modeled with a large value for n, and smaller values are used for duller surfaces. For a perfect reflector, n_s is infinite. For a rough surface, such as chalk or cinderblock, n_s would be assigned a value near 1. Figures 8.3 and 8.4 show the effect of n_s on the angular range for which we can expect to see specular reflections.

The intensity of specular reflection depends on the material properties of the surface and the angle of incidence, as well as other factors such as the polarization and color of the incident light. We can approximately model monochromatic specular intensity variations using a specular-reflection coefficient, $W(\theta)$, for each surface. Figure 8.5 shows the general variation of $W(\theta)$ over the range $\theta = 0^0$ to $\theta = 90^0$ for a few materials. In general, $W(\theta)$ tends to increase as the angle of incidence increases. At $\theta = 90^0$, $W(\theta) = 1$ and all of the incident light is reflected. The variation of specular intensity with angle of incidence is described by Fresnel's laws of Reflection. Using the spectral-reflection function $W(\theta)$, we can write the Phong specular-reflection model as

$$\text{Ispec} = W(\theta)\ Il\ cos^{ns}\ \phi$$

where Il is the intensity of the light source, and ϕ is the viewing angle relative to the specular-reflection direction R.

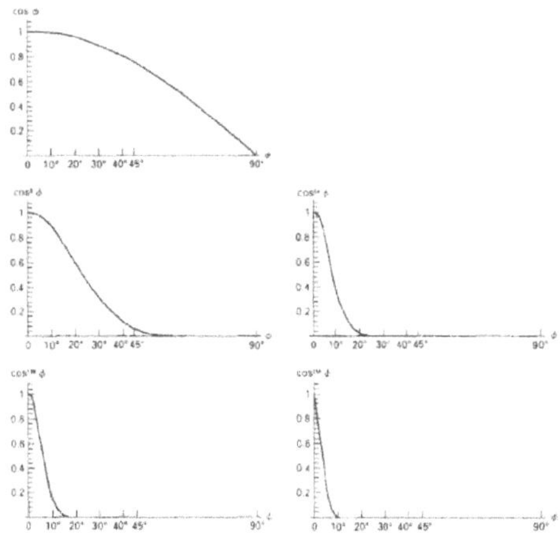

Figure 8.4: PLOTS of $\cos^{ns}$ for Several Values of Specular Parameter n_s

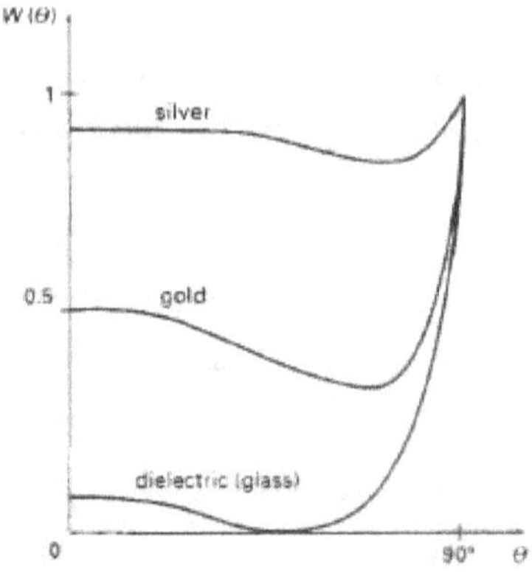

Figure 8.5: Approximation Variation of the Specular Reflection Coefficient as a Function of Angle of Incident

8.1.4. *Combined Diffuse and Specular Reflections with Multiple Light Sources*

For a single point light source, we can model the combined diffuse and specular reflections from a point on an illuminated surface as

$$I = I_{diff} + I_{spec}$$
$$= k_a I_a + k_d \, Il \, (N \cdot L) + k_s \, Il(N \cdot H)^{ns} \tag{8.1}$$

If we place more than one point source in a scene, we obtain the light reflection at any surface point by summing the contributions from the individual sources:

$$I = k_a I_a + \sum_{i=1}^{n} I_{li}[k_d(N \cdot L) + k_s(N \cdot H)^{ns}] \tag{8.2}$$

To ensure that any pixel intensity does not exceed the maximum allowable value, we can apply some type of normalization procedure. A simple approach is to set a maximum magnitude for each term in the intensity equation. If any calculated term exceeds the maximum, we simply set it to the maximum value. Another way to compensate for intensity overflow is to normalize the individual terms by dividing each by the magnitude of the largest term. A more complicate procedure is first to calculate all pixel intensities for the scene, then the calculate intensities are scaled onto the allowable intensity range.

8.1.5. *Warn Model*

The Warn model provides a method for simulating studio lighting effects by controlling light intensity in different directions. Light sources are modeled as points on a reflecting surface, using the Phong model for the surface points. Then the intensity in different directions is controlled by selecting values for the Phong exponent In addition, light controls, such as "barn doors" and spotlighting, used by studio photographers can be simulated in the Warn model. Flaps are used to control the amount of light emitted by a source in various directions. Two flaps are provided for each of the $x, y,$ and z directions. Spotlights are used to control the amount of light emitted within a cone with apex at a point-source position.

8.1.6. *Shadows*

Hidden-surface methods can be used to locate areas where light sources produce shadows. By applying a hidden-surface method with a light source at the view position, we can determine which surface sections cannot be "seen" from the light source. These are the shadow areas. Once we have determined the shadow areas for all light sources, the shadows could be treated as surface patterns and stored in pattern arrays. *Figure 8.6* illustrates the generation of shading patterns for two objects on a table and a distant light source. All shadow areas in this figure are surfaces that are not visible from the position of the light source.

The scene shadow effects produced by multiple light sources. Shadow patterns generated by a hidden-surface method are valid for any selected viewing position, as long as the light-source positions are not changed. Surfaces that are visible from the view position are shaded according to the lighting model, which can be combined with texture patterns. We can display shadow areas with ambient-light intensity only, or we can combine the ambient light with specified surface textures.

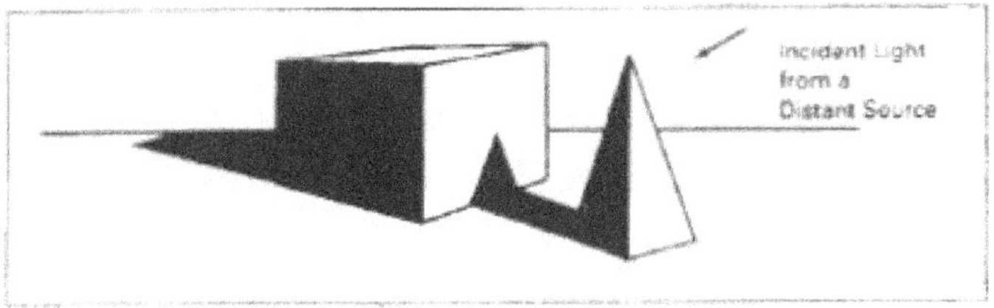

Figure 8.6: Objects Modeled with Shadow Regions

8.1.7. *Polygon – Rendering Methods*

The application of an illumination model to the rendering of standard graphics objects: those formed with polygon surfaces. The objects are usually polygon-mesh approximations of curved-surface objects, but they may also be polyhedra that are not curved-surface approximations. Scan line algorithms typically apply a lighting model to obtain polygon surface rendering in one of two ways. Each polygon can be rendered with a single intensity, or the intensity can be obtained at each point of the surface using an interpolation scheme.

8.1.8. Constant-Intensity Shading

A fast and simple method for rendering an object with polygon surfaces is constant - intensity shading, also called flat shading. In this method, a single intensity is calculated for each polygon. All points over the surface of the polygon are then displayed with the same intensity value. Constant shading can be useful for quickly displaying the general appearance of a curved surface.

In general, flat shading of polygon facets provides an accurate rendering for an object if all of the following assumptions are valid,

- The object is a polyhedron and is not an approximation of an object with a curved surface.
- All light sources illuminating the object are sufficiently far from the surface so that N. L and the attenuation function are constant over the surface.
- The viewing position is sufficiently far from the surface so that V. R is constant over the surface.

Even if all of these conditions are not true, we can still reasonably approximate surface-lighting effects using small polygon facets with flat shading and calculate the intensity for each facet, say, at the center of the polygon.

8.1.9. Gouraud Shading

This intensity-interpolation scheme, developed by Gouraud and generally referred to as Gouraud shading, renders a polygon surface by linearly interpolating intensity values across the surface. Intensity values for each polygon are matched with the values of adjacent polygons along the common edges, thus eliminating the intensity discontinuities that can occur in flat shading.

Each polygon surface is rendered with Gouraud shading by performing the following calculations:

- Determine the average unit normal vector at each polygon vertex.
- Apply an illumination model to each vertex to calculate the vertex intensity.
- Linearly interpolate the vertex intensities over the surface of the polygon.

At each polygon vertex, we obtain a normal vector by averaging the surface normals of all polygons sharing that vertex, as illustrated in *Fig. 8.7*. Thus, for any vertex position *V*, we obtain the unit vertex normal with the calculation

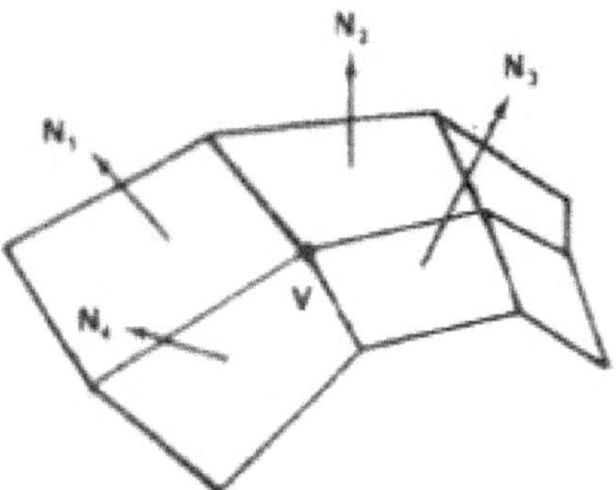

Figure 8.7: The Normal Vector at Vertex V is Calculated as the Average of the surface Normals for each Polygon Sharing that Vertex

$$N_V = \frac{\sum_{k=1}^{n} N_k}{\left| \sum_{k=1}^{n} N_k \right|}$$

(8.3)

Once we have the vertex normals, we can determine the intensity at the vertices from a lighting model. Fig 8.8 demonstrates the next step: interpolating intensities along the polygon edges. For each scan line, the intensity at the intersection of the scan line with a polygon edge is linearly interpolated from the intensities at the edge endpoints. For the example in Fig. 8.8, the polygon edge with endpoint vertices at positions 1 and 2 is intersected by the scan line at point 4. A fast method for obtaining the intensity at point 4 is to interpolate between intensities I_1 and I_2 using only the vertical displacement of the scan line:

$$I_4 = \frac{y_4 - y_2}{y_1 - y_2} I_1 + \frac{y_1 - y_4}{y_1 - y_2} I_2$$

(8.4)

Similarly, intensity at the right intersection of this scan line (point 5) is interpolated from intensity values at vertices 2 and 3. Once these bounding intensities are established for a scan line, an interior point (such as point p in Fig. 8.8) is interpolated from the bounding intensities at points 4 and 5 as,

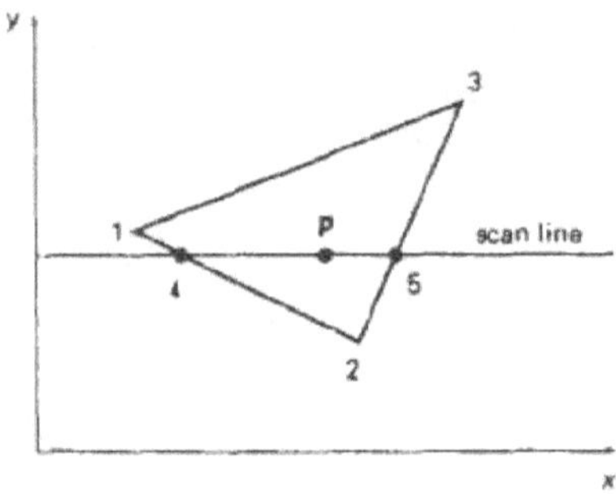

Figure 8.8

Incremental calculations are used to obtain successive edge intensity values between scan lines and to obtain successive intensities along a scan line. As shown in Fig. 8.9, if the intensity at edge position (x, y) is interpolated as,

$$I = \frac{y - y_2}{y_1 - y_2} I_1 + \frac{y_1 - y}{y_1 - y_2} I_2 \qquad (8.6)$$

then we can obtain the intensity along this edge for the next scan line, y – 1, as

$$I' = I + \frac{I_2 - I_1}{y_1 - y_2} \qquad (8.7)$$

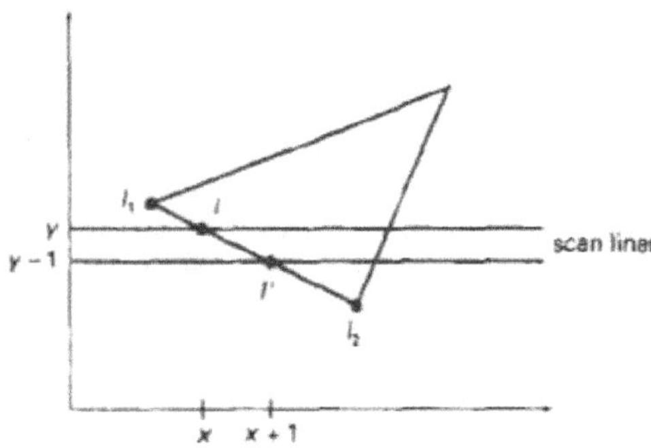

Figure 8.9: Incremental Interpolation of Intensity Values along a Polygon Edge for Successive Scan Lines

8.1.10. Phong Shading

A more accurate method for rendering a polygon surface is to interpolate normal vectors, and then apply the illumination model to each surface point. This method, developed by Phong

Bui Tuong, is called Phong shading,or normal vector interpolation shading. It displays more realistic highlights on a surface and greatly reduces the Mach-band effect.

A polygon surface is rendered using Phong shading by carrying out the following steps:

- Determine the average unit normal vector at each polygon vertex.
- Linearly interpolate the vertex normals over the surface of the polygon.
- Apply an illumination model along each scan line to calculate projected pixel intensities for the surface points.

Interpolation of surface normals along a polygon edge between two vertices is illustrated in Fig. 8.10. The normal vector N for the scan-line intersection point along the edge between vertices 1 and 2 can be obtained by vertically interpolating between edge endpoint normals:

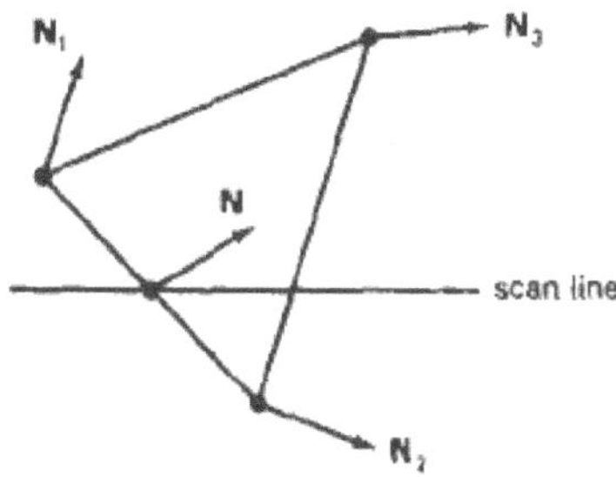

Figure 8.10: Interpolation of Surface Normal along a Polygon Edge

$$N = \frac{y - y_2}{y_1 - y_2} N_1 + \frac{y_1 - y}{y_1 - y_2} N_2 \tag{8.8}$$

Incremental methods are used to evaluate normals between scan lines and along each individual scan line. At each pixel position along a scan line, the illumination model is applied to determine the surface intensity at that point.

8.1.11. Fast Phong Shading

Surface rendering with Phong shading can be speeded up by using approximations in the illumination model calculations of normal vectors. Fast Phong shading approximates the intensity calculations using a Taylor series expansion and triangular surface patches.

Since Phong shading interpolates normal vectors from vertex normals, we can express the surface normal N at any point (x, y) over a triangle as

$$N = A_x + B_y + C \tag{8.9}$$

where vectors A, B, and C are determined from the three vertex equations

$$N_K = A x_k + B y_k + C, \quad k = 1, 2, 3 \tag{8.10}$$

with (x_k, y_k) denoting a vertex position.

$$
\begin{aligned}
I_{\text{diff}}(x, y) &= \frac{\mathbf{L} \cdot \mathbf{N}}{|\mathbf{L}||\mathbf{N}|} \\
&= \frac{\mathbf{L} \cdot (\mathbf{A}x + \mathbf{B}y + \mathbf{C})}{|\mathbf{L}|\,|\mathbf{A}x + \mathbf{B}y + \mathbf{C}|} \\
&= \frac{(\mathbf{L} \cdot \mathbf{A})x + (\mathbf{L} \cdot \mathbf{B})y + \mathbf{L} \cdot \mathbf{C}}{|\mathbf{L}|\,|\mathbf{A}x + \mathbf{B}y + \mathbf{C}|}
\end{aligned}
\tag{8.11}
$$

We can rewrite this expression in the form

$$I_{\text{diff}}(x, y) = \frac{ax + by + c}{(dx^2 + exy + fy^2 + gx + hy + i)^{1/2}} \tag{8.12}$$

where parameters such as a, b, c, and d are used to represent the various dot products. For example,

$$a = \frac{\mathbf{L} \cdot \mathbf{A}}{|\mathbf{L}|} \tag{8.13}$$

Finally, we can express the denominator in Eq. 8.12 as a Taylor-series expansion and retain terms up tosecond degree in x and y. This yields

$$I_{\text{diff}}(x, y) = T_5 x^2 + T_4 xy + T_3 y^2 + T_2 x + T_1 y + T_0 \tag{8.14}$$

where each T_k is a function of parameters a, b, c, and so forth.

CHAPTER IX

9. Computer Animation

9.1.   Introduction

The term computer animation generally refers to any time sequence of visual changes in a scene. In addition to changing object position with translations or rotations, a computer-generated animation could display time variations in object size, color, transparency, or surface texture. Advertising animations often transition one object shape into another: for example, transforming a can of motor oil into an automobile engine. Computer animations can also be generated by changing camera parameters, such as position, orientation, and focal length.

9.1.1.   *Design of Animation Sequences*

In general, an animation sequence is designed with the following steps:

- Storyboard layout
- Object definitions
- Key-frame specifications
- Generation of in-between frames

Real-time computer animations produced by Bight simulators, for instance, display motion sequences in response to setting on the aircraft controls. And visualization applications are generated by the solutions of the numerical models. For frame-by-frame animation, each frame of the scene is separately generated and stored. Later, the frames can be recoded on film or they can be consecutively displayed in "real-time playback" mode.

The *storyboard* is an outline of the action. It defines the motion sequence as a set of basic events that are to take place. Depending on the type of animation to be produced, the storyboard could consist of a set of rough sketches or it could be a list of the basic ideas for the motion.

An *object definition* is given for each participant in the action. Objects can be defined in terms of basic shapes, such as polygons or splines. In addition, the associated movements for each object are specified along with the shape.

A *keyframe* is a detailed drawing of the scene at a certain time in the animation sequence. Within each key frame, each object is positioned according to the time for that frame. Some key frames are chosen at extreme positions in the action; others are spaced so that the time interval between key frames is not too great. More key frames are specified for intricate motions than for simple, slowly varying motions.

In-between are the intermediate frames between the key frames. The number of in-betweens needed is determined by the media to be used to display the animation. Film requires 24 frames per second, and graphics terminals are refreshed at the rate of 30 to 60 frames per second. Typically, time intervals for the motion are set up so that there are from three to five in-betweens for each pair of key frames. Depending on the speed specified for the motion, some key frames can be duplicated. For a 1-minute film sequence with no duplication, we would need 1440 frames.

9.1.2. *General Computer-animation Functions*

Some steps in the development of an animation sequence are well-suited to computer solution. These include object manipulations and rendering, camera motions, and the generation of in-betweens. Animation packages, such as Wave-front, for example, provide special functions for designing the animation and processing individual objects.

One function available in animation packages is provided to store and manage the object database. Object shapes and associated parameters are stored and updated in the database. Other object functions include those for motion generation and those for object rendering. Motions can be generated according to specified constraints using two-dimensional or three-dimensional transformations. Standard functions can then be applied to identify visible surfaces and apply the rendering algorithms.

Another typical function simulates camera movements. Standard motions are zooming, panning, and tilting. Finally, given the specification for the key frames, the in-between can be automatically generated.

9.1.3. *Raster Animations*

On raster systems, we can generate real-time animation in limited applications using raster operations. A simple method for translation in the xy plane is to transfer a rectangular block of pixel values from one location to another. Two dimensional rotations in multiples of 900 are also simple to perform, although we can rotate rectangular blocks of pixels through arbitrary angles using antialiasing procedures. To rotate a block of pixels, we need to determine the percent of area coverage for those pixels that overlap the rotated block. Sequences of raster operations can be executed to produce real-time animation of either two-dimensional or three-dimensional objects, as long as we restrict the animation to motions in the projection plane. Then no viewing or visible-surface algorithms need be invoked.

We can also animate objects along two-dimensional motion paths using the color-table transformations. Here we predefine the object at successive positions along the motion path, and set the successive blocks of pixel values to color-table entries. We set the pixels at the first position of the object to "on" values, and we set the pixels at the other object positions to the background color. The animation is then accomplished by changing the color-table values so that the object is "on" at successively positions along the animation path as the preceding position is set to the background intensity (Fig 9.1).

Figure 9.1: Real-time Raster Color - table Animation

9.1.4. *Computer-animation Languages*

Design and control of animation sequences are handled with a set of animation routines. A general-purpose language, such as C, Lisp, Pascal, or FORTRAN, is often used to program the animation functions, but several specialized animation languages have been developed. Animation functions include a graphics editor, a key-frame generator, an in-between generator, and standard graphics routines. The graphics editor allows us to design and modify object shapes, using spline surfaces, constructive solid-geometry methods, or other representation schemes.

A typical task in an animation specification is scene description. This includes the positioning of objects and light sources, defining the photometric parameters (light-source intensities and surface-illumination properties), and setting the camera parameters (position, orientation, and lens characteristics). Another standard function is action specification. This involves the layout of motion paths for the objects and camera. And we need the usual graphics routines: viewing and perspective transformations, geometric transformations to generate object movements as a function of accelerations or kinematic path specifications, visible-surface identification, and the surface-rendering operations.

Key-frame systems are specialized animation languages designed simply to generate the in-betweens from the user-specified key frames. Usually, each object in the scene is defined as a set of rigid bodies connected at the joints and with a limited number of degrees of freedom. Parameterized systems allow object-motion characteristics to be specified as part of the object definitions. The adjustable parameters control such object characteristics as degrees of freedom, motion limitations, and allowable shape changes.

Scripting systems allow object specifications and animation sequences to be defined with a user-input script. From the script, a library of various objects and motions can be constructed.

9.1.5. Key-frame Systems

Morphing

Transformation of object shapes from one form to another is called morphing, which is a shortened form of metamorphosis. Morphing methods can he applied to any motion or transition involving a change in shape. Given two key frames for an object transformation, we first adjust the object specification in one of the frames so that the number of polygon edges (or the number of vertices) is the same for the two frames. This pre-processing step is illustrated in Fig. 9.2. A straight-line segment in key frame k is transformed into two line segments in key frame *k + 1*. Since key frame *k + 1* has an extra vertex, we add a vertex between vertices *1* and *2* in key frame *k* to balance the number of vertices (and edges) in the two key frames. Using linear interpolation to generate the in-betweens. We transition the added vertex in key frame k into vertex 3' along the straight-line path shown in Fig. 9.2. An example of a triangle linearly expanding into a quadrilateral is given In Fig. 9.4.

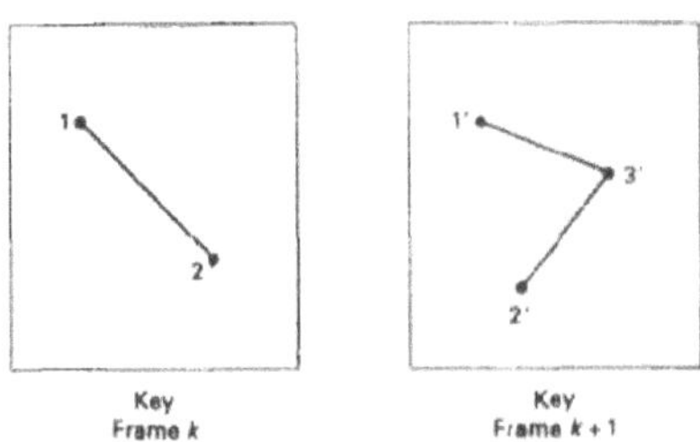

Figure 9.2: An Edge with Vertex Positions 1 and 2 in Key Frame k Evolves into Two Connected Edges in Key Frame k + 1 in Key Frame k + 1

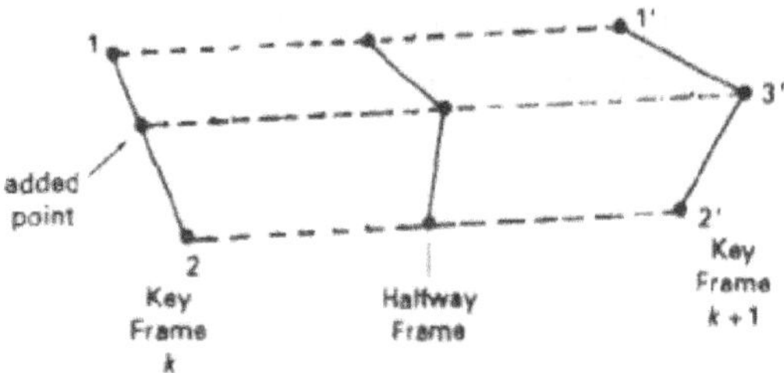

Figure 9.3: Linear Interpolation for Transforming a Line Segment in Key Frame k into Two Connected Line Segments

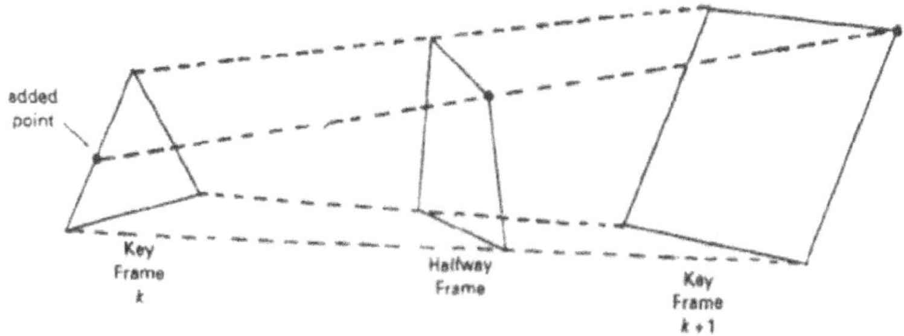

Figure 9.4: Linear Interpolation for Transforming a Triangle into a Quadrilateral

We can state general pre-processing rules for equalizing key frames in terms of either the number of edges or the number of vertices to be added to a key frame. Suppose we equalize the edge count, and parameters L_K and L_{K+1} denote the number of line segments in two consecutive frames. We then define

$$L_{max}= max(L_k , L_{k+1}), \qquad L_{min}= min(L_k , L_{k+1}) \qquad (9.1)$$

and

$$N_e= L_{max} \bmod L_{min}$$

$$N_s = int \left(\frac{L_{max}}{L_{min}}\right) \qquad (9.2)$$

Then the preprocessing is accomplished by,

1. Dividing N_e edges of *keyframe_min* into $N_s + 1$ sections.
2. Dividing the remaining lines of *keyframe_min* into N_s sections.

As an example, if $L_k = 15$ and $L_{k+1}= 11$, we would divide 4 lines of *keyframe_{k+1}*, into 2 sections each. The remaining lines of *keyframe_{k+1}*, are left intact.

If we equalize the vertex count, we can use parameters V_k and V_{k+1} to denote the number of vertices in the two consecutive frames. In this case, we define,

$$V_{max}= \max(V_k , V_{k+1}), \quad V_{min}= \min(V_k , V_{k+1}) \qquad (9.3)$$

and

$$N_{l\,s} = (V_{max} - 1) \bmod (V_{min} - 1)$$

$$N_p = \text{int}\left(\frac{V_{max} - 1}{V_{min} - 1}\right) \qquad (9.4)$$

Preprocessing using vertex count is performed by,

1. Adding N_p points to N_{ls} line sections of $keyframe_{min}$
2. Adding N_p - 1 points to the remaining edges of $keyframe_{min}$

For the triangle-to-quadrilateral example, $V_k = 3$ and $V_{k+1} = 4$. Both N_{ls} and N_p are 1, so we would add one point to one edge of $keyframe_k$ No points would be added to the remaining lines of $keyframe_{k+1}$.

Simulating Accelerations

Curve-fitting techniques are often used to specify the animation paths between key frames. Given the vertex positions at the key frames, we can fit the positions with linear or nonlinear paths. Figure 9.5 illustrates a nonlinear fit of key-frame positions. This determines the trajectories for the in-betweens. To simulate accelerations, we can adjust the time spacing for the in-betweens.

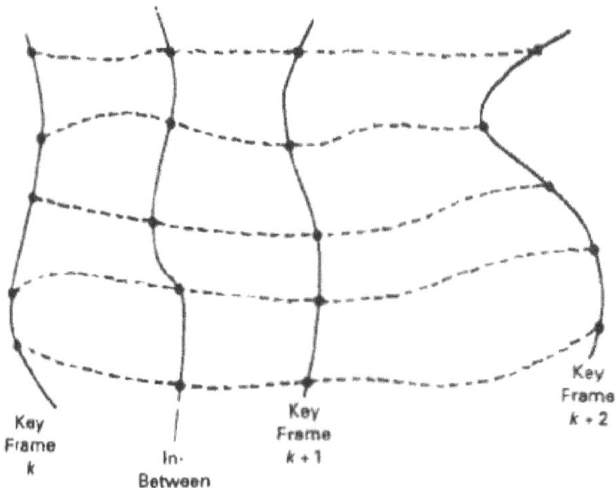

Figure 9.5: Fitting Key-frame Vertex Positions with Nonlinear Splines

For constant speed (zero acceleration), we use equal-interval time spacing for the in-betweens. Suppose we want n in-betweens for key frames at times t_1 and t_2 (*Fig. 9.6*). The time interval between key frames is then divided into $n + 1$ subintervals, yielding an in-between spacing of

$$\Delta t = \frac{t_2 - t_1}{n+1} \qquad\qquad (9.5)$$

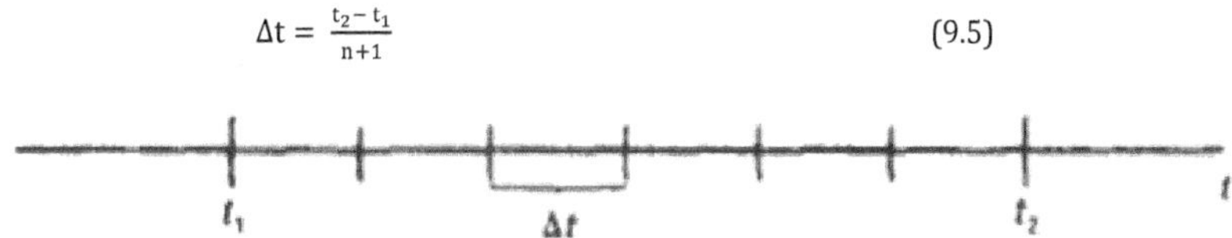

Figure 9.6: In-between Positions for Motion at Constant Speed

We can calculate the time for any in-between as

$$tB_j = t_1 + j\,\Delta t, \qquad j = 1, 2, 3, \ldots\ldots n \qquad (9.6)$$

and determine the values for coordinate positions, color, and other physical parameters.

Nonzero accelerations are used to produce realistic displays of speed changes, particularly at the beginning and end of a motion sequence. We can model the start-up and slowdown portions of an animation path with spline ortrigonometric functions. Parabolic and cubic time functions haw been applied to acceleration modeling, but trigonometric functions are more commonly used in animation packages.

To model increasing speed (positive acceleration), we want the time spacing between frames to increase so that greater changes in position occur as the object moves faster. We can obtain an increasing interval size with the function

$$1 - \cos\theta, \qquad\qquad 0 < \theta < \pi/2$$

For n in-betweens, the time for the jth in-between would then be calculated as,

$$tB_j = t_1 + \Delta t \left[1 - \cos\frac{j\pi}{2(n+1)}\right], \qquad j = 1, 2, \ldots\ldots n \qquad (9.7)$$

where Δt is the time difference between the two key frames. *Figure 9.7* gives a plot of the trigonometric acceleration function and the in-between spacing for n= 5.

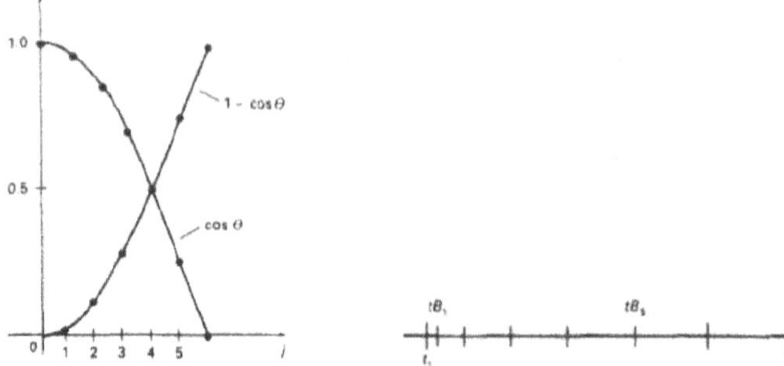

Figure 9.7: Atrigonometric Acceleration Function and the Corresponding in-between Spacing

We can model decreasing speed (deceleration) with $sin\theta$ in the range $0 < \theta < \pi/2$. The time position of an in-between is now defined as

$$tB_j = t_1 + \Delta t \sin\left[\frac{j\pi}{2(n+1)}\right], \qquad j = 1, 2, ...n \qquad (9.8)$$

A plot of this function and the decreasing size of the time intervals is shown in *Fig. 9.8* for five in-betweens.

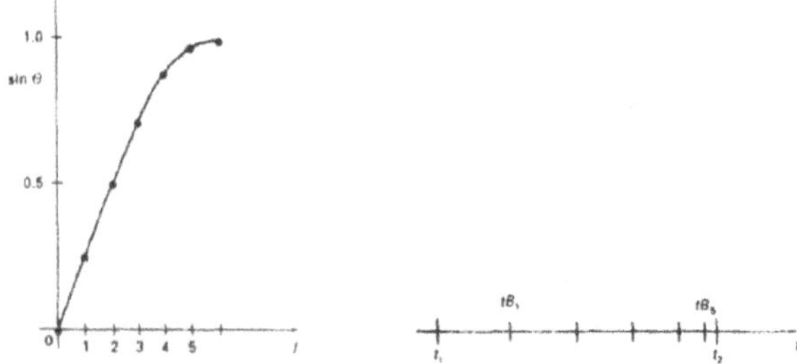

Figure 9.8: Atrigonometric Deceleration Function and the Corresponding in-between Spacing

A trigonometric accelerate-decelerate function and the corresponding in-between spacing for *n = 5*.

$$\frac{1}{2}(1 - \cos\theta), \qquad 0 < \theta < \pi/2$$

The time for the jth in-between is now calculated as

$$tB_j = t_1 + \Delta t \left[\frac{1-\cos\left[\frac{j\pi}{(n+1)}\right]}{2}\right], \qquad j = 1, 2, ...n \qquad (9.9)$$

with Δt denoting the time difference for the two key frames. Time intervals for the moving object first increase then the time intervals decrease, as shown in Fig. 9.9.

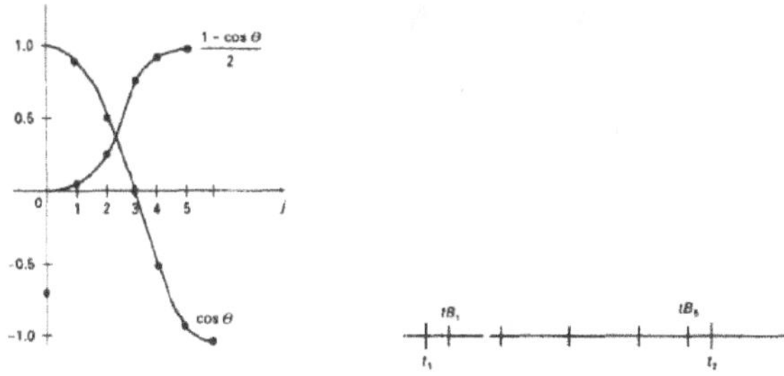

Figure 9.9: A Trigonometric Accelerate-decelerate Function and the Corresponding in-between Spacing

9.1.6. Motion Specifications

There are several ways in which the motions of objects can be specified in an animation system. We can define motions in very explicit terms, or we can use more abstract or more general approaches.

Direct Motion Specification

The most straightforward method for defining a motion sequence is direct specification of the motion parameters. Here, we explicitly give the rotation angles and translation vectors. Then the geometric transformation matrices are applied to transform coordinate positions. Alternatively, we could use an approximating equation to specify certain kinds of motions. We can approximate the path of a bouncing ball, for instance, with a damped, rectified, sine curve (Fig. 9.10):

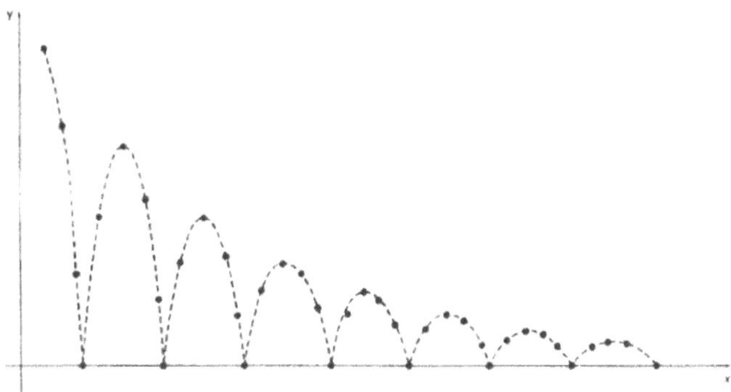

Figure 9.10: Approximating the Motion of a Bouncing Ball with a Damped Sine Function

$$y(x) = A\,|\sin(\omega x + \theta_0)|\,e \qquad\qquad (9.10)$$

Where A is the initial amplitude, w is the angular frequency, θ_0 is the phase angle, and k is the damping constant. These methods can be used for simple user-programmed animation sequences.

Goal-Directed Systems

At the opposite extreme, we can specify the motions that are to take place in general terms that abstractly describe the actions. These systems are referred to as goal directed because they determine specific motion parameters given the goals of the animation. For example, we could specify that we want an object to "walk" or to "run" to a particular destination. Or we could state that we want an object to "pick up" some other specified object. The input directives are then interpreted in terms of component motions that will accomplish the selected task. Human motions, for instance, can be defined as a hierarchical structure of submotions for the torso, limbs, and so forth.

Kinematics and Dynamics

We can also construct animation sequences using kinematic or dynamic descriptions. With a kinematic description, we specify the animation by giving motion parameters (position, velocity, and acceleration) without reference to the forces that cause the motion. For constant velocity (zero acceleration), we designate the motions of rigid bodies in a scene by giving an initial position and velocity vector for each object.

An alternate approach is to use inverse kinematics. Here, we specify the initial and final positions of objects at specified times and the motion parameters are computed by the system. For example, assuming zero accelerations, we can determine the constant velocity that will accomplish the movement of an object from the initial position to the final position. This method is often used with complex objects by giving the positions and orientations of an end node of an object, such as a hand or a foot. The system then determines the motion parameters of other nodes to accomplish the desired motion.

Dynamic descriptions on the other hand, require the specification of the forces that produce the velocities and accelerations. Descriptions of object behavior under the influence of forces are generally referred to as a physically based modeling.

Object motions are obtained from the force equations describing physical laws, such as Newton's laws of motion for gravitational and friction processes, Euler or Navier-Stokes equations describing fluid flow, and Maxwell's equations for electromagnetic forces. For example, the general form of Newton's second law for a particle of mass m is

$$F = \frac{d}{dt}(mv)$$

(9.11)

With F as the force vector, and v as the velocity vector If mass is constant, we solve the equation $F = ma$, where a is the acceleration vector. Otherwise, mass is a function of time, as in relativistic motions or the motions of space vehicles that consume measurable amounts of fuel per unit time. We can also use inverse dynamics to obtain the forces, given the initial and final positions of objects and the type of motion.

COMPUTER GRAPHICS UNIT – I

PART – A

1. Define Computer Graphics.

Computer graphics is an art of drawing pictures, lines, charts, etc. using computers with the help of programming. Computer graphics is made up of number of pixels. Computer graphics may be defined as a pictorial representation or graphical representation of objects in a computer.

2. What is meant by scan code?

When a key is pressed on the keyboard, the keyboard controller places a code carry to the key pressed into a part of the memory called as the keyboard buffer. This code is called as the scan code.

3. What is meant by refreshing of the screen?

Some method is needed for maintaining the picture on the screen. Refreshing of screen is done by keeping the phosphorus glowing to redraw the picture repeatedly. (i.e.) By quickly directing the electronic beam back to the same points.

4. Define Random scan/Raster scan displays.

Random scan is a method in which the display is made by the electronic beam which is directed only to the points or part of the screen where the picture is to be drawn. The Raster scan system is a scanning technique in which the electrons sweep from top to bottom and from left to right. The intensity is turned on or off to light and unlight the pixel.

5. List out the merits and demerits of Penetration techniques.

The merits and demerits of the Penetration techniques are as follows, It is an inexpensive technique.

It has only four colors.

The quality of the picture is not good when it is compared to other techniques. It can display color scans in monitors x Poor limitation etc.

6. List out the merits and demerits of DVST.

The merits and demerits of direct view storage tubes [DVST] are as follows, It has a flat screen.

Refreshing of screen is not required.

Selective or part erasing of screen is not possible. It has poor contrast.

Performance is inferior to the refresh CRT.

7. What do you mean by emissive and non-emissive displays?

The emissive display converts electrical energy into light energy. The plasma panels, thin film electroluminescent displays are the examples. The Non emissive are optical effects to convert the sunlight or light from any other source to graphic form. Liquid crystal display is an example.

8. List out the merits and demerits of Plasma panel display.

Merits

- Refreshing is not required
- Produce a very steady image free of Flicker
- Less bulky than a CRT.

Demerits

- Poor resolution of up to 60 d.p.i
- It requires complex addressing and wiring
- It is costlier than CRT.

9. What is persistence?

The time it takes the emitted light from the screen to decay one tenth of its original intensity is called as persistence.

10. What is resolution?

The maximum number of points that can be displayed without an overlap on a CRT is called as resolution.

11. What is Aspect ratio?

The ratio of vertical points to the horizontal points necessary to produce length of lines in both directions of the screen is called the Aspect ratio. Usually the aspect ratio is ¾.

12. What is meant by Addressability?

The Addressability is the number of individual dots per inch (d.p.i) that can be created.

If the address of the current dot is (x, y) then the next dot will be (x+y), (x+y+1) etc.

13. List some applications of graphics.

CAD – Computer Aided Design

Presentation

Image Processing

Entertainment

14. Define pixel.

Pixel is shortened forms of picture element. Each screen point is referred to as pixel or pel.

15. What is frame buffer?

Picture definition is stored in a memory area called frame buffer or refresh buffer.

16. What is bitmap and what is pixmap?

The frame buffer used in the black and white system is known as bitmap which take one bit per pixel. For systems with multiple bits per pixel, the frame buffer is often referred to as a pixmap.

17. What is a Vector display or stroke writing or calligraphic display?

Random scan monitors draw a picture one line at a time and for this reason are also referred as vector displays.

18. Where the video controller is used?

A special purpose processor, which is used to control the operation of the display device, is known as video controller or display controller.

19. What do you mean by scan conversion?

A major task of the display processor is digitizing a picture definition given in an application program into a set of pixel-intensity values for storage in the frame buffer. This digitization process is called scan conversion.

20. What is an output primitive?

Graphics programming packages provide function to describe a scene in terms of these basic geometric structures, referred to as output primitives.

21. What do you mean by 'jaggies'?

Line with stair step appearance is known as jaggies.

22. What is point in the computer graphics system?

The point is a most basic graphical element & is completely defined by a pair of user coordinates (x, y).

23. Write short notes on lines.

A line is of infinite extent can be defined by an angle of slope, and one point on the line $P=P(x,y)$. This can also be defined as $Y=mx+C$ where C is the Y- intercept.

24. Define Circle.

Circle is defined by its center xc, yc and its radius in user coordinate units. The equation of the circle is $x^2+y^2-r^2=0$.

25. Define Ellipse

An ellipse can use the same parameters xc, yc, r as a circle, in addition to the eccentricity e. the eqn of an ellipse is: $(x-xc)2/a2 + (y-yc)2/b2 = 1$.

26. Define polygon.

A polygon is any closed continues sequence of line segments i.e., a polyline whose last node point is same as that of its first node point. The line segments form the sides of the polygon and their intersecting points from the vertices of the polygon.

27. Distinguish between convex and concave polygons.

If the line joining any two points in the polygon lies completely inside the polygon then, they are known as convex polygons. If the line joining any two points in the polygon lies outside the polygon then, they are known as concave polygons.

28. What is seed fill and soft fill?

One way to fill a polygon is to start from a given point (seed) known to be inside the polygon and highlight outward from this point i.e. neighbouring pixels until encounter the boundary pixels, this approach is called seed fill. Soft fill is a filling method in which fill coloris combined with the background colors.

29. What is scan line algorithm?

One way to fill the polygon is to apply the inside test. i.e. to check whether the pixel is inside the polygon or outside the polygon and then highlight the pixel which lie inside the polygon. This approach is known as scan-line algorithm.

30. Define coherence properties.

A coherence property of a scene is a part of a scene by which relate one part of the scene with the other parts of the scene.

31. What is an active edge list in the scan line algorithm?

The active edge list for a scan line contains all edges crossed by that scan line.

32. What is an attribute parameter?

Any parameter that affects the way a primitive is to be displayed is referred to as an attribute parameter.

33. What are the various attributes of a line?

The line type, width and color are the attributes of the line. The line type include solidline, dashed lines, and dotted lines.

34. What is pixel mask?

Pixel mask is a string containing the digits 1 and 0 to indicate which positions to plot along the line path. The mask 1111000, could be used to display a dashed line with a dash length of 4 and inter dot spacing of three.

35. What is Color Look up table?

In color displays, 24 bits per pixel are commonly used, where 8 bits represent 256 entries to pixel values in RGB format. This look up table is commonly known as colour table.

36. Define bundled attributes.

Individual attribute commands provide a simple and direct method for specifying attributes when a single output device is used. When several kinds of output device are available at a graphics installation, it is convenient to set up a table for each output device that lists set of attribute values that are to be used on that device to display each primitive type. Attribute specified in this manner is known as bundled attribute.

37. What is aliasing and antialiasing?

In the line drawing algorithms, all rasterized locations do not match with the true line and have to represent a straight line. This problem is severe in low resolution screens. In such screens line appears like a stair-step. This www.studentsfocus.com effect is known as aliasing. The process of adjusting intensities of the pixels along the line to minimize the effect of aliasing is called antialiasing.

38. What is pixel phasing?

Pixel phasing is an antialiasing technique, stair steps are smoothed out by moving the electron beam to more nearly approximate positions specified by the object geometry

39. List the types of graphics.

Interactive Graphics

Non-Interactive Graphics

Part-B

1. Explain refresh cathode ray tube.

2. Explain color CRT monitors.

3. Explain direct view storage tubes and liquid crystal displays.

4. Write short notes on Raster scan systems.

5. Describe in detail about the DDA scan conversion algorithm?

6. Explain in detail about Bresenham's (mid-point) circle generating algorithm. Give an example.

7. Explain in detail about Bresenham's (mid-point) ellipse generating algorithm. Give an example.

8. Explain in detail about Bresenham's line generating algorithm. Give example.

9. Explain in detail about graphics input devices.

10. Write short notes on parallel line algorithm.

11. Explain in detail about video display devices.

12. Explain in detail about raster and random scan systems.

Computer Graphics Unit-II

Two Dimensional Graphics

Part - A

1. What is Transformation?

Transformation is the process of introducing changes in the shape size and orientation of the object using scaling rotation reflection shearing & translation etc.

2. Write short notes on active and passive transformations.

In the *active transformation* the points x and y represent different coordinates of the same coordinate system. Here all the points are acted upon by the same transformation and hence the shape of the object is not distorted.

In a *passive transformation* the points x and y represent same points in the space but in a different coordinate system. Here the change in the coordinates is merely due to the change in the type of the user coordinate system.

3. What is translation?

Translation is the process of changing the position of an object in a straight-line path from one coordinate location to another. Every point (x, y) in the object must undergo a displacement to (x',y'). The transformation is: $x' = x + t_x$, $y' = y+t_y$

4. What is rotation?

A two-dimensional rotation is applied to an object by repositioning it along acircular path in the xy plane. The original coordinates of the point in polar coordinates are,

$$x = r \cos \emptyset, \quad y = r \sin \emptyset$$

5. What is scaling?

The scaling transformations changes the shape of an object and can be carried out by multiplying each vertex (x, y) by scaling factor S_x, S_y where S_x is the scaling factor of x and S_y is the scaling factor of y.

6. What is shearing?

The shearing transformation actually slants the object along the X direction or the Y direction as required.ie; this transformation slants the shape of an object along arequired plane.

7. What is reflection?

The reflection is actually the transformation that produces a mirror image ofan object. For this use some angles and lines of reflection.

8. Distinguish between window port & view port?

A portion of a picture that is to be displayed by a window is known as window port. The display area of the part selected or the form in which the selected part is viewed is known as view port.

9. Define clipping? And types of clipping.

Clipping is the method of cutting a graphics display to neatly fit a predefined graphics region or the view port.

- Point clipping
- Line clipping
- Area clipping
- Curve clipping
- Text clipping

10. What is covering (exterior clipping)?

This is just opposite to clipping. This removes the lines coming inside the windows and displays the remaining. Covering is mainly used to make labels on the complex pictures.

11. What is the need of homogeneous coordinates?

To perform more than one transformation at a time, use homogeneous coordinates or matrixes. They reduce unwanted calculations intermediate steps saves time and memory and produce a sequence of transformations.

12. Distinguish between uniform scaling and differential scaling.

When the scaling factors s_x and s_y are assigned to the same value, a uniform scaling is produced that maintains relative object proportions. Unequal values for s_x and s_y result in a differential scaling that is often used in design application.

13. What is fixed point scaling?

The location of a scaled object can be controlled by a position called the fixedpoint that is to remain unchanged after the scaling transformation.

14. Write down the shear transformation matrix.

A transformation that distorts the shape of an object such that the transformed shape appears as if the object were composed of internal layers that had been caused to slide over each other is called a shear.

15. What is the use of clipping?

Clipping in computer graphics is to remove objects, lines or line segments that are outside the viewing volume.

16. How will you clip a point?

Assuming that the clip window is a rectangle in standard position, we save a point $P=(x,y)$ for display if the following inequalities are satisfied:

$$xwmin \leq x \leq xwmax, \quad ywmin \leq y \leq ywmax$$

where the edges of the clip window (xwmin, xwmax, ywmin, ywmax) can be either the world-coordinate window boundaries or viewport boundaries. If any oneof these inequalities is not satisfied, the points are clipped (not saved for display).

17. Define viewing transformation.

The mapping of a part of world coordinate scene to device coordinates are called viewing transformation. Two dimensional viewing transformation is simply referred to as window to viewport transformation or the windowing transformation.

PART-B

1. Explain reflection and shear?
2. Explain Sutherland Hodgeman polygon clipping
3. Explain about clipping operations
4. Explain in detail about window to viewport coordinate transformation.
5. Write a detailed note on the basic two dimensional transformations.
6. Explain with an example the Cohen-Sutherland line clipping algorithm.
7. Compare Cohen-Sutherland line clipping algorithm and Cyrus-Beck line clipping algorithm.

COMPUTER GRAPHICS UNIT III

THREE DIMENSIONAL GRAPHICS

PART - A

1. What are the various representation schemes used in three dimensional objects?

- *Boundary representation (B-res)* – describe the 3 dimensional object as a set of surfaces that separate the object interior from the environment.

- *Space-portioning representation* – describe interior properties, by partitioning the spatial region containing an object into a set of small, no overlapping, contiguous solids.

2. What is Polygon mesh?

Polygon mesh is a method to represent the polygon, when the object surfaces are tiled, it is more convenient to specify the surface facets with a mesh function. The various meshes are,

- *Triangle strip* – (n-2) connected triangles.

- *Quadrilateral mesh* – generates (n-1) (m-1) Quadrilateral.

3.   **Define B-Spline curve.**

A B-Spline curve is a set of piecewise (usually cubic) polynomial segments that pass close to a set of control points. However the curve does not pass through these control points, it only passes close to them.

4. What is a spline?

To produce a smooth curve through a designed set of points, a flexible strip called spline is used. Such a spline curve can be mathematically described with a piecewise cubic polynomial function whose first and second derivatives are continuous across various curve section.

5. What is the use of control points?

Spline curve can be specified by giving a set of coordinate positions called control points, which indicates the general shape of the curve, can specify spline curve.

6. What are the different ways of specifying spline curve?

- Using a set of boundary conditions that are imposed on the spline.

- Using the state matrix that characteristics the spline.

- Using a set of blending functions that calculate the positions along the curve path by specifying combination of geometric constraints on the curve.

7. **What are the important properties of Bezier Curve?**

It needs only four control points

- It always passes through the first and last control points.
- The curve lies entirely within the convex half formed by four control points.

8. **Differentiate between interpolation spline and approximation spline.**

When the spline curve passes through all the control points then it is called interpolate. When the curve is not passing through all the control points then that curve is called approximation spline.

9. **Define Octrees.**

Hierarchical tree structures called octrees, are used to represent solid objects in some graphics systems. Medical imaging and other applications that require displays of object cross sections commonly use octree representation.

10. **Define Projection.**

The process of displaying 3D into a 2D display unit is known as projection. The projection transforms 3D objects into a 2D projection plane. The process of converting the description of objects from world coordinates to viewing coordinates is known as projection.

11. **What do you mean by view plane?**

A view plane is nothing but the film plane in camera which is positioned and oriented for a particular shot of the scene.

12. **What is view-plane normal vector?**

This normal vector is the direction perpendicular to the view plane.

13. **Define translation.**

In a three-dimensional homogeneous coordinate representation, a point is translated from position $P = (x, y, z)$ to position $P' = (x', y', z')$.

14. **What is the matrix representation of a translation vector in 3D.**

$$\begin{bmatrix} x' \\ y' \\ z' \\ 1 \end{bmatrix} = \begin{bmatrix} 1 & 0 & 0 & t_x \\ 0 & 1 & 0 & t_y \\ 0 & 0 & 1 & t_z \\ 0 & 0 & 0 & 1 \end{bmatrix} \cdot \begin{bmatrix} x \\ y \\ z \\ 1 \end{bmatrix}$$

15. **What are the translation equations?**

$$x' = x + t_x$$
$$y' = y + t_y$$
$$z' = z + t_z$$

16. Write down the 3D rotation equation about z-axis and its equivalent matrix form.

$$x' = x \cos \theta - y \sin \theta$$

$$y' - x \sin \theta + y \cos \theta$$

$$z' = z$$

$$\begin{bmatrix} x' \\ y' \\ z' \\ 1 \end{bmatrix} = \begin{bmatrix} \cos\theta & -\sin\theta & 0 & 0 \\ \sin\theta & \cos\theta & 0 & 0 \\ 0 & 0 & 1 & 0 \\ 0 & 0 & 0 & 1 \end{bmatrix} \begin{bmatrix} x \\ y \\ z \\ 1 \end{bmatrix}$$

17. Write down the 3D scaling equation and its equivalent matrix form.

$$x' = x \cdot S_x$$

$$y' = y \cdot S_y$$

$$z' = z \cdot S_z$$

$$\begin{bmatrix} x' \\ y' \\ z' \\ 1 \end{bmatrix} = \begin{bmatrix} s_x & 0 & 0 & 0 \\ 0 & s_y & 0 & 0 \\ 0 & 0 & s_z & 0 \\ 0 & 0 & 0 & 1 \end{bmatrix} \cdot \begin{bmatrix} x \\ y \\ z \\ 1 \end{bmatrix}$$

18. Write notes on reflection.

A three-dimensional reflection can be performed relative to a selected reflection axis or with respect to a selected reflection plane. In general, three-dimensional reflection matrices are set up similarly to those for two dimensions. Reflections relative to a given axis are equivalent to 180^0 rotations about that axis. Reflections with respect to a plane are equivalent to 180^0 rotations in four-dimensional space.

19. Write down the matrix representation of a reflection w.r.t z-axis.

$$RF_z = \begin{bmatrix} 1 & 0 & 0 & 0 \\ 0 & 1 & 0 & 0 \\ 0 & 0 & -1 & 0 \\ 0 & 0 & 0 & 1 \end{bmatrix}$$

20. Write down the matrix representation of a shearing w.r.t z-axis.

$$SH_z = \begin{bmatrix} 1 & 0 & a & 0 \\ 0 & 1 & b & 0 \\ 0 & 0 & 1 & 0 \\ 0 & 0 & 0 & 1 \end{bmatrix}$$

21. List some three dimensional transformation functions.

```
translate3 (translateVector, matrixTranslate
rotateX (thetaX, xMatrixRotate)
rotateY (thetaY, yMatrixRotate)
rotateZ (thetaZ, zMatrixRotate)
scale3 (scaleVector, matrixScale)
```

22. Write about view reference point.

To establish the viewing-coordinate reference frame, we first pick a world-coordinate position called the view reference point. This point is the origin of our viewing-coordinate system. The view reference point is often chosen to be close to or on the surface of some object in a scene.

23. What is view-up vector.

The up direction for the view by specifying a vector V, called the view-up vector.

24. What are the types of projections?

- **Parallel Projection** - coordinate positions are transformed to the vied plane along parallel lines.
- **Perspective Projection** - The projected view of an object is determined by calculating the intersection of the projection lines with the view plane.

25. Define projection reference point.

Object positions are transformed to the view plane along lines that converge to a point called the projection reference point (or center of projection).

26. Define projection vector.

A parallel projection with a projection vector that defines the direction for the projection lines.

27. Define orthographic and oblique parallel projection.

When the projection is perpendicular to the view plane, we have an orthographic parallel projection. Otherwise, we have an oblique parallel projection.

28. Define axonometric orthographic projection.

A orthographic projections that display more than one face of an object. Such views are called axonometric orthographic projections.

29. What is frustum?

With a perspective projection, the front and back clipping planes truncate the infinite pyramidal view volume to form a frustum.

30. What is normalized projection coordinate system?

The parallelepiped is mapped into the unit cube, a normalized view volume called the normalized projection coordinate system.

31. Write down the region code values in 3D clipping?

$$\text{bit } 1 = 1, \quad \text{if } x < xv_{min} \text{ (left)}$$
$$\text{bit } 2 = 1, \quad \text{if } x > xv_{max} \text{ (right)}$$
$$\text{bit } 3 = 1, \quad \text{if } y < yv_{min} \text{ (below)}$$
$$\text{bit } 4 = 1, \quad \text{if } y > yv_{max} \text{ (above)}$$
$$\text{bit } 5 = 1, \quad \text{if } z < zv_{min} \text{ (front)}$$
$$\text{bit } 6 = 1, \quad \text{if } z > zv_{max} \text{ (back)}$$

Unit IV

1. Define computer graphics animation.

Computer graphics animation is the use of computer graphics equipment where the graphics output presentation dynamically changes in real time. This is often also called real time animation.

2. What is tweening?

It is the process, which is applicable to animation objects defined by a sequence of points, and that change shape from frame to frame.

3. Define frame.

One of the shape photographs that a film or video is made of is known as frame.

4. What is solid modeling?

The construction of 3 dimensional objects for graphics display is often referred to as solid modeling.

5. What is Fractals?

A Fractal is an object whose shape is irregular at all scales.

6. What is a Fractal Dimension?

Fractal has infinite detail and fractal dimension. A fractal imbedded in n-dimensional space could have any fractional dimension between 0 and n. The Fractal Dimension D= LogN / Log S Where N is the No of Pieces and S is the Scaling Factor.

7. What is random fractal?

The patterns in the random fractals are no longer perfect and the random defects at all scale.

8. What is geometric fractal?

A geometric fractal is a fractal that repeats self-similar patterns over all scales.

9. Viewing pipeline

Introduction: A world-coordinate area selected for display is called a window. An area on a display device to which a window is mapped is called a viewport. The window defines what is to be viewed; the viewport defines where it is to be displayed. Often, windows and viewports are rectangles in standard position, with the rectangle edges parallel to the coordinate axes. Other window or viewport geometries, such as general polygon shapes and circles, are used in some applications, but these shapes take longer to process. In general, the mapping of a part of a world-coordinate scene to device coordinates is referred to as a viewing transformation. Sometimes the two-dimensional viewing transformation is simply referred to as the window-to-viewport transformation or the windowing transformation. But, in general, viewing involves more than just the transformation from the window to the viewport.

10. View volume

The *view volume* (sometimes called the display volume) is the volume of the design cube that is displayed in a 3D view.

11. 3d Transformation (All types with equation and diagrams)

12. Projections and its types

UNIT V

1. What is color model?

A color model is a method for explaining the properties or behavior of color within some context.

2. List out the properties that are perceive in a light source. Hue

Brightness (luminance)

Purity (saturation)

3. How is the color expressed in XYZ color model? Any color is expressed as C1=XX+YY+ZZ

X,Y, and Z represent vectors in 3D.

X,Y, and Z designate the amounts of the standard primaries.

4. What is RGB color model?

The RGB color model is an additive color model in which red, green and blue light is added together in various ways to reproduce a broad array of colors.

5. How is RGB model represented?

RGB model is represented by a unit cube. The color is expressed as an RGB triplet, each component of which can vary from 0 to 1.

6. What is YIQ color model?

YIQ is the color space used by the National Television System Committee color TV system. It was designed to separate chrominance from luminance. The Y,I,Q components are assumed to be in the [0,1] or [0,255] range.

7. How is RGB converted to CMY?

The conversion from RGB to CMY representation is done using the following matrix transformation.

$$[C\ M\ Y]=[1\ 1\ 1]-[R\ G\ B]$$

Where [1 1 1] represents white.

8. How is CMY converted to RGB?

The conversion from CMY to RGB representation is done using the following matrix transformation.

$$[R\ G\ B]=[1\ 1\ 1]-[C\ M\ Y]$$

Where [1 1 1] represents black.

9. What is HSV color model?

HSV stands for Hue, Saturation and Value. Hue-The color we see (red, green, purple) Saturation-How far is the color from gray Values (Luminance)-How bright is the color.

10. What does Computer animation refer?

Computer animation refers to any time sequence of visual changes in scene. It display time variations in object size, color, transparency & surface texture.

11. What is Frame-by-Frame animation?

Frame-by-Frame animation is an animation in which each frame of the scene is separately generated and stored.

12. What does story board define?

The story board is an outline of the action. It defines the motion sequence as a set of basic events that are to take place.

13. What is Graphics editor?

The graphics editor allows designing and modifying object shapes, using spline surfaces, constructive solid geometry methods, or other representation schemes.

14. What is Morphing?

Transformation of object shapes from one form to another is called morphing.

15. What is OPENGL?

OpenGL stands for Open graphics library. OpenGL provides a set of commands to render a 3D scene i.e., the data is provided in an OpenGL usable form and OpenGL will show this data on the screen.

16. Write down the Skeleton of an event driven program using OpenGL?

```
Void main()
{
Initialize things
Set the display mode
Create a screen window
Register the call back functions
Perhaps initialize other things
Enter the unending main loop
}
```

17. Give the format OpenGL vertex command? The OpenGL vertex command contains

The prefix "gl" indicates a function from the OpenGL library.

The basic command root.

The number of arguments being sent to the function.

The type of argument.

18. What is the use of glPointSize()?

The glPointSize() is used to set the size of a point which takes one floating point argument.

Syntax

glPointSize(Glfloat size)

where,

size specifies the diameter of rasterized points the default is 1.0

19. What is the Modelview Matrix?

The modelview matrix is the CT. It combines the following 2 effects.

Modelling tranformations on objects the transformation that orients and positions the camera in space.

20. What is the Viewport Matrix?

The viewport matrix maps the standard cube into a 3D viewport

21. Types of hidden surface detection algorithms

1.   Object space methods

2.   Image space methods

Object space methods: In this method, various parts of objects are compared. After comparison visible, invisible or hardly visible surface is determined. These methods generally decide visible surface. In the wireframe model, these are used to determine a visible line. So these algorithms are line based instead of surface based. Method proceeds by determination of parts of an object whose view is obstructed by other object and draws these parts in the same color.

Image space methods: Here positions of various pixels are determined. It is used to locate the visible surface instead of a visible line. Each point is detected for its visibility. If a point is visible, then the pixel is on, otherwise off. So the object close to the viewer that is pierced by a projector through a pixel is determined. That pixel is drawn is appropriate color.

22. VSD

When we view a picture containing non-transparent objects and surfaces, then we cannot see those objects from view which are behind from objects closer to eye. We must remove these hidden surfaces to get a realistic screen image. The identification and removal of these surfaces is called Hidden-surface problem.

There are two approaches for removing hidden surface problems– Object-Space method and Image-space method. The Object-space method is implemented in physical coordinate system and image-space method is implemented in screen coordinate system.

23. Methods

1. Scan line method
2. Z buffer method
3. BSP method
4. Back face detection method.

प्रलेख प्रक्रियाकरण एवं व्यवस्थापन
(DOCUMENT PROCESSING AND ORGANISATION)

(बी.एल.आई.आई.-012)

पुस्तकालय और सूचना विज्ञान में
प्रमाणपत्र [सी.एल.आई.एस.] के लिए
For Certificate in Library and Information Science [CLIS]

Useful For

Delhi University (DU), IGNOU, Berhampur University (Odisha), University of Kashmir, Sambalpur University (Odisha), University of Kalyani (West Bengal), Gurukula Kangri Vishwavidyalaya (Uttarakhand), Himachal Pradesh University, Cooch Behar Panchanan Barma University (West Bengal), Ranchi University, and other Indian Universities

---

Closer to Nature  We use Recycled Paper

गुल्लीबाबा पब्लिशिंग हाउस प्रा. लि.
आई.एस.ओ. 9001 एवं आई.एस.ओ. 14001 प्रमाणित कं.

Published by:
GullyBaba Publishing House Pvt. Ltd.

Regd. Office:	**Branch Office:**
2525/193, 1st Floor, Onkar Nagar-A, Tri Nagar, Delhi-110035 (From Kanhaiya Nagar Metro Station Towards Old Bus Stand) Call: 9991112299, 9312235086 WhatsApp: 9350849407	1A/2A, 20, Hari Sadan, Ansari Road, Daryaganj, New Delhi-110002 Ph.011-45794768 Call & WhatsApp: 8130521616, 8130511234

E-mail: hello@gullybaba.com, **Website:** GullyBaba.com

New Edition

ISBN: 978-93-89601-01-5
Author: Gullybaba.com Panel

HOME DELIVERY of GPH Books

You can get GPH books by VPP/COD/Speed Post/Courier.
You can order books by Email/SMS/WhatsApp/Call.
For more details, visit gullybaba.com/faq-books.html
Our packaging department usually dispatches the books within 2 days after receiving your order and it takes nearly 5-6 days in postal/courier services to reach your destination.